"A Good Poor Man's Wife"

Harriet Jane Hanson at eighteen, about 1843.
By courtesy of the Trustees of the Boston Public Library.

"A Good Poor Man's Wife"

Being A Chronicle of Harriet Hanson Robinson and Her Family in Nineteenth-Century New England

Claudia L. Bushman

University Press of New England
Hanover and London, 1981

University Press of New England

Brandeis University
Brown University
Clark University
Dartmouth College
University of New Hampshire
University of Rhode Island
Tufts University
University of Vermont

Copyright © *1981* by *Claudia L. Bushman*
All rights reserved
Library of Congress Catalog Card Number *80-54470*
International Standard Book Number *0-87451-193-3*
Printed in the United States of America
Library of Congress Cataloging in Publication data
will be found on the last printed page of this book.

Publication of this volume has been aided by a grant from
the NATIONAL ENDOWMENT FOR THE HUMANITIES.

CONTENTS

ILLUSTRATIONS

ACKNOWLEDGMENTS

One memorable day I discovered a treasure trove of manuscript materials of the Robinson family at the Arthur and Elizabeth Schlesinger Library on the History of Women in America, at Radcliffe College. I was drawn to work on these materials for many reasons, among them that Schlesinger Library is the pleasantest of archives in which to work and only ten minutes away from my home at that time. More important, Harriet Robinson's character has value for me in working out my own destiny, and my life has been bound up with hers for ten years.

The Schlesinger staff was unfailingly gracious in providing materials and assistance. I am grateful to them and to the staffs of other repositories, including the Boston Public Library, the Merrimack Valley Textile Museum Library, the Baker Library of Harvard University, the Malden Public Library, and the Concord Public Library. I appreciate the permission to quote from manuscript collections granted by the courtesy of the Trustees of the Boston public Library, Baker Library of Harvard University, and the Schlesinger Library.

For permission to publish the photographs that serve as illustrations for this volume, I wish to acknowledge the Schlesinger Library, Zivan Simonian, and the courtesy of the Trustees of the Boston Public Library.

David D. Hall who advised this project provided a steady and critical voice. Though I was never able to align the manuscript to his vision, his suggestions were invaluable during the many times the chapters were rewritten.

Zivan Simonian, who was married to Harriet Robinson's late granddaughter Martha Abbott, cordially invited me to a family home and shared his memories. He searched his shelves and came up with a valuable find: three more volumes of Harriet Robinson's diaries. As her living descendant, he granted me the privilege of publication and quotation from the manuscript materials, a favor I greatly appreciate. Our several communications on this subject have been so pleasant that I consider him a good friend.

I would like to acknowledge the assistance of a group of scholars whose support at regular meetings was mutually helpful. Polly Kaufman, Betty Reinhardt, Barbara Hobson, Lynn Weiner, Anne Farnam, Laurie Crumpacker, Susan Walton, Eugenia Kaledin, Susan Porter, Louise Stevenson, the late Hannah Bewick, and others who came and went during that time, read and discussed chapters and shared their references and insights.

Finally, the help of Richard Bushman, who served as patron throughout, must be acknowledged. He sustained this work financially and emotionally, often laying aside his own scholarship to give advice. Harriet was grateful that her "life companion" gave her the "exact help that [she] needed for continued education." I too am grateful for that help and am equally pleased that my work is now useful to him.

INTRODUCTION

I dont know as it pays for me to be so particular about writing, for who will ever read it, unless I should live to be a forlorn lonely old woman* which I much dread and fear. Then it would certainly be pleasant for me to read and remember what I once was, as if one ever forgets! So I am like the squirrel who lays up his stores of nuts in an old hollow tree. When the munching days of winter comes he is glad enough of them. Then if my presentiment of a sudden death should be realized, and my darling is left alone he will like to hear me "still speak" here.

*in 1876 it came

So wrote Harriet Hanson Robinson on April 17–18, 1866, when she was a matron of forty-one. She kept a diary to preserve her life for her husband, but she outlasted him. He died only ten years after this entry, as she indicates in the asterisked note. Still she stored up her "nuts in an old hollow tree" for winter munching and left behind a rich record.

A narrative of the lives of an ordinary family holds considerable significance in this day of growing interest in family history and plain people. The lives of Harriet Hanson Robinson (1825–1911) and her husband, William Stevens Robinson (1818–76), who were second-echelon social reformers, and of their ancestors and descendants, are useful in understanding the nonrich, nonfamous people of the past. The Robinsons were both lifelong residents of Middlesex County, Massachusetts, moving a dozen times between Boston, Lowell, Concord, and Malden. This study stresses Harriet because she was the longest-lived and central figure of the family group and because she kept the records.

Harriet Hanson was a child of six when her carpenter father died, leaving his wife with four children. Mrs. Hanson moved to

Lowell, the bustling industrial textile town, where she supported her family by running a company boarding house. The children worked in the mills as well as attending school, and justification of this early labor was a recurrent theme of Harriet's.

At the age of twenty-three Harriet married Robinson, who had come from a similarly poor family in Concord, Massachusetts, and whose bright mind and facile pen had earned him some success as a newspaperman. Together Harriet and William had four children, and they made a home for their widowed mothers. The family lived respectably, though on the edge of destitution, as Robinson's outspoken articles made it difficult for him to hold a job. Later they knew relative prosperity for eleven years when he was employed as the clerk of the Massachusetts House of Representatives. They bought a house in Malden. When a political disagreement with Benjamin Butler, the demagogic political boss who wanted to be the state's governor, led to the loss of the clerkship, Robinson began the long decline that ended with his early death, at fifty-eight, in 1876.

Reordering her life as a widow with three children and a mother to support, Harriet showed the stuff she was made of. She wrote her husband's history, published the book, and peddled it on the road to pay the costs. She used her house as capital and rented rooms to pay living expenses. Along with her daughters, she immersed herself in women's rights and became well known as a suffrage figure and clubwoman. She studied the classics and repeatedly tried to write something that would become one. Having long struggled with the concept of organized religion, she finally made peace with the church, and with her fellow man, and died at the age of eighty-six. Family members lived on in the house for another generation.

Harriet was a strong-minded woman who made a good life from very little. A model of the nineteenth-century woman who emerged from household seclusion to a public position, she combined domestic skill and motherly devotion with literary achievement.

Often dissatisfied with her lot, Harriet strove to better herself and to appear better than she was. A portrait taken at eighteen shows a haughty young lady, her regal gaze accentuated by heavy

dark brows; the narrow black ringlets of her elaborate coiffure
fall to the waist of her homemade black silk dress. At the time of
the photograph this slim and fashionable beauty had been working in the mills for seven years. She matured into an efficient
housewife and then a handsome matron, graying early and characteristically preferring her natural color to artificial attempts to
stay time's ravages; she stood somewhat over five feet tall and
by then weighed about 160 pounds. Distinguished in expression,
portly in figure, fashionable in dress, Harriet was a commanding
presence.

She wrote her diaries for public consumption as well as for her
own pleasure. According to her comments, she did not tell all. In
her uncorrected shorthand—which in this book is faithfully reproduced—she repeatedly apologizes for keeping a diary at all
and assures her readers that she amounted to more than she
recorded.

I often think that this Diary business dont amount to much for how little
of ones *real* life gets told of, or written about but perhaps it will interest
somebody after me—if anyone ever takes pains to read it. Yet after all it is
only the scum of the real life within.
                              —HHR Diary, 2 December 1864
This little book wont hold what I am, after all a few skimmings to speak
after the manner of cooking, is all that it contains.
                              —HHR Diary, 7 March 1867
And by the way this keeping a dairy is growing to be more and more of a
tax on my time, and then I do so little that is really worthy of mention.
What is the *real* things of my life I do not write.
                              —HHR Diary, 4 November 1888

Never confessional, Harriet's diaries chronicle her opinions
and the facts of her life. When she could not present a confident
public face, she cut off the record. She wrote no diaries for the
twelve years following her husband's death. The daily notes were
resumed in 1888, when she realized how useful the entries had
been in compiling her books and when she saw the historical
value of a daily record.

She preserved the materials for reclaiming the rest of her life.
The Schlesinger Library on the History of Women in America, at
Radcliffe College, houses Harriet Robinson's twenty-seven daily

diaries, the thirty-nine scrapbooks, and hundreds of letters that she saved, as well as the scrapbooks and diaries of her daughter Harriette Lucy (Hattie) Robinson Shattuck. Harriet deposited the papers of her husband in the Boston Public Library. Harriet and William's courtship letters have recently surfaced in a private collection. It was this woman's remarkable urge to pickle the remains of her life for future sampling that has provided a hundred-year record of a lower-middle-class American family, its relationships, household routines, and financial stresses.

As interesting and important as the family records are Harriet Robinson's salty comments on contemporary social and political issues—abolition, suffrage, labor reform, Massachusetts politics—in which she and her relatives were involved. The papers shed light on the petty aspects of internal squabbles and personality conflicts, rather than on strategy or theory. Sometimes infighting involving the Robinsons affected the outcome of important issues; often it did not. Because Harriet's published writing serves as source and commentary on the women's-history topics of work, suffrage, and club activity, an effort has been made to evaluate her facts and opinions. Understanding the context in which she wrote her books explains much of her passions and bias. It should be pointed out that Harriet affiliated herself with various groups for social association and status: ideology was less compelling than the identity realized from connection with an organization.

With her husband and with her daughter Hattie, Harriet Robinson formed units that moved on the edges of important reform groups. Defining themselves against more acceptable norms, they were anticlerical and politically liberal. Intellectually and culturally advanced, they aspired to influence opinion, but they lacked the financial backing and social ease to move in higher circles. They were known and respected, but not accepted.

In rapidly industrializing Massachusetts, Harriet and William Robinson occupied a marginal position. Discontented with the farmer and artisan class they came from, and unwilling to leave the state to try their luck on the Western frontier, they moved into the city. They lived by their wits. Skilled with words, they achieved a prominence in print they could not match in their real lives, where they moved more comfortably with newspaper writers than with statesmen and with suburban housewives than with movement leaders. This Yankee family had left behind Puritan rigor, though they retained a belief in the virtues of thrift, hard work, and self-reliance. Sundered by early male death and financial failure—as were many such families—the Robinsons were martriarchal. Uprooted from ancestral homes, they lived in no one's memory but their own. The families were forgotten even as the widows lived on.

In the face of financial instability, the members of families like the Robinsons often cooperated to help one another. Familiar relationships remained strong despite financial disruption— probably because of it. The family worked well as an emotional unit when it failed financially. The literary evidence of the Robinsons serves to counter claims that similarly uprooted, unstable families were anxious and desperate. The Robinson family perceived itself as successful despite reverses.

Much of the writing of family history in recent years has depended on new techniques of social history that rely heavily on the quantification of official records. Philip Greven has transferred the records of Andover, Massachusetts, to computer cards and arrived at data on family size, fertility and ages at the time of distribution of property; these data have forced some rethinking of historical assumptions. John Waters has similarly mined wills for their wealth of information. Tamara Hareven has used company records in connection with vital statistics to reconstitute families and family patterns in Manchester, New Hampshire. John Demos has employed court records and artifacts to theorize on the otherwise almost dumb society of seventeenth-century Plymouth, Massachusetts. In most of this recent work scholars have analyzed documents previously considered fruitless for the gathering of family history.

By contrast, the following story of the Robinsons is an old-fashioned work, based as it is primarily on diaries, letters, and scrapbooks—the literary sources scholars wish were more often available for the common people. As such, it is closer in type to *The Family Life of Ralph Josselin*, by Alan MacFarlane, and even more so to *Yankee Family*, by James R. McGovern, a fine study of the Poors. Both of these are histories of a single family over time, each using that group of kin to answer the questions that demographers raise about family life in the past and to illustrate the way that family relationships can answer such questions. In both cases the books suffer from overconceptualization. MacFarlane's model, though very neat in the way concentric circles of relatives and friends relate to the central figure, loses something of subtlety in its working out. McGovern also suffers from a too rigid attempt to force his material into the categories demographers and family historians have set up because their documents lead them toward and limit them to certain questions.

This study of the Robinsons attempts to answer the questions outlined by the current study of family history: questions on social and geographical mobility, life-cycle patterns, nuclear and extended households, fertility and child-rearing patterns, care for the aged, changing gender roles as a family moves from agricultural to urban life. But the answers to these questions that tend to be statistical in nature have not been the primary concern of the work.

The rich literary materials available on the Robinsons have made it possible to concentrate on more human themes, on the love, the duties, and the resentments of family life. Central to this study is one woman's perception of her female role and the tension she felt between being a traditional supportive wife—which she enjoyed—and her compulsive need for personal power. Other major themes are the nineteenth century's middle-class striving for success, with its attendant high hopes and shattered dreams, and the rebelliousness of the times, which stemmed from a Revolutionary War heritage and worked itself out against organized religion, political enemies, and social injustices; in Harriet Robinson it finally abated and came to serenity with the end of the century. Above all, the effort here is to portray real life, to stay close to the facts and to dignify common lives by respecting daily living.

"A Good
Poor Man's
Wife"

I

Ancestry and Childhood

❧Did you tell him who you are?
—Diary of Harriette Robinson Shattuck, 11 June 1915

Harriet Hanson's mother told her always to remember that she had been born the year the cornerstone was laid for the Bunker Hill Monument.[1] That important event in 1825 bound her into the history of her country and her people, for her grandfather had distinguished himself in that famous battle of the Revolutionary War. Her mother's lesson was well learned; Harriet spent much of her life writing a place for herself into the history of her times.

This drive to place herself in history led Harriet when she grew up to research her genealogy and to join the New England Historical Genealogical Society as soon as women were admitted as members. She collected family information, asking her mother for anecdotes, and assembled it in a little book. She searched out the family heirlooms—her grandfather's flintlock, a clock marked "Browne" (her mother's maiden name), a Browne coat of arms, her great-grandfather William Browne's moccasins from the French and Indian Wars, the Bible with family names and old doodling in it.[2] Gradually she came to know a great deal about the members of her family who had gone on before.

The family from which Harriet had sprung was respectable and hard-working, but not distinguished. There were no ministers, no university graduates, no military officers, no political-office holders after the first American generation, in the seventeenth century, and few landholders. No brilliant ornaments hung on this family tree.

Harriet was able to trace her mother's father's line back through seven generations of Brownes to Edward Browne and his wife, Jane Lide, the ancestors from Inkborrow, Worcestershire, England, who fathered Nicholas Browne (d. 1673), the first American ancestor. This Browne line was notable for mobility, for large families disrupted by death, and for steadily falling fortunes. The family groups lost their land, lost their breadwinners, and several times even lost their status as families as the members broke apart and went to live with others. The landowners and farmers of the first few American generations gave way to landless artisans whose children had little chance of rising above their fathers' status. Descended through a long line of younger sons, Harriet was born at the nadir of family fortunes.

The Browne family had, however, begun its American phase in a promising way. Nicholas Browne, along with his wife, Elizabeth, was one of the early "planters" of Lynn, Massachusetts, having been granted 210 acres of land by the town in what is now Saugus. Made a freeman in 1638, he served as a deputy to the General Court in 1641, 1655, 1656, and 1661, a public office that none of his descendants attained. Not content with his Lynn acres, Browne moved to Reading, then an adjoining town, where he was granted 200 more acres, and where he owned considerable other property. He also served as commissioner "to try small causes," and as selectman of the town.

Besides his American property, Nicholas Browne fell heir to his father-in-law's property in England. He sent his son John there in 1660 to call one William Rand to account "what of shops, houses, lands and monies he hath received for rents, profits and sheep-rent, heretofore and of late due, arising, growing and properly belonging unto the heirs of the said Lide."

Nicholas, a man of property, good judgment, and community stature, joined the First Church in Reading in 1663. He and his wife produced seven children, six of whom lived to marry. When

Nicholas died, his estate was valued at £1,232 9s.[3] He was an ancestor to be proud of.

The line continued through Cornelius (m. 1665, d. 1701), the fourth son and fifth child of Nicholas. Cornelius was one of fifty-nine householders listed in Reading in 1669, and was granted an additional lot valued at 12s. 8d. in 1666. He paid an assessment to the Indians for the purchase of land for the town and subscribed to the new meetinghouse in 1688. On December 13, 1670, he was "owned by the Church," and became a member.

Cornelius and his wife, Sarah Lamson, had eleven children in twenty-two years, at least three of whom died young. Sarah herself died in 1683, just surviving the birth of her youngest child. Seven years later, on July 18, 1690, Cornelius sold his farm to his seventh child and second living son, Samuel, "out of fatherly love and good affection." Samuel was to pay his father the sum of £3 a year and reserve room for him in his "now dwelling-house while I [Cornelius] am a widower." So in his late forties, Cornelius, who may well have been in ill health, gave up being the head of his household in favor of Samuel, who would have been just fifteen if the dates are correct. Cornelius died insolvent in 1701. The son of a rich man died a poor man in a single room of his son's house.

William Browne (1682–1768), Cornelius's youngest son and Harriet's great-grandfather, inherited some of his father's "common rights in Reading" and also a piece of pine swamp and meadow. These he apparently sold when he moved closer to Boston, where he bought "for a valuable sum of money" some real estate in Watertown. This land was sold on September 20, 1705, to Thomas Brattle, Esq., of Boston, treasurer of the society known as "the President and Fellows of Harvard College in Cambridge." Harriet liked to think that the sixty acres were important in the development of the college.

When he was just twenty-one, in 1703, William Browne married Deborah, the widow of Thomas Squire. Perhaps some of the money used in the real estate transaction was hers. He was admitted to "full communion" in the "First Church in Little Cambridge" (now Brighton) on April 18, 1714.

William was a carpenter and builder; the inventory of his estate included a long list of carpenter's tools. But Harriet imagined him primarily in connection with his service against the French

and Indians during Queen Anne's War and for the Indian moccasins from Canada that his great-grandchildren played with for
many years.

William lived a life of interesting shape and confusing generations. Left motherless at one year, he fathered fifteen children by
two wives over an incredible sixty-four-year period. His first wife,
Deborah, bore six children, five of whom are recorded as mar-
rying. The children came at two-year intervals except for a four-
year period when William was away at war. The last was born
sometime in 1717–18. Much later, after Deborah's death, William
married Mary Bailey, on October 13, 1744. He then produced his
second family, consisting of nine children, the last born in 1768,
the year William died, at eighty-six. All fifteen of the children
were mentioned in his will, evidence against there being any
mistake in the record of births.[4]

The generations got out of hand in William Browne's family.
He first married a widow, who predeceased him by more than
twenty years. When he married again, a woman much younger
than himself, he produced children young enough to be the
grandchildren of their older half brothers and sisters. A year
after William died, his wife Mary married Peter Bray, a mariner,
and dismantled the household: she sold all her property, found
guardians for her children, and sailed away with her new husband to England. According to family tradition, Harriet recorded, Mary took all she could of her first husband's property,
"silver, heirlooms, deeds of land, etc."[5] How poignant to think of
little Abijah, Susannah, Lucy, and Josiah—the last just over a year
at the time of his mother's remarriage—abandoned by their
mother to the care of others. The older children scattered. One
brother went to Canada, another to Cape Cod. Jonathan was lost
at sea, Thaddeus moved out to Concord. Seth Ingersoll settled in
Charlestown, Massachusetts.[6]

Seth Ingersoll Browne (bap. 1750–1809), William's sixth son
and Harriet's grandfather, was nineteen when his mother, Mary,
married again. Harriet was proudest of this ancestor, a man she
never knew, because of his participation in the Revolutionary
War. Like his father, Seth was a carpenter, and in the early 1770s
he kept a shop near Warren Bridge in Charlestown. He was one

of the "Mohawks" who helped throw the tea into Boston Harbor and a minuteman at the Battle of Bunker Hill. Seth often relived those glorious days for his little daughters, holding their hands and singing verses of "Yankee Doodle" that probably originated in postwar pubs. Harriet recorded some of these verses, which are bad enough to be genuine.

> We marched down to the Long Wharf
> With officers and soldiers,
> And as good troops as England had
> Not a foe that dared confront us.

> We marched down to Charlestown Ferry,
> And there we had our battle:
> The shot it flew like pepper & salt
> And made the old town rattle.

Seth, a thick-set man with a fierce look—called by his descendents the Browne scowl—had white, even "double" teeth, which he gritted in his sleep. He had black hair and light eyes, one blinded by the battle, and when "He used to talk about the cruel scenes which he had witnessed and the children whimpered, he would tell them not to cry for we whipped [the British] when we were boys and we can now we are men."[7] This was some comfort to the little girls who feared a new invasion by redcoats.

Some of the powder used at the Battle of Bunker Hill was secreted in Seth's shop, and the place was destroyed when Charlestown was burned by the British. Seth was sleeping the morning of the battle when Charlestown began to blaze. An Irishman called him: "Get up, Mr. Brune. The barracks will all be afire." Seth fought for some time and then helped in rolling barrels of stone down the hill to make the British think the patriots had plenty of gunpowder. He told his daughters he would never forget the cry of "No ammunition, No ammunition!," which forced the patriots to retreat.[8] When Major Andrew McClary, his commanding officer, was wounded, Browne took over and superintended the retreat across the Mystic River. While the patriots were crossing in open boats, Major McClary was killed by a shot from a frigate.

Seth continued his Revolutionary service as assistant camp commissary under General Washington at Cambridge, and he was chosen one of a company of select men to transport the packages of specie the Marquis de Lafayette was sending from Newport, Rhode Island, to White Plains, New York. Seth was a patriot, a man to be trusted. But he was not a man of property.

Family legend held that Seth was paid off after the war with a large sheaf of Continental bills. By then the money had depreciated so far as to be worthless, and his angry wife threw the whole stack into the fire. Having sacrificed his livelihood, his health, and his fortune to the patriot cause, Browne supported his family precariously by keeping a tavern in Roxbury, Massachusetts, called The Punch Bowl. Harriet's mother, Harriet Browne, was born in this public house. Seth later ran a riding school and stable.[9]

Like his father, Seth Ingersoll Browne had fifteen children by two wives. Like his father's family, his own became disrupted and dispersed. His first wife, Lucy Brown Browne, (m. 1777) produced four children, who scattered to the winds: William went to sea and died in South Carolina; Daniel, a sea captain, died in Havana, of yellow fever; Seth, Jr., also a sailor, signed a quit claim to his father's estate in 1805, went away, and was never heard from again; and the fourth child, Elizabeth, died young. Daniel, the only one of the group to marry, wed Sarah Piper. A young woman from Concord, Sarah lived in infamy in Harriet's mind, because she and the other Piper siblings dispatched their mother to the Concord poorhouse and let her die there.[10]

Seth Ingersoll Browne married again in 1786, and began a second family. His wife Sarah Godding, thirteen years his junior, bore him eleven children, nine of whom lived to marry. Sarah Godding was called handsome in her youth. She used to wear a short, loose white gown over a black skirt with a blue-and-white checked apron. She had deep-set eyes and a low, broad forehead, white skin, and long, straight black hair, which she wore covered with a high-crowned shift cap tied with a black ribbon around her head. Very smart and quick-stepping, Sarah was called by her neighbors "an extra good woman."

This Mrs. Browne was a firm mother. At one time when the family was living near Boston's Lewis Wharf in a brick house with a steep roof, she had occasion to demonstrate her concern for her children. She was entertaining company at tea when a neighbor ran in to say that the children were playing on the roof. "Almost frightened to death," Sarah Browne used her softest, sweetest voice to call the children to come for cake; when the last child had landed safely she soundly spanked the older ones. This mother showed more regard for her children than her mother-in-law who had sailed away had done for hers, yet she died at the age of thirty-eight, leaving them just as surely. Sarah Browne's survivors included her husband and nine of the eleven children she had borne, ranging from Jane, six months old, to thirteen-year-old Sally.[11]

Little Jane was put out to nurse and almost starved. Sally took her back and abused her until their sister Harriet (Harriet Robinson's mother) became indignant. Harriet, who was then only seven or eight and was at service at the time, walked from Boston to Waltham—about twelve miles—to take the baby to the widow of an older half brother; that afternoon she walked back to Boston again.[12] Such were the vagaries of the disrupted family.

The children, probably lonely without their kind mother, recorded seeing her after her death. Sarah Godding Browne sometimes became visible in a bedroom, brushed her long black hair, and walked out. Her presence may have been of some comfort to the bereft children.

Seth Ingersoll Browne died of consumption in Charlestown in 1809, at the age of fifty-nine. On his last day he was so much worse that his daughter Harriet was sent to get the doctor. The March streets were slippery, and she was obliged to climb one of Charlestown's steep hills on her hands and knees in order to reach the doctor's house. She did not get back in time to see her father alive again. Seth Ingersoll Browne—a genuine patriot, but a poor one—was buried in someone else's tomb in Boston's Granary Burial Ground, resting place for Revolutionary heroes. Presumably he still lies there in anonymous glory. His participation in the Tea Party was later proclaimed on a marble monument in the Mt.

Hope Cemetery in Worcester, Massachusetts. After his death his
and Sarah's children were dispersed and sent to live among
strangers.[13]

Harriet knew less about her father's family, but the brief records show similar mobility and disruption. At least two generations of Hanson men fathered families and died young. The
Hansons came from a long line of English Quakers who had
settled in Dover, New Hampshire.[14] Not much is known of those
men beyond their repeated given names—William, John, John,
John, Thomas, Thomas—stretching back over the generations.

Harriet's grandfather John Hanson lived with his wife, Sally
Getchel, in Milton, New Hampshire. In 1803, when his son William was only eight, John was crushed by a load of stone while
working out his taxes on the highway. A family legend records
Sally Getchel Hanson's premonition of her husband's death. She
was washing some clothes at the brook that afternoon when a
drop of blood appeared in a clean place. She rinsed it off, but
another drop appeared and was scarcely washed away when a
third appeared. Filled with presentiments, Sally ran toward home
and demanded that an approaching neighbor tell her the bad
news. Like many another widow in succeeding generations of the
Hanson family, Sally Hanson then struggled on alone, and after
her household broke up she moved in with some of her children.
She lived to a very old age.[15]

Sally Hanson's son William, Harriet's father, left the family
home to apprentice himself as a carpenter with a man named
Whitehouse in Milton, New Hampshire. When he had learned
his trade, at the age of twenty-one, he moved to Boston and went
to work for Peter Cudworth on Merrimack Street, near the corner of Causeway. At some point he met Harriet Browne, the sister
of his boss's wife, and married her. Both bride and groom were
twenty-seven years old. They rented a house in Leverett Court,
later called Cotting Street, close to the Mill Pond that had not yet
been filled in.[16]

William Hanson was something of a dandy, a stout young man
with blue eyes, very small hands, a large head, and curly auburn
hair; he called himself Sorrel Top. Harriet remembered her
father dressed in white pants and vest, with a ruffled shirt and

bosom pin. He wore white stockings, and the shiny black pumps with large bows on his small feet were "the admiration of [her] childhood." She remembered her pride in him as they walked hand in hand on the Boston Common.[17]

The Hansons were soon the parents of a fine son, John Wesley (1823–1901), and on August 2, 1825, Harriet Jane (1825–1911), the protagonist of this drama, made her advent. Of her premature birth (after seven months) Harriet characteristically commented: "[My] little face could be covered with a common teacup."[18] Harriet was followed by Benjamin Piper Browne (b. 1826) and by William, who died in infancy. Another William was then born (1829–36), completing the family.

When Harriet was just six, with brothers eight, five, and two, her father died. Harriet's mother, Harriet Browne Hanson, was then a thirty-six-year-old widow without money-earning skills. Motherless at six and orphaned at fourteen, Mrs. Hanson had had a "hard experience in her youth in living amongst strangers."[19] Now she faced the dissolution of her own family.

The nuclear family of that time worked well as an economic unit if the father was present and earning money. But when he died and there were no land, no money, no grown-up children, and no prospects of remarriage for the widow, the household dissolved. This theme had been played out repeatedly in the history of Harriet's family.

It is sobering to consider the annals of this one early family and to realize that the pattern of family dissolution was very common in early America. Generation after generation of helpless mothers and children were thrown on the mercy of relatives or into the cruel world. It was not only the death of the husband that dispersed a family. Frequently husbands migrated off to set up new households or went to war, as William Browne had done. William Hanson had to leave home to find work. And always death hung over these fragile family groups. Workers might suffer violent death on the job, as the senior William Hanson had done. Poorly treated ailments or incurable diseases, such as Seth's consumption, incapacitated and carried away breadwinners. Often women died of the complications of childbirth, leaving vulnerable young families.

Women were unprepared by skill or tradition to support their families once their husbands were gone. Children had to be farmed out as apprentices or domestics, as Mrs. Hanson had been. Widows and children thus lost the protection of the nuclear household's operation as an economic unit.

Second marriages could reunite scattered members, but the emotional bonds that tied the blood group would be difficult to forge again with a new partner. Mary Bailey Browne, William's second wife, showed no interest in the first wife's children; although perhaps an extreme case, in that she showed little interest in her own children, she sailed away from them all, never to see them again. Disruption of family groups was common, and practical people adjusted to new circumstances

The fraternal bond among siblings born over many years could not be strong. When men sired children young enough to be the grandchildren of their half brothers and sisters, as William Browne did, these siblings could scarcely be acquainted, let alone close. Even in families with fewer children, who were born closer together, the older ones would often leave home long before the younger ones, making the family an amorphous, ill-defined unit.

The hard economic facts of American life argued against maintaining the family circle in adverse circumstances. Only fortunate groups, with stable breadwinners and ample finances, could afford what was essentially a luxury: to live as a group with those bound most tightly by blood and emotion. Several generations of the Browne family had broken up because of financial straits.

Against this background Harriet Browne Hanson made a dramatic and defiant stand. She refused to break up her family. She was determined to keep her children together whatever the difficulty.

In so doing she reflected a changed cultural attitude toward family life that was consistent with the evolution of nineteenth-century sentiments. As children took on a greater emotional worth, and parental training and home unity became increasingly desirable, the loving family assumed a higher value in society.[20] Harriet Browne Hanson maintained her family at heavy cost, laboring the rest of her days to preserve it.

With the help of some of her husband's fellow carpenters, she opened a shop in Boston, where she sold food, candy, and kindling. The small shop was in the front of the building, where the jars of striped candy and loaves of bread were displayed. The family lived in a room behind the shop, where young John sawed the kindling. Mrs. Hanson did not complain of her poverty, but she could not earn a living from the store. The family lasted through one cold winter there, sleeping together for warmth.

Seeing the family's struggle, a neighbor who was better off looked with "longing eyes" on little Harriet, whom she offered to adopt and give more advantages than the mother could provide. Mrs. Hanson refused: "No; while I have one meal of victuals a day, I will not part with my children."[21] When a teacher at charity sewing classes referred to Harriet as a "poor little girl," Mrs. Hanson proudly withdrew her daughter from the school.[22] This early training in family unity and pride was to influence Harriet Hanson Robinson throughout her life.

Help came the next year, in 1832, from Mrs. Hanson's sister, also a carpenter's widow, who managed a factory boarding house in Lowell, Massachusetts, the booming textile town. Angeline Cudworth advised Mrs. Hanson to come to Lowell, and applied to one of the corporations for a house for her. This is how the Hansons came to rent the old Tremont No. 5, a neat brick row house among many exact counterparts in four blocks of chunky houses with green doors and window blinds.[23] Here Mrs. Hanson could remain the head of the household, with her children around her, while cooking, cleaning, and washing for forty boarders, mostly the well-behaved and brotherly sons of farmers. Although Mrs. Hanson's family could not afford to support her, a family connection did help her to a position where she could support herself. Relatives and friends, such as the fellow carpenters, helped one another as they could.

By the 1830s, as illustrated by Harriet Browne Hanson, a widow could manage to maintain a family if it was important enough to her to do so. The period's growing sentimental attachment to families justified, in fact required, sacrifice in order to protect dependent children. Harriet's mother and later Harriet herself felt a desperate need to avoid the loneliness, suffering, and shame of a breakup. They had to maintain their families.

In the past generations of this family, relationships had been more casual, broken as they were by death and circumstance. But to Mrs. Hanson and later to Harriet, family was all in all. Family had placed Harriet in the world, and she passed the same attitude on to her children. Many years later, when Harriet's daughter Hattie spoke to the daughter of an old suffrage-worker friend, Hattie "told her who I was." Harriet Hanson Robinson "always used to say" to her children, "Did you tell him who you are?"[24]

II

Work

⌁ I wanted to earn money.

—Loom and Spindle

⌁ Help was too valuable to be ill-treated.

—Early Factory Labor in New England

Harriet Hanson Robinson painted a rosy picture of her life as a
child worker in the Lowell mills. She defended the experience as
wholesome and educational.

According to Harriet, she had entered mill work at age ten at
her own "urgent request." For I wanted to earn *money* like the
other little girls." Mrs. Hanson "allowed" her daughter to take
this step. Harriet presented her employment as her own idea, but
quietly prefaced her decision with the fact that her mother felt
obliged to have some household help and needed extra money to
pay for it:[1] childish enterprise may well have masked stern necessity.

Considered practically, Harriet's work in the mills was probably easier than her work at home. To keep her family together
Mrs. Hanson took on unrelenting household labor. As the mistress of a boarding house "on the corporation," she became a
minor entrepreneur in a patriarchal system. She bought the
furniture and the provisions, paid rent, and ran the house
according to her tastes. The corporation paid her $1.25 a week
for each boarder. The possible margin of profit was never gener-

ous, and without past experience managing a large establishment, Mrs. Hanson had to work very hard to get by. For the first
four years the children provided all the household help Mrs.
Hanson had, and with the demands of shopping and cooking for
forty-five people three times a day, as well as doing their laundry
and keeping the crowded house in order, their help was sorely
needed. Harriet's specific duties as the only daughter of the
house were to wash all the dishes—when she was still so small she
had to stand on a cricket to reach the sink—and to scour the
mountain of flatware each week. Even as a young child Harriet
would have been working almost continuously when she was not
in school.

By contrast, her job at the mill as a "doffer"—a worker who
replaced filled bobbins with empty ones for about a quarter of
each hour—seemed less demanding. She later recalled the
leisurely sociability of her factory work. During their long free
periods the doffers could read, knit, play outside, or run home to
help their mothers. They sang and told stories. When work was
over they had warm food, loving mothers, and comfortable
homes awaiting them. For this pleasant life they received wages.
Harriet proudly lined up and stood on the bobbin box to collect
her $2 each week.[2] Compared with work at home, factory life
offered entertainment, leisure time, friends, and money. For the
next five years young Harriet spent nine months of each year
working in the mills and three months in school, as required by
the corporation.

The rapid growth of Lowell—named for the man who had
conceived the idea of this industrial center where raw cotton
would be turned into finished cloth, Francis Cabot Lowell—
amazed the world. Until the water privileges at Pawtucket Falls on
the Merrimack River were secured, in 1821, the area had been
part of the farming community of Chelmsford. The Merrimack
Manufacturing Company, highly capitalized and employing
many young women rather than the families employed in existing Rhode Island mills, was incorporated in 1822 and produced cloth in 1823. By the time Harriet arrived with her family,
in 1832, the town was humming. In 1821 five families had lived
on the land, five years later 2,500 people lived in the same area,
and ten years later there were 18,000.[3]

The textile industry created the town, whose development was marked with much commentary on its social value. Harriet herself described the "Lowell factory system" as meaning that "corporations should have souls, and should exercise a paternal influence over the lives of their operatives."[4] This attitude, which had wide acceptance—as well as the fact that Lowell had no native aristocracy, no old institutions, and no town history—led to an open and welcoming tone. Lowell in the 1830s was a place of "frank friendliness and sincerity in the social atmosphere."[5]

One reason for the open atmosphere was that the power figures—the stockholders and the treasurers who set company policy, handled finances, bought raw materials, and arranged for the sale of the finished product—lived in Boston. An agent, working under the treasurer, supervised day-to-day activities on the site, but made no important decisions; this person was to be the paternal, kindly figure, but he had little power. The companies were run from a distance, their major aim being, despite their altruistic propaganda, to pay the highest possible return to the stockholders.[6] This contradiction between the "paternal influence" and the profit-making goal was later to lead to difficulties.

The hierarchical structure was based on people's current status rather than past connections. The working population of Lowell that Harriet perceived broke down into four major groupings. The eight agents ran the eight corporations and formed the town's aristocracy. Well-educated gentlemen, though not necessarily wealthy, they lived in large houses set some distance from the mills. Next down the scale came the overseers, who supervised individual workrooms and the skilled workers. These machinists might well work their way up to be overseers. They lived in tenements in the blocks of girls' boarding houses or in row houses built for them. Harriet had little to do with these skilled workers who serviced the machinery. The operatives, or working girls, came next, forming the bulk of the working population, more than seventy percent of whom in 1830 were between the ages of fifteen and twenty-nine.[7] The girls lived in company houses that looked like boarding schools, and their status was above the fourth class, who were "lords of the spade and the shovel."[8] These laborers who dug the canals and put up the factory buildings were generally Irish, even as early as the 1830s, and a small stone Catholic church was built in the midst of their shanties in the "Acre," to give some community feeling to the slum.

Although there were differences in attitude among the people, all of Lowell looked to the factories for support. A modified feudal subjection to the corporations unified the town. The operatives, particularly, felt themselves under the promised protection and patriarchal care of the management, and offered their loyalty in return.

An attitude of sentimental self-sacrifice, of meeting challenges gladly with a brave heart, characterized the articulate early mill girls. Harriet and her friend Lucy Larcom, later a noted poet, remembered their factory days from this point of view. They discounted tensions with overseers, recognizing only the conflict between the job before them and their ability to perform it with grace. In this spirit they accepted the fourteen-hour workdays. They sandwiched their reading, writing, mending, studying, and other self-improvement activities into their two free evening hours and short weekends.

The mill girls accepted their lot because the work was no worse than alternative work at home and because it was a means to an improved life. Harriet described the money earned as going into barren homes "like a quiet stream, carrying with it beauty and refreshment."[9] Lucy Larcom in her romantically titled poem "An Idyl of Work" listed the idealistic reasons girls worked in the mills:

> Not always to be here among the looms,—
> Scarcely a girl she knew expected that;
> Means to one end, their labor was—to put
> Gold nest-eggs in the bank, or to redeem
> A mortgaged homestead, or to pay the way
> Through classic years at some academy;
> More commonly to lay a dowry by
> For future housekeeping.[10]

Larcom stressed that the girls of the late 1830s and '40s pursued a purpose beyond the work itself: they sought "an opening into freer life." A mill girl's daughters would never toil in the mill, she predicted, but would be teachers. The accumulation of sufficient money would raise the family to a higher financial plane.[11]

This model of proper behavior was made available to mill workers in the prescriptive literature and sentimental fiction of the time. The story of "Susan Miller," written by "F. G. A., a Lowell Operative," and published in the Lowell *Offering*, a periodical containing poems and stories written by the working girls, graphically illustrates the correct conduct of a mill girl. In the story Susan, the eldest child of a ruined family, attempts to put things to rights after the death of her drunken father. Susan outlines to Deacon Rand, who holds the mortgage on the family farm, her intention to work in the Lowell mills and pay off the family debt. The classic debate about mill problems and advantages follows and underscores Susan's determined self-sacrifice in the face of the deacon's mature wisdom.

Susan counters the prejudice against factory girls with the nobility of all labor. The deacon's complaint that the place is full of wickedness, corruption, and immoral girls is answered by Susan's statement that her virtuous cousin works there. When he suggests that difficult working conditions, noise, and long hours might cost her her health, Susan assures him that she is strong and will eat carefully. Rumors of girls who have had their hands torn off by machinery and concern that girls might be mistreated by their overseers do not stay Susan. The deacon's final, generous offer—that Susan help his wife as a daughter might and perhaps marry into the family—is rejected: "delicacy forbade" her to take this false position.

Sad but brave, Susan goes off to Lowell to take up the difficult work and master it. Thanks to her efforts the family is eventually comfortably settled again, and she finally goes home, a full year after the last dollar is paid. Although she is now looked upon as an old maid and begins to consider herself one, she is happy, "Happy in the success of her noble exertions, the affection and gratitude of her relatives, the esteem of her acquaintances, and the approbation of conscience." She is happy to be a martyr for others as long as they recognize her sacrifice. "Those who see the factory girls in Lowell," she chides her readers, "little think of the sighs and heart-aches which must attend a young girl's entrance upon a life of toil and privation, among strangers."[12] She can bravely say "It's nothing" as long as observers realize "It's too much."

Lucy Larcom commented in words that might have been Susan Miller's: "Certainly we mill-girls did not regard our own lot as an easy one, but we had accepted its fatigues and discomforts as unavoidable, and could forget them in struggling forward to what was before us. . . . We trod a path full of commonplace obstructions, but there were no difficulties in it we could not hope to overcome, and the effort to conquer them was in itself a pleasure."[13] Harriet called the mill her "*Alma Mater*," and felt that its "incentive to labor" and the discipline of the work were of great value. "We were taught daily habits of regularity and of industry; it was, in fact, a sort of manual training or industrial school.[14]

Girls in this position did not see themselves as members of the working class—the term and concept *working class* was an invention of industrialism that was still in formation in the 1830s.[15] Group consciousness was absent from these girls, who viewed their stay in the mills as temporary, a stepping-stone to a better life or else a deliberate sacrifice for others. Rather than improve the lot of all workers, they hoped to rise above it, individually.

One early evening, Harriet, weary after her labor in the mills, passed by an agent's house. The gate in the high fence was open, and the house with its beautiful gardens appeared like paradise, compared with the noisy mill. Harriet could look in with "longing eyes" and see the agent's wife, a handsome woman, reading by an astral lamp. The image had great power over her: she yearned to have a parlor of her own and leisure to read good books, lighted by an astral lamp.[16] To be such a privileged wife did not seem impossible to Harriet; she did not see herself cut off from such niceties by class distinction. Harriet saw herself, rather, as a junior member of the same group.

Harriet asserted that the girls were treated with consideration by their employers, that there was a feeling of "respectful equality" between supervisors and workers. "The rights of the early mill girls were secure." "Their life in the factory was made pleasant to them." She declared that "*Help was too valuable to be ill-treated.*"[17] Harriet maintained that her loyalty to the management was purchased by their respect for her, even though more recent writers have demonstrated that factory paternalism was largely a myth perpetuated by the management in order to control workers.[18] Harriet had to deny that factory managers disregarded their help, because if she had accepted the assertion, it would have reflected on her worth as an individual. Her experiences were generally positive and she remembered her mill-girl time with happiness.

Nevertheless, her reminiscences also show another side of mill life, contradictory to the dominant complacency of her writings. As a young girl Harriet led a strike, and her reputation as a militant worker has lived after her. The incident suggests a dark underside to mill life that is hard to reconcile with her narrative of satisfaction and pleasant time.

As a nine-year-old schoolgirl in 1834, when the first strike occurred, Harriet had no idea of the mills' financial trouble. After a decade of growth and high profits the textile industry had reached a crisis in the early 1830s. Rapid production satisfied the demand, and as a surplus began to accumulate, the price of finished goods dropped steadily. The cost of raw materials dropped at the same rate, but in order to maintain the profits per yard, the cost of production had to be lowered. As working hours could not practically be increased beyond the fourteen-hour day, the management decided to lower the wage paid per piece of work done, meanwhile speeding up the work by running the machinery faster and requiring the girls to tend more equipment, in an effort to gain back what they had lost.[19]

Although the wages were certainly cut back, the workers' actual loss of earning at each reduction was soon overcome. Robert Layer's extensive analysis of mill records makes clear that the workers suffered only a slight dip in take-home pay before their wages climbed back to the previous level and up again.[20] The differential could be accounted for by increased effort and by steady improvements in the machinery. While Harriet knew of girls who sat idle for twenty or thirty minutes at a time without a supervisor's cross word or admonition to be up and doing,[21] the spare time was gradually filled until the girls were stepping lively for the entire day. Needless to say, girls who made as much money by working harder for it felt they were being short-changed. However, without these measures for increased production it is quite possible that the entire textile industry might have foundered. Earlier experiments had failed. The stockholders had invested tremendous sums of money, and to operate those vast plants without a steady stream of sales would soon be very costly. Although those early industrialists are frequently condemned for their callousness, their position is understandable.

Nevertheless, by 1834 conflict was inevitable. The companies' financial retrenchment through the lowering of wages aroused the revolutionary zeal of the operatives. Angered that their "protectors" had become their tyrants, the girls defied public opinion and struck the mills.[22]

To go back to the events leading up to the strike, the announcement of the pending reduction in wages was issued in a joint circular by the agents of the eight corporations:

The unparalleled pressure of the times,—the immense quantity of manufactured goods accumulating in the hands of the manufacturers, unsold,—and the consequent depression of the prices of said goods, have caused many manufacturing establishments to close their works, and others materially to diminish the number of their operatives.—Taking this into consideration, together with the reduction of the protective duties, which has recently taken place, the Proprietors of the Mills in Lowell, co-operating with other large establishments in New England, to prevent the disagreeable necessity of stopping their works, and discharging their hands, have decided, that a simultaneous movement to equalize, and in some cases reduce the wages now paid, shall take effect the first of March next.

LOWELL, JAN'Y 30, 1834.[23]

The circular urged cooperation, acceptance of the "equalization," and "in some cases," a small reduction for the mutual good. Dismissal was threatened in only the faintest tones.

The correspondence between the agents in Lowell and the treasurer, who served three related corporations in Boston, is particularly helpful in understanding the strain between the old bond of attachment the company seemed to promise and the cash nexus that was closer to reality. That the corporations were duplicitous is evident. Treasurer Henry H. Hall demanded a wage reduction of twenty-five percent. Agent William Austin of the Lawrence Corporation feared that no more than twelve percent could be managed without "much murmuring & very baneful effects."[24] Abbott Lawrence, a major stockholder and potentate, wrote that a full reduction of from one-quarter to one-third of the workers should be made at once; he was "willing to take the risk of stopping the mills."[25] In private, the proprietors were ready to write off a number of the girls under their "protection"; indeed, they thought it necessary to do so.

Austin, closer to the situation, questioned whether the best interests of the manufacturing establishment were prompted by the wage reduction. He reported that the girls were not accepting the decree from above in the docile spirit expected. The operatives were meeting together. "Threats are manifested with a truly Amazonian Spirit and I doubt not that many of the best girls will leave the mills."[26]

When the high spirits he admired in the "best girls" were seditiously exercised, Austin began to see the dangers. His letter two days later expressed sorrow, but no forgiveness, for the misguided zealots. "A spirit of evil omen to the ultimate well being of [the girls] has prevailed, & overcome the judgement & discretion of too many. . . . I anticipate much suffering on the part of those who have thus from evil communication or whatever cause, thrown themselves out of employment. & placed themselves in a position so averse to good order & their best interest."[27]

At the writing of this letter about half of the girls in Austin's mill had walked out. Stung by the insubordination, he was determined to make the disloyal pay. Hall, who watched the Lowell scene from a distance, in Boston, found the behavior of the operatives inexplicable—"unless they suppose[d] by a *show* of resistance, that the proprietors [would] be intimidated & induced to continue *old* prices."[28]

The tone of this correspondence makes the operatives' position clear. As early as 1834 the management had effectively abandoned paternal protection. Yet the owners demanded continued loyalty from the girls, punishing any lapses in it. The girls had depended on their employers for fair treatment and felt justified in demonstrating against what they saw to be inequity. But they received reprisals rather than understanding for so doing. The owners took no responsibility for mistreating their help, and punished them for objecting to the mistreatment. As Hall wrote to Austin, the "deludons or ring leaders—should be made to feel that they have done wrong—& ought to be excluded from the mills."[29]

Austin attempted to discharge Julia Wilson, the ringleader in his mill. She declared that every girl in the room should leave with her, made a signal, and they all marched out to the clang of the quitting bell. The striking girls were quickly fired. The next day the strikers marched and countermarched the mills, and soon a procession of seven hundred was seen perambulating the streets. Julia Wilson, Austin balefully reported, delivered several "extempore addresses with great effect being elevated to the top of pumps." She figured as the "heroine of the disgraceful drama."[30] In keeping with their sense of American history, the girls made heavy rhetorical use of their status as "daughters of freemen," independent of those whose "avarice would enslave" them.[31]

Confident of their cause, the girls played out their ritualistic "Amazon parade." An overseer of one of the weaving rooms remembered the girls as quiet and determined rather than unruly. As the strikers came in sight of the mill windows, they waved their handkerchiefs, sang "their liberty effusions," and urged the girls crowding the windows to turn out. "The light-headed ones easily got interested, and had an itching to share in the fun," said the old overseer[32]

This overseer, by the way, was successful in keeping his girls in the room by reasserting his paternal interest in them, which had some truth to it. He reorganized the weaving room into quarters with supervisors who kept every loom in running order, so that the hands could make as much money as they had made before. They were satisfied by his concern and their pay, and he lost only two weavers, whereas some other rooms were emptied.[33]

The fired girls were put out of the company boarding houses and planned to leave town. Because two weeks' notice was required to withdraw their savings—the bank had to send to Boston for specie—the girls rented a big house and helped one another. In a fortnight the "trouble-makers" had hired all the hacks, wagons, and carts in town so that they could take themselves back home. (The old overseer kept his room quietly at work and said little about the fuss, but he was "tickled all over with fun to see the women carry so much sail and manage it so well, too."[34]) If the management was no longer protective, the girls were no longer dependent.

All in all, the directors were pleased with the strike, or "turn-out," and its results. Hall wrote to John Aiken, the agent for the Tremont Corporation, that there was no question in his mind that Aiken would find "a salutary influence from the 'Rebellion'—which will have a lasting influence."[35] Still, the offending operatives who had been "so unwise and indelicate as to engage in that frantic and ill advised project" must be punished. The turnout, Austin urged, should be understood as "wounding to the heart of the larger majority who remained firm to their engagements."[36] This final condemnation harked back to the old relationship. The strikers were faithless to their "true natures" and the "loving fathers" who had engaged them. Austin even refused forgiveness to the penitent, commenting that the few "old hands" who offered themselves for employment were "contaminated with the 'turn out' fever," and so could not be rehired.[37]

On March 1, when the wage reductions actually took place, the ringleaders were long gone. The day passed as any other. Aiken lost between seventy and a hundred girls, a figure that might be multiplied by the eight corporations, as the exact number of strikers is unknown.[38] Many looms were still idle a year and a half later.[39] The girls who remained went to work at the new wages, which were set to allow them something over $1.50 a week above their $1.25 board cost. The wage reduction that resulted in the strike meant less money per piece of work completed, but in general, as described earlier, the total wages were still on the rise.[40]

The Lowell strike of 1834 was notable for being among the first instances of organized opposition in the history of the textile industry. The mill girls had demonstrated their independence to all those watching when they staged an orderly retreat rather than backing down on their demands. The dissident operatives returned home with their pride intact.

Although not in the mills in 1834, Harriet was there working as a doffer in 1836 when another turnout, more bitter and longer-lasting than the first, took place. Again the issue was money: the corporations proposed to raise the price of board.

When the mills were established, respectable boarding houses were opened and regulated as an inducement for proper New England girls to take up factory life. The boarding-house keepers were allowed $1.25 per girl per week to pay for the cost of meals. The money was withheld from the girls' wages and paid directly to the housekeepers.

The board allowance had never been generous, and as inflation raised the cost of staples, the housekeepers were hard put to feed their charges for the sum. Lucy Larcom's mother, who was used to setting a nice table, could not make the compromises necessary to keep her household solvent. In order to feed her boarders, she sent her two young daughters to work in the mills.[41] The complaints of other keepers finally provoked the corporations' management to ease their financial strain. The solution fixed upon was to lower the keeper's rent 12½¢ per week per boarder and to deduct an additional 12½¢ per week from each girl's wages. This solution divided the necessary increase equally between the girls and the corporations. The amount in question represented about five percent of the girls' take-home pay.

Perhaps the girls could see some justice in this new demand, if they understood it. But the managers acted in an overbearing way, undercutting the respectful attitude they supposedly felt for the operatives. Despite the suggestions of the agents that the management give two weeks' notice of any contemplated change—as the girls were required to do—treasurer Henry Hall proclaimed in a haughty directive that the 12½¢ charge would be added at once. With his characteristic condescension, Hall told agent Robert Means that he would be "quite anxious to know how the new rate of Board is rec'd by the *Ladies of Your Family*. I hope there is good sense enough among them to see the necessity of the case."[42]

On October 1, 1836, agent John Aiken seized a moment to advise his superiors that the "Lawrence Mills [were] in a state of rebellion." A third of the girls were out and the operations at a standstill. Between twelve hundred and fifteen hundred girls paraded through the steets singing that they would not be slaves.[43] Aiken reported that the spirit manifested was of a "decidedly more resolute and determined character than that which prevailed in 1834 & of course must be expected to hold out longer."[44]

A newspaper account pictured two thousand striking girls assembled in a grove on Chapel Hill, along with several hundred men and boys. The event seemed to be a general muster, and all enjoyed the "fine holiday." Again the revolutionary tradition was made explicit. An unnamed striker declared, "As our fathers resisted unto blood the lordly avarice of the British ministry, so we, their daughters, never will wear the yoke which has been prepared for us."[45] The girls had traded one acceptable tradition—that of dutiful daughters—for another—that of righteous patriots. (In an appeal for public support, they did temper their revolutionary behavior; after holding one evening meeting, they determined that it was "more becoming the character of their sex" to meet in the daytime.[46])

Despite the appeal, sympathy for the girls was in short supply. The Boston *Evening Transcript* chided the "very [un]grateful girls [for kicking] up this bobbery." The managements had set up their "small convenient tenements" to "*protect the female* operatives from the rapacity of the keepers." The paper considered the girls unjustified in resisting the corporations' attempt to help the housekeepers, whose costs had risen nearly fifty percent from the earlier days.[47] As the girls could not refute the additional costs of the keepers, the strike indicated that accumulated anger had spilled over to this one case of seeming injustice.

Two weeks later the girls were still out. John Aiken reported that of about 420 who had struck only 75 or 80 had returned to work. The rest manifested "good 'spunk.'" He coolly concluded that "wisdom learnt from experience has always been called the best, but theirs will be rather dearly bought."[48]

While the eleven-year-old Harriet was working in a spinning

room at the Tremont Corporation, according to her later account, the parade of striking girls snaked by her building, urging the other workers out. Harriet had heard the strike discussed and had been an "ardent listener" to the arguments against the injustice of the management. She sided with the strikers. But while many operatives marched from the mill, the girls in Harriet's room stood irresolute, uncertain what to do. They asked one another:

"Would you?" or "Shall we turn out?" and not one of them having the courage to lead off, I, who began to think they would not go out, after all their talk, became impatient, and started on ahead, saying, with childish bravado, "I don't care what you do, *I* am going to turn out, and was followed by the others.[49]

She felt great pride as she looked back at the long line of girls following her.

This incident, quoted from Harriet's *Loom and Spindle, Or Life Among the Early Mill Girls, with a Sketch of "The Lowell Offering" and Some of Its Contributors*, tells a great deal about the young Harriet Hanson. Decisive and intolerant of indecision in others, she was quick to anger. She liked to be the leader. Had she considered the issues rationally, she might have stayed in the mill. Her family stood to benefit from the increase in board payments, and they badly needed the board increase and her own salary. Harriet's reactions were emotional rather than ideological. The passion of the moment swept her up and took her to the front of the line.

Harriet's discussion of the incident illustrates her perception of historical events. Even according to her own description, Harriet did very little in this strike. She led girls from only one room, and perhaps she only seemed to make the move that started the group out. Someone must have taken similar action in two hundred other mill rooms. She was only "an ardent listener" and spoke with "childish bravado." Yet her account, with its tension and vividness, is presented as central to the strike. The selection is frequently quoted, and Harriet gets credit for being a prime mover. In her book she gave further importance to the incident by tying it to a larger issue. She was prouder of the strike success, she said, than she would ever be again "until my own beloved

State gives to its women citizens the right of suffrage."[50] What was at best a child's daring has been presented as a major incident along the road to increased women's rights. Harriet was writing herself a place in history.

The strike experience can be found twice in her papers before the *Loom and Spindle* account. At the first telling Harriet was over fifty and the little girl was anonymous. While the facts were the same, the fervor and fire had not yet developed:

In one room some indecision was shown among the girls. After stopping their work they discussed the matter anew, and could not make up their minds what to do, when a little girl of eleven years old said, "I am going to turn out whether any one else does or not," and marched out, followed by all the others. The "turn-outs" all went in procession to the grove on "Chapel Hill" and were addressed by sympathizing speakers. Their dissatisfaction subsided or burned itself out in this way, and though the authorities did not accede to their demands, they returned to their work, and the corporations went on cutting down the wages.[51]

Twelve years later Harriet had taken this incident for her own, and while attending the International Council of Women in Washington, D.C., in 1888, she made her part very clear. A newspaper interviewer reported that "Mrs. Robinson was probably one of the earliest strikers in the country. In 1836–'37 she led the girls in the room in which she worked and encouraged them to strike, saying . . . . She was then about twelve years old." The reporter commented that Harriet's "individuality causes her to occupy a unique position among the women who are gathered [here]."[52]

The *Loom and Spindle* account, written fifty years after the event, still bristles with the tension Harriet had felt between obedience and rebellion, a tension so characteristic of her whole life that she was never to resolve it. Whatever the origin of the strike incident, Harriet learned to manage her material effectively and to make something important out of something relatively minor—she used her past to bolster her future.

In *Loom and Spindle* she continued her story, describing the results of the strike. Her mother was punished for harboring a miscreant.

The agent of the corporation where I then worked took some small revenges on the supposed ringleaders; on the principle of sending the weaker to the wall, my mother was turned away from her boarding-house, that functionary saying, "Mrs. Hanson, you could not prevent the older girls from turning out, but your daughter is a child, and *her* you could control.[53]

The paragraph has a nice irony, for if Mrs. Hanson had been able to control her own daughter, she might well have suggested that Harriet act differently. As it was, the long-suffering Widow Hanson was punished both by her daughter, who demonstrated against her interests in having board fees raised, and by the corporation, which apparently turned her out of her boarding house.

One result of the strike was a reconsideration of the board system. Since boarding houses had been instituted as an inducement for the girls to come to Lowell, if the girls were unhappy with the houses, perhaps the system should be abolished. Already at the time of the strike more than half of the Tremont girls were boarding outside the corporation, while the Merrimack and Boott companies had discontinued paying the board allowance to the houses and had received no complaints.[54] Apparently the corporations were willing to relinquish this manifestation of their paternalism as early as 1836, and the boarding houses were gradually phased out.

Working-class consciousness was sufficiently aroused during this strike for the workers to organize a union, the Factory Girls' Association. Although membership reached a high of 2,500 in short order, the union accomplished little. The oversupply of workers, their short-term commitment to mill life, their lack of bargaining power, and the fact that the natural leaders had been forced out of the mills all tended to diminish any of the union's potential power. Impotent dissatisfaction remained.

Despite her rebelliousness, Harriet kept her job in the Tremont Mills until she was thirteen, when she took two years off to go to high school. Her mother apparently continued to take in boarders outside the company system. At fifteen, Harriet returned to the mill to work as a spinner until she came into her job as a drawing-in girl. Soon after this, Harriet's mother "had some financial difficulties," and in order to keep her daughter's wages from being trusteed, or appropriated by her creditors, she gave Harriet her "time," a document disavowing financial responsibility for her daughter. In this way Mrs. Hanson relinquished any claim to Harriet's wages. The document, which Harriet later explained was to save the two women "from annoyance," calmly dissolved the financial responsibility between the generations:

> Be it known that I, Harriet Hanson, of Lowell, in consideration that my minor daughter Harriet J. has taken upon herself the whole burden of her own support, and has undertaken and agreed to maintain herself henceforward without expense to me, do hereby release and quitclaim unto her all profits and wages which she may hereafter earn or acquire by her skill or labor in any occupation,—and do hereby disclaim all right to collect or interfere with the same. And I do give or release unto her the absolute control and disposal or her own time according to her own discretion, without interference from me. It being understood that I am not to be chargeable hereafter with any expense on her account.
>
> (Signed) Harriet Hanson
>
> JULY 2, 1840.[55]

The letter seemed to echo the end of paternalism in the mills as parent and child each went his or her way without obligation to the other. But in the Hansons' case, responsibility for the family was now in fact reversed, rather than dissolved, as Harriet and her brother John, a clerk in another corporation, took over the support of their mother and brother. They prevailed upon Mrs. Hanson to "give up keeping boarders," feeling that she had worked long enough, and the two maintained their mutual home with their mill earnings.[56]

Labor unrest continued and picked up momentum. The Lowell Female Labor Reform Association bought the presses that published Lowell's labor newspaper, *Voice of Industry*, and factory operatives were urged to agitate for better wages and hours. Sarah G. Bagley, an outspoken new operative who did some editing for the liberal *Voice of Industry*, challenged the assumption that all was well. Though she was not in the mills at the time of the strikes, Bagley has come to personify that period of labor agitation to today's students, for she provided a rallying point for the dissatisfied and made Lowell the center for the ten-hour movement in the mid-1840s.[57] She testified before the Massachusetts legislature, taught mill workers in evening school, and wrote briefly for the Lowell *Offering*.

Curiously, it is only in this last activity that Sarah Bagley is mentioned in Harriet's book *Loom and Spindle*. Harriet's account of her own life in the mills during the twelve years from the 1836 strike to her final departure, in 1848, shows her oblivious to Bagley, and in fact records no more involvement in labor activities. Although Harriet reported that conditions continued to deteriorate and that piecework wages were cut again and again, she apparently took no further part in the opposition to the mill owners.

Significantly, Harriet found herself a niche where she was protected from the worst conditions of factory labor. As a drawer-in she stood apart from the automation of mill employment. One of only a dozen or so drawers-in in each building, Harriet prepared the beams for each new piece of weaving by drawing the warp threads one by one through the harness reed. Drawing-in was a craft, meticulous handwork rather than machine work, and Harriet felt pride and identity in her occupation. Her hooks were the "badge of all my tribe."[58] Lucy Larcom found a similarly protected niche; she measured finished pieces of fabric in the cloth room and recorded their lengths in a ledger.[59] Neither Harriet's nor Lucy's job was associated with close air, noise, or muscle strain.

Harriet steadily maintained throughout *Loom and Spindle* that mill life had been good but went downhill after she left in 1848, when immigrant labor almost entirely replaced native operatives. Yet Harriet's praise of her idyllic, uncharacteristic factory life is frequently belied by her own evidence. The circumstances of the early strikes indicate that the downward cycle—which is to say, the end of paternalism and respect—had already begun before Harriet came into the mills. The workers were disillusioned with the management before Harriet was a doffer.

Used to hard work and cheerful acceptance of her lot, Harriet was insensitive to the changing scene around her. Somewhat defensively admitting that there might have been another side to the mill picture than her own, she asserted that she gave the side she knew best, "the bright side."[60] Despite Harriet's growing reputation as an early agitator, she was closer in spirit to Susan Miller than to Sarah Bagley.

Her handling of her mill-life experience seen from a perspective far in the future tells more about Harriet than about mill-life realities. For one thing, it was important to her that she differentiate her own experience as an innocent child working in an industrial garden from the grim factory experience of girls working during her maturity. Mill work did change, and she emphasized the point in order to foreclose identification with downtrodden and listless mill girls of the later part of the century.

Harriet Robinson's account of the Lowell strike experience of the thirties is somewhat lacking in accuracy; she combines the two strikes considering them as a single event. But for Harriet history was less important than the myth she was creating of the early mill girls and of herself. The happy minions in the mills were not robots but thoughtful people with a revolutionary heritage that at times required disobedient behavior. She portrayed the girls as she had come to think of herself, as a submissive, happy person with a latent capacity for independence and truculence. Retelling the story through the years helped her to locate and bring forward elements of herself that during childhood and marriage had been largely submerged—a capacity for resentment of injustice and for taking pleasure in swimming against the tide.

III

Education

✦ *Improve your mind, try and be somebody.*

—Loom and Spindle

As Harriet Hanson worked in the mill as a drawing-in girl, seated on a high stool, she kept a book in her lap. She was paid by the piece, rather than by the hour, and felt justified in pausing to read her book or to note down the poetic phrases she had worked out. "I dont remember that I ever *lived* in the mill much," she said of the years when she had spent fourteen hours a day within its brick walls. Her mind was full of "fairy stories and things." The whizzing of the spinning became "tunes and all sorts of melodies."[1] She called the two drawing-in hooks she preserved from that time "companions of many a dreaming hour."[2] She dismissed mill life by not thinking about it.

Harriet's mother enjoined her to "Improve your mind, try and be somebody."[3] Proper speech and written expression would qualify her to write memorable poetry. Genteel language would form the genteel woman. Someday she knew she would have a better life, and learning was the only way to get there.

The high value placed on education in the Lowell of the 1830s and '40s reflected the middle-class work ethic of the populace. Powered by an intense desire for respect and recognition, families sacrificed to send their children to school in order to raise them above the poor. The educational facilities in Lowell reflected this upward striving. Although the buildings were primitive and the teachers frequently punitive, public support for education in the face of mill opposition testified to a high belief in the power of education to improve the people. A confrontation dramatizing this conflict occurred in 1832, the year the Hansons arrived in Lowell.

The Lowell school committee proposed floating a $20,000 loan to buy land and construct two new schools consolidating the five ungraded district schools. The conflict pitted the school committee's most visible member, Theodore Edson, minister of St. Anne's Episcopal Church—the established religious body in early Lowell—against Kirk Boott, the agent of the first Lowell mill and Edson's employer and patron. Boott, an English-educated autocrat who, according to Harriett, was a "great potentate" who "exercised almost absolute power over the mill-people," had "imbibed the autocratic ideas of the mill-owners of the mother country." Boott did not believe in the saving power of universal free education and on behalf of the mills he opposed the school appropriations.[4] At the town meeting, Boott's arguments were based on economy. He contended that Lowell was but an experiment, for which it was folly to incur massive expenses. Why, a traveler visiting the place in a few years might find only a "heap of ruins."[5] Edson coolly answered that any traveler picking over the ruins of Lowell would know the cause of its downfall when he found no schoolhouse.

The new plan would mean long-term economy. Though the taxes to pay for the schools would fall most heavily on the corporations, which held most of the land, the taxes would still be lower than for equivalent land in Boston. The discussion was "not without warmth, and somewhat protracted."[6] Individually every man in town but Edson would have bowed to the authority Boott represented. Collectively, behind a strong leader such as Edson, they stood firm. The school appropriation passed by twelve votes.

When the corporations called for a special town meeting to rescind the vote and engaged two lawyers to represent the business interests of the mills, Edson again stood as the sole spokesman against the opposition. This time he won his case by thirty-eight votes. The town thereby risked powerful corporate displeasure to support improved public education.

Boott never again darkened the door of St. Anne's, so great was his wrath.[7] And neither he nor any other mill agent would have anything to do with the two sturdy brick school buildings that rose the next year. He did, however, deign to show off the schools to Henry Clay and Massachusetts governor Levi Lincoln, along with other sites of interest, when they toured Lowell in October of 1833. The visitors were impressed.[8]

So keen was the displeasure of the mill owners that when the lease on St. Anne's Church expired, the corporations launched a lawsuit demanding that the religious society buy the property—which had been widely advertised as a gift to the community—at a sum considerably higher than the original cost. In 1842 the church people managed to buy the church, but Edson was evicted from the parsonage in 1843 and had to live elsewhere until the congregation was able to buy it back, in 1866.[9]

The schools Edson fought so hard for were not the answer to an educator's dream. Each had but one large room, with 250 pupils in it; one or two smaller recitation chambers opened off the large room.[10] The educational experience frequently failed to enlighten the students. When she entered school at Lowell, Lucy Larcom was immediately promoted to a higher grade, because of her superior reading ability. But as no one had ever taught her any arithmetic, and she was too shy to ask the monitor for help, she was reduced to having another girl do her sums. She felt like a miserable cheat. She was terrified of the tall, gaunt master, who punished the children by sticking pins in them and beating them with leather straps. The master strode about the room, some-times stepping right over the desk tops, looking for mischief makers.[11] Had timid little Lucy been caught cheating on her arithmetic, she would have been scarred indeed. The fact that such an experience did not discourage her in her schooling demonstrates the strength of the popular myth of the power of education.

Young Harriet Hanson suffered similar difficulties at Lowell's North Grammar School in 1835. Whipping was an everyday occurrence and performed publicly during class hours. Master Hills would go secretly behind a boy playing at his desk and strike him across the back with a leather strap. A more serious offender was made to lie across a chair and be whipped—not always through his clothing.[12]

When she was ten years old, Harriet was accused by a classmate of tearing up the girl's one-cent multiplication table. Harriet was innocent of this insignificant crime and denied the charge, but Master Hills dismissed her denials and proceeded to punish her by striking her palm with a leather strap. "He punished her till she could not see, for pain and terror, and then she gave in, *whipped into a lie*, and said she did it."[13] She crept away to her desk, thinking that the incident was at least over, but found that she must continue to lie to explain why she had denied the crime in the first place. Heartily sick of the whole matter, Harriet "wished that she had stuck to the truth, even if the master had killed her."[14]

This experience made her appreciative of Master Hills's successor, Jacob Graves, who used moral suasion and instilled a sense of honor in his pupils. He never punished the children physically, but his "kind, remonstrating voice was more powerful than any whipping."[15]

Though Master Graves's methods were certainly preferred, what was a small child to learn from such inconsistent school experiences? The remonstrating voice was as painful as the whip, and the notoriety of punishment transcended the benefit of learning daily lessons. Education might be a privilege and a way up from poverty, but threading the maze through school was confusing and threatening.

Working children were required by their corporations to attend classes for three months of the year. When Lucy Larcom returned to school after her first year in the factory, she found the teachers kind and thorough in their instruction: her mind seemed to have been "ploughed up during that year of work, so that knowledge took root in it easily." Study delighted her, and after three months the master told her that she was ready for the high school.[16] But the wages she earned in the mill were essential to keep her family's household running so she could not quit her job in order to go to high school. Hungry for learning, she had looked through "an open door" that closed before her.[17] Working in the mills intensified Lucy's desire for schooling.

Harriet's education was similarly interrupted. She labored in the mills while her older brother, John, completed the grammar school and took two years in high school, after which, at the age of fourteen, he went to work in the counting room of the Tremont Corporation. Then, with John earning money, Harriet could go to school.

In 1829 the state law requiring a high school for every hundred households was relaxed so that such a school was obligatory only where there were five hundred households. But though a census of Lowell's homes showed that the requisite population was lacking, the town established a high school all the same—another example of the popular support for education there. This school opened in December of 1831, giving it the honor of being the first permanent coeducational high school in Massachusetts.[18] The stated purpose of the school was to "perfect the English education . . . begun in the Primary and Grammar Schools, and also to fit young men for College."[19]

The high school shone as a beacon for young Harriet. She studied and worried for weeks before she "ran the gauntlet" of the entrance examination, with twenty or more others. Only five were accepted into the school, and Harriet went home feeling the world had "nothing else to offer." Only later did she discover that there was room for just five students, so that five would have been taken even if a hundred had qualified. She had run the gauntlet for nothing, she felt.[20] The next year, however, she competed successfully, and for two years attended the high school regularly.

When Harriet entered, in 1840, the high school met in a wooden building over a butcher shop. The school committee had high hopes for the institution, reporting that the school served as an "incentive to exertion" for all the public schools in the city.

Its object is to place within reach of the poorest citizen such means of preparing his children for college, or for giving instruction for any branch of active business, as the richest shall be glad to avail themselves of, for their own children. This object has been realized.[21]

Later that year the high school moved to its own permanent building, where the fifty-seven boys and fifty girls were segregated on their own floors for study, joining for mixed recitations. A special female principal was hired to supervise the girls.[22]

Harriet learned a little of everything, including French and Latin. English was the major course of study, with classes in grammar, composition, rhetoric, and spelling. Harriet drank it all in. Words, not just education, were important to her as a claim to respectability. When one day she said, "I done it," her pedantic brother John seized her by the shoulders and looking severely in her face declared, "Don't you ever let me hear you say *I done it* again, unless you can use *have* or *had* before it."[23] His intensity taught her that much was at stake.

Harriet preserved a number of her school compositions, neatly written on folded sheets of paper in a fine, spidery script affecting long hanging letters and flourishes. Her teachers had penciled in a few stylistic corrections in the margins and ranked them "10," which was probably the highest grade. Literate and forceful, the compositions were good work for a thirteen-year-old girl, revealing her thought as well as her expository skill.

For the young Harriet, the aim of education was personal respect. She hoped to attain status with schooling:

The stations of men in society, are generally more dependant on education than on birth, or fortune, as fortune can descend to us from others but education can only be acquired by ourselves; and while we have the good chances that we do now to acquire an education, ought we not to improve it, to the best of our ability? and shall we not! we certainly shall, when we recolect that the superiority of one person over another is more owing to education, than to nature.

That Harriet was not happy with her lot and felt it necessary to strive toward a better condition in life she made clear in a composition entitled "Poverty Not Disgraceful." She insisted that in the eyes of God the earnest efforts of the poor equaled those of the rich.

But how much difference there is in the sight of the world between a rich man and a poor man. if a man enters a public place, the first enquiry is "Is he rich" and if he is, all are ready to tender their services. no matter whether he has wit, brains, or not if he a *fool*, no matter if he is rich, but if the man is *poor* no notice is taken of him. he is suffered to pass on without a word, or a bow, or even a nod.

Hotly indignant about the injustices of life, Harriet articulated her ambiguous feelings about wealth, running on her sentences and forgetting her normally careful punctuation. She cynically concluded that though conditions on earth would never be fair, she would persevere, "for I hope that by persevereance, and Good-behaviour, I may be as much respected in after life, as if I was rich."

Respect was what she sought, and she was willing to work for it. In an imaginative piece called "Indolence and Industry" she described a vivid dream:

Methought I saw a chariot, drawn by tigers rush past me, and in there was a most horrid looking female, clothed in black. And on her forehead, in letters of blood I saw written "Indolence." And in her train was Despair, Misery, Want, and Intemperance. Onward the Chariot rushed. . . .[24]

Again she was lashed on by the values she had internalized, the threatening language foretelling the terrors awaiting the lazy. Work! Work! her demons commanded her, lest you become a similar scarlet woman. By contrast, the white-clothed "Industry" was drawn by milk-white horses followed by "Peace, Plenty, Happiness and Temperance." Hard work and education would give her standing in life and compensate for her lack of wealth.

When she was fifteen, Harriet left the high school to return to the mill, her formal schooling over. But she continued her education, through lending libraries, night schools, church societies, and finally the mill itself. She found the regularity of her work of great value. The precise comings and goings, punctuated by the clanging of bells, disciplined the girls, whose hands became deft, their fingers nimble, their feet swift; the habits of industry were to remain with them a lifetime.[25] Harriet made a virtue out of the mill effort to automate her activities.

Books were forbidden in most mill rooms, where they might get caught in the whirling belts and cause accidents, as well as distracting girls from their labors. Some girls found a way around the ban on printed matter by pasting poems cut from the newspaper all over the window frame or the loom.[26] Girls who attempted to sneak a little religion into the spinning room by bringing in their Bibles were chastised and had their Scriptures

confiscated: "I did think you had more conscience than to bring
that book here," scolded one overseer, who had collected a
drawerful of Bibles.[27] The bringing in of reading material can be
seen as resistance to the overseers' efforts to control the girls'
minds as well as their bodies.

Perhaps because of the mills' prohibition of reading, books
abounded in Lowell's after-work life, serving as a major factor in
self-education. Lucy Larcom wanted to study English literature
historically and, finding no teacher, she went to the city library—
established in 1844—to write down extracts of Chaucer, Spenser,
Milton, and Shakespeare.

Private circulating libraries made books widely available for
6¼¢ a week. One of Mrs. Hanson's boarders, a farmer's daughter
from Maine, had taken a job in Lowell just so she could get books
to read. She read from two to four volumes a week, and the young
Hansons were allowed to read them all in exchange for running
to the library. The children sped home from school to snatch
up Richardson, Fielding, Smollett, Cooper, Scott, and many
others—the books were "as good as a fortune to us,"[28] wrote
Harriet.

Novels appealed to the romantic girls. When *Jane Eyre*, the
story of a poor girl who married well (the girls called her "Jane
Erie"), was discovered, it "ran through the mill-girl community
like an epidemic."[29] Harriet noted that she read such books as
John Lloyd Stephens's *Incidents of Travel in Central America,
Chiapas, and Yucatán*, Tasso's *Jerusalem Delivered*, and *Lights and
Shadows of Scottish Life* while she breakfasted before work.[30] Her
brother John, the clerk of the Tremont Corporation's agent,
Charles L. Tilden, was allowed to borrow overnight or for the
weekend any book Tilden left on his desk. John and Harriet read
late into the night and on Sunday, memorizing poetry they might
not get the chance to see again. In this way Harriet learned by
heart most of Longfellow's published work.[31]

Night schools sprang up as a result of the philanthropic efforts
of individuals or organizations such as the Lowell Missionary
Association. Classes met in the basements of school buildings, in
church halls, or in boarding houses, in rooms that were often ill
lighted, unventilated, and unsanitary. Pupils sat or stood around

long tables, with a teacher at each table. Sometimes several hundred students were taught in a single room. Going to school under these conditions testified to the students' strong motivation.

Classes were organized in response to demand rather than according to an established curriculum. Arithmetic and reading lessons were available for working children and others who needed basic skills. Harriet took an evening course in geography, in which the lessons were sung out in unison. She also studied rhetoric in a class where those who "fancied they had thoughts" were taught to express them in writing; the teacher faltered a little on subjects and predicates, but he firmly fixed in the minds of his pupils that they must never mix a metaphor or confuse a simile.[32] After her high-school years, Harriet took private lessons in German, drawing, and dancing, an incredible course of study for a factory laborer. Lowell's diverse and growing population and the strong desire of the people for self-improvement created a lively demand for teachers, both volunteer and paid. Sarah G. Bagley was not untypical in that she both worked in a mill and taught evening school.

All this educational activity was crammed into the mill workers' two free evening hours, from the time supper was over until bedtime, at 10 p.m. As their bedrooms were frequently too cold to sit in, the girls crowded the dining rooms, where they studied, read, wrote, and sewed—their clothes had to be made and mended as well as their schoolwork done.[33] Bagley, who worked as a weaver on the Hamilton Corporation for eight years, testified to the Massachusetts legislature that her working hours were too long and did not allow enough time for eating or for cultivating her mind. But though her health was impaired by her activities, she nevertheless continued her heavy schedule of weaving and teaching for years.[34]

Lectures were epidemic in New England from 1825 to 1850. They were available from many sources. In Lowell, the churches, the Lowell Lyceum, the Lowell Institute, the Mercantile Library Association, the Mechanics Institutes, the Middlesex Mechanics' Association, and other high-toned bodies offered a little learning to eager listeners.[35]

The lecturers were as impressed with their audiences as the audiences were with their lecturers. Andrew Preston Peabody, the Unitarian clergyman and later Harvard professor who lectured constantly for more than thirty years, considered mill girls his most earnest and diligent listeners. In Lowell he found the lecture hall crowded with operatives who had come for instruction rather than amusement. When he arrived every girl had a book in her hand and was reading intently; as he rose to speak the books were laid aside and the note taking began. Peabody claimed he had never seen such assiduous note taking—"No, not even in a college class"—"as in that assembly of young women, laboring for their subsistence."[36] A heavily subscribed course of lectures cost 75¢, the equivalent of half a week's board.[37]

Education eased the tension between the workers' new life of the mechanized, disciplined, regimented factory and their old life of the farm, which seemed free and noble by comparison. A high value was placed on obedience in the mill, and the girls proved themselves generally docile and willing to work, but to maintain their identity as individuals they had to surround their workday with another way of life that defined them as more than factory workers.[38] Harriet's desire for learning resulted from the conflict between an idealization of her culture, in which she felt she had standing as the granddaughter of a patriot, and her real position as an anonymous cog in the industrial machine, a position she perceived but denied. A similar conflict in others partially accounts for the general intellectual ferment in early Lowell. One casual survey indicated that in the 1840s 290 girls, or about a third of the workers of one corporation, spent their winter evenings in night school.[39] This figure still allowed for the other 500 or so girls who squirreled away their wages or spent them on finery.

Literary groups, known as improvement or self-improvement circles, also furthered education. In these, girls were encouraged to express their thoughts in poetry and prose and to bring their work to the groups to be criticized. The circles sprang up spontaneously. Emmeline Larcom, Lucy's motherly elder sister, organized a dozen friends, cousins, sisters, and boarders into such a group in 1837, when Lucy was thirteen. They produced a little

magazine called *The Diving Bell*, which ran twelve issues in manuscript. The group later merged with some neighbors and, with
Emmeline as its first president, became an organized society
called The Improvement Circle.[40]

In 1839 Abel C. Thomas and his colleague Thomas B. Thayer,
pastors of the First and Second Universalist Churches in Lowell,
organized groups of young people who belonged to their respec-
tive parishes. The young men and women were to practice their
public speaking, but as many of them persistently declined, they
were invited instead to write out their comments to be read
anonymously. So many modest young people submitted these
written comments that the reading and discussion of them came
to dominate the meetings.[41] These bimonthly meetings—which
considered "fiction and fact, poetry and prose, science and letters, religion and morals," as well as humor—excited, according
to Thomas, a "remarkable impulse to the intellectual energies of
our population."[42]

Some of the more notable pieces produced for these improvement circles found their way into print in October 1840 as the first
issue of the Lowell *Offering*. The sixteen-page paper of working-
girls' poetry and prose sold for 6¼¢ a copy, helped toward
solvency by two pages of advertisements. Four numbers were
published with great success, and a new series of double-sized
monthly issues appeared the next year. The paper served several
educational needs for the community: encouraging the girls'
writing, providing criticism at the circle meetings, and rewarding
the girls' efforts with publication.

The First Congregational Church as well as the Universalist
churches held literary meetings for its mill girls and published its
own *Operatives Magazine*. Apart from their religious differences,
the groups were very similar. *The Offering, Operatives Magazine*,
and the later *New England Offering* were all eventually edited by
former mill girls. Rising from the spinning frame to the desk of
the lady editor must have seemed the apotheosis of success to the
self-educated mill girls.

Harriet was neither an early nor a constant contributor to *The
Offering*, although she was later its historian.[43] She attended a
meeting of one of the five circles operating in 1845 and remem-

bered the occasion with indignation. The publication office of *The Offering* was filled with operatives "with quaking hearts and conscious faces," waiting to hear their compositions read. Harriet Farley, the imperious coeditor, presided and selected the pieces most worthy of consideration. Harriet's poem was chosen, and the couplet

> It took the tall trees by the hair,
> And as with besoms swept the air

was read, exciting a good deal of mirth among the circle's members. Trees with hair were just too funny. When invited to do so, Harriet did submit two more pieces, which were published, but she never again laid a written contribution on the altar for group judgment.[44] Presenting her literary work for her peers' criticism entailed too great a risk.

Harriet's *Offering* poems are typical of her writing, meticulously crafted and based on some genuine feeling. "Song," published in 1847, is a guarded piece, just the sort of poem to give to an editor who had criticized her poetry.

Song

> Evening is weeping
>   On vale and lea,
> Moonlight is sleeping
>   Soft on the sea.
> Sinless eyes glisten,
>   Loved forms to see;
> Happy hearts listen,
>   Not so with me.
>
> Quiet is stealing
>   Soft to each breast;
> Soothing each feeling,
>   Balmlike, to rest.
> Lonely I languish—
>   Come, come to me!
> Waiting in anguish,
>   Lost one, for thee.[45]

This grim tone characterized much of the poetry of the period. Lucy Larcom later noted that in her early poems "[I] continued to dismalize myself at times, quite unnecessarily." She affected unhappiness for poetic purposes, and though she was healthier than the average girl, she found the idea of an early death rather picturesque. She wrote lines like "And must I die? The world is bright to me" and "Weave me a shroud in the month of June."[46] Though perhaps melodramatic, these lines, like many of Harriet's, served to express the discouragement that it was considered poor form to complain of. The girls' poetry may have helped them deal with their reality by translating it into a poetic realm, where they could resolve it. Poetry was a legitimate way to "share secret sorrows."[47]

Harriet took "some pieces of poetry" to the Lowell *Journal,* where she met the subeditor, William Stevens Robinsons—later to be her husband. He agreed to publish those of good quality, but rejected some, as he said it would not do "to let the editor step aside to make way for the friend."[48] He accepted her narrative, "The Dying Boy," which was a harmonization of a tragic incident in the Hanson family. The angel child here is "Little Willie" Hanson, Harriet's youngest brother, "the brightest and the best of us," who "drownded" in the Merrimack River November 8, 1836. While his busy mother ran her boarding house, the seven-year-old boy had fallen into the river; no one noticed the little body that floated downstream until it was washed ashore on Plum Island, forty miles from Lowell. The family lacked the money and time to go claim the body, which was buried on the island in a nameless grave.[49] The pathetic reality of a mother too busy to watch her child and too poor to bury him, of ten years of grief and guilt, was transformed by Harriet into the glorification of a child's death.

The Dying Boy

'T was eve. The beams of parting day
Gilded the earth; the shadows gray
Stole from their haunts by woodland stream,
Like the dim phantoms of a dream.

A boy lay low; upon his cheek
Death's hand was pressed; his forehead meek
Was marked with pain, and in his eye
So dark and clear, there seemed to lie
A shadow, like the cloudlets white
That dot the moonlit blue of night!
But still he lay, save when he raised
His heavy lids and fondly gazed
On a fair face, grown sadly dim
With anxious, ceaseless care for him.
The evening waned; with boat-like grace,
The moon sailed forth, and on his face
She shed her beams like silver spray,
And washed the dews of death away!
From his young eye the shadow fled—
A lustre o'er his brow was spread—
His outstretched arms a welcome spoke,
While gladly from his pale lips broke,
A gushing sound, like the mellow chime
Of silver bells in the cool night-time:

"Oh, mother! see there! a white-winged boat,
    From the far-off spirit-land;
It comes like a lily-cup afloat,
    Or a sea-bird o'er the sand.

"My sister is there, and father too!
    He beckons, I cannot stay!
And shows a cross to my eager view,
    That he holds to guide the way.

"The dove that we lost so long ago,
    Flies over my sister's head;
The one that unfurled its wings of snow,
    For the land of death, you said!

"And music around them seems to break,
    Like sunshine on flowers bright,
While Cherub forms afar in their wake,
    Make a living line of light.

"I go, dear mother! Oh! do not weep,
　For I long to lay my hand
In my sister's dear, and fall asleep,
　And sail to the Happy Land.

Do you know when we staid so long at play,
　And you pined to see your own,
You came to us? So you'll come one day,
　When you're tired of living alone."

Silent in death was the music-strain;
　And low drooped the boy's fair head;
For the silver chain was rent in twain,
　And the white-winged boat had fled.

'T was autumn—and the snow-flakes began to float—
　On an evening calm and mild,
The mother embarked in the spirit-boat,
　And followed her angel child.

　　　　　　　　　　—Lowell *Journal*, 1846

Death here is pictured as uniting rather than separating. The child is happy to go and all anticipate a better life. The mother's role, her "anxious, ceaseless care," is honorable, the drowning is changed to illness. As she was to do many times, Harriet recreated the universe to turn a failure into a tale of triumph and joy.

　The poems Harriet wrote to qualify herself as a literary figure were carefully crafted but derivative, motivated more by ambition than literary talent, notwithstanding their genuine feeling. She was spurred on by her brother John, who also wrote poetry. But though her poems are not dazzling, her output is not to be dismissed. Her finished poetry was good enough to be published, and her repeated themes reveal much of her striving to better herself and her world.

　Her youthful poetry and that of other *Offering* contributors echoed the work of Mrs. Sigourney, Mrs. Hemans, Miss Landon, and Mrs. Barbauld. That the girls imitated the writing of the well-known ladies of letters of the period is significant: these poets served as models of genteel self-support.

The life of Lydia Huntley Sigourney, the "Sweet Singer of Hartford," is a case in point. As her father was the gardener of a wealthy widow, young Lydia's position was no higher than that of a carpenter's orphan. She educated herself through wide reading and such schooling as was available, much as Harriet did with lending libraries, public schools, and private lessons in German and dancing. Lydia Huntley was a successful schoolteacher and had published a book when she married a well-to-do widower with three children. Her husband was averse to her publishing under his name, as Mrs. Sigourney, but when he suffered financial reverses "conciliation and duty alike succumbed to economic pressure," and she set out to make a living by her pen.[50] The quality of her work was not particularly high, but she was amazingly prolific, publishing fourteen volumes of "dilute saccharine verses"[51] between 1840 and 1850, when Harriet was writing her poetry. Although Mrs. Sigourney did not make a fortune, she was a personage of great note, much admired for her literary work. At the same time, she was practical, considering the secret of her success the combining of the "good and the useful."[52] This "poor girl who had grown famous" was a figure that a self-educated young working woman could emulate.[53]

Harriet's poetry failed to carry her to greatness, or even to fame, but she was a competent writer. Although she produced very little verse in her middle years, her powers continued to grow, and when she was sixty-four she wrote a dramatic sonnet about her inner conflicts. Despite the demanding form, her message is immediate and unconstricted:

The Inward Voice

I said unto my soul, "Be still, nor haunt
   Me longer with they voice divine, nor urge
   Me yet to do the thing I ought, nor scourge
My follies. Off! Thou shalt not rule and taunt

Me thus. I'll eat and drink and die, and vaunt
   My purpose still." Then evil thoughts did surge,
   Usurp her place, and desperate to the verge
Of darkest night I came, that well might daunt

A stronger one. Then I recalled my soul,
  And pleading to the voice that once was mine
I said: "Come yet again and have control;
  Come back, I'll welcome thee and ne'er repine.
But do they will and bravely speak the whole,
  Whate'er betide. In life and death be thine."

—*Magazine of Poetry*, 1889

Education was available to Harriet. She took what she could from the public schools, the libraries and periodicals, the evening schools and private classes, the lectures and self-improvement circles, the examples of older girls and accomplished writers, and she made herself a cultivated person. She was ambitious. Her mother said of her when she was eighteen that she "would defy the universe," so sure was Harriet of her own gifts.[54] She wanted to be somebody, to be considered worthy of notice. She directed her education to that end.

IV

Religion

⌛ I do not believe.

—Loom and Spindle

Harriet Hanson Robinson was raised in the Congregational
Church, in which she remembered being taught to believe in a
literal devil, in a "lake of brimstone and fire," and in the "wrath of
a just God." These "monstrous doctrines," as she later called
them, brought "terrors" that could "hardly be described" to her
young mind.[1] The gloomy doctrinal remains of Puritan orthodoxy still hung heavy over her childhood world.

But if this was the faith of her people, it was not strictly the faith
of her fathers. Both parents had a history of religious deviation.
John Hanson, the carpenter, came from a long line of New
Hampshire Quakers. Harriet identified herself with these shadowy ancestors, imagining them as people of peace, who fought
for the Indians rather than against them, though she never
learned much of the doctrines nor allied herself with the sect.

Harriet's mother, Harriet Browne Hanson, was raised as a
Congregationalist, but as a young woman she had drifted away
from the church. Nevertheless, she sent her children to the traditional church, not wishing, Harriet thought, to take the same
chances with her children's souls that she might be taking with
her own.[2]

For herself, Mrs. Hanson cast her lot with the controversial and
despised Universalists. Though the sect preached the mild, lov-

49

ing doctrine of universal salvation and the brotherhood of man, Universalism aroused powerful antipathy, and with cause. The sect undercut the very basis of religion and morality as they were then understood. If all people were to be saved, then reigning Calvinism, with its central tenets of election and reprobation, was attacked at the core. If Hell was to be denied, the incentive to live a good life disappeared. Universalists, it was said, free from traditional morality, might well be guilty of the lowest behavior. Why should they not cheat, steal, lie, even murder, if eternal horrors did not threaten?

The traditionalists had reason to fear and despise the Universalists. While the Universalists preached love and brotherhood, the movement was revolutionary at the base. It dismissed claims of authority in existing churches. Founded and promulgated by lower-class, uneducated preachers, the sect was democratic and reasonable, whereas the Calvinists were authoritarian and punitive. Universalism threatened the power structure of the traditional church, removing the sting from God's commandments and even humanizing Christ. Universalists refused to take their place in the ordained order of society. Their agitation rattled the framework of life.

Another reason for the traditionalists' concern was the belligerent stance of the Universalists. Not content to go their way in peace and love, they felt obliged to criticize the establishment and to enter into disputations with clergymen of other sects. They pictured their religious work as a battle, adopting a military jargon to talk about it. Sermons and editorials were peppered with references to "watchmen and sentinels of God," "armies of the Living God," "weapons of truth, love, justice," cowards who "shrink from duty," "abandon posts," or "surrender ground." In an effort to win the souls of humankind they fought an opposing army of "black coats and flowing robes," pitting themselves against other ministers rather than sin, indifference, or "genuine" forces of evil.[3] Though the Universalists were not alone among religions in waging this war for souls against other sects, they battled at least as well as any other.

Harriet's mother sat under the preaching of Paul Dean, the dynamic young minister called to assist and then replace Universalism's great minister John Murray. Dean had pronounced the marriage of the Hansons in 1822. Dean's "love of social and religious excitement," "abundant command of language," and ease of delivery fitted him exquisitely for the wants of the denomination. "He must travel much, visit much; and of course, study little. He must preach often—preach doctrinal sermons. . . . He must do battle before the public, with the champions of opposing sects; and his ready command of words enabled him to talk and conciliate, if he failed to convince."[4] This description by a colleague, S. R. Smith, while generous in its praise, also suggests that Dean might have been hasty, unprepared, facile, perhaps a little unstable.

Although Harriet never officially allied herself with Universalism, her mother's chosen religion, any more than she did with Quakerism, the style of Universalism greatly influenced her relations with organized religion. Even more, her brushes with this militant sect seem to have shaped her combative personal style.

༄ༀ༄ༀ༄ༀ

Religion was a major preoccupation of the young women of Lowell in the 1830s and '40s. Many were far from home and felt the need of religious consolation to help them through the day and protect them from evil. Going to church provided a familiar note in a strange new life, and religious societies absorbed much of the spare time available to the girls. The aggressiveness of the opposing sects as they went after the membership—the souls—of the uncommitted workers provided a good share of the liveliness of the town life.

Lowell's founders had recognized the need for religious services and decreed that they should be conducted in the town. In 1826 the first Lowell mill, the Merrimack Manufacturing Company, appropriated $5,000 for the building of a church and rectory. It happened that Kirk Boott, the mill's agent, was an Episcopalian, which is why that minority denomination was chosen for the official church. He named the church St. Anne's, in honor of his wife (unfortunately no Kirk had been canonized). The corporation's board of directors, primarily Unitarians, doubted that an Episcopal church would be supported. To guarantee that it would, church attendance was required of all operatives. They were also required to pay 37½¢ quarterly toward its upkeep.[5] The newly ordained Episcopal minister, Theodore Edson, was engaged as rector.

The second church in Lowell to receive official corporation support was a Catholic chapel. Large numbers of Irish laborers had moved to Lowell to put up the buildings, dig the canals, and build the roads. These "lords of the spade" were the only mill workers not equipped with company housing, and they huddled together in squalid huts on "the Acre." The Irish children often fought with the other children. John Hanson, tough and contentious, was known as "the Bully," and Harriet, who "run scared to school," was "the Bully's Sister";[6] their confrontations with the Irish children were indicative of the tension between the two cultures. Perhaps in the hope of discouraging violence and forging good relations, Boott offered the bishop of the Catholic diocese the use of the old schoolhouse for the Catholics to meet in and a piece of land on which they could build their church. In 1831 they erected a chapel in the Gothic style. Anti-Catholic attempts to wreck the new building were unsuccessful.[7]

Other denominations soon established themselves in Lowell. The Congregational Church had long had a building nearby, in Dracut, but organized another meeting place in Lowell in one of the corporation boarding houses, in 1826. A church was built the next year. Lowell's Baptists had been visited by itinerant preachers before they organized, in 1825. They first baptized converts in 1826, dedicating their first building later that year. The Free Baptist Church started holding prayer meetings in 1830 and was organized with twenty members in 1833; a fine church edifice was erected in 1837, built largely with the savings of more than a hundred factory girls.[8] The first Methodist Episcopal church was organized in the home of James R. Barnes in 1824, with eleven people; a meetinghouse was dedicated in 1827. The Unitarians began meeting in 1829, dedicating their church in 1832. The Universalists first met when Dr. Thomas Whittemore preached a sermon at Carter's Public House in 1826; regular meetings began in their new church in 1828. All of these congregations were established in their buildings and in lively order when seven-year-old Harriet Hanson first came to Lowell, in 1832.

Twenty-six churches were built in Lowell before the Civil War. In the five years between 1827 and 1832 ten were built, establishing most of the active denominations in that growing town. After a pause of a few years, twelve more churches were built between 1837 and 1846, many of which were additional meeting places for already established denominations. Four more churches were built in the early fifties.[9] And there were other groups, which were still meeting in private houses.

Girls who had grown up in isolated villages were exposed to a new richness of religious expression in this open town. They lived in proximity to girls whom they might previously have avoided on the street. One operative wrote of the religious diversity of the thirteen people, including eleven boarders, in her house: these included one Calvinist Baptist, one Unitarian, one Congregationalist, one Catholic, one Episcopalian, one "Mormonite," two Universalists, two Methodists, and three Christian Baptists. Members of the household subscribed to a total of fifteen newspapers and other periodicals, many of religious intent, and they regularly borrowed five others.[10] The religious scene in Lowell was vigorous and competitive. Girls who had grown up in one sect could easily move to another.

Lucy Larcom, who eventually became an Episcopalian, expressed her growing disillusion with Congregationalism in a poetic way. "The religion of our fathers overhung us children like the shadow of a mighty tree against the trunk of which we rested, while we looked up in wonder through the great boughs that half hid and half revealed the sky. Some of the boughs were already decaying, so that perhaps we began to see a little more of the sky than our elders."[11] The many competing sects in Lowell persuaded Lucy that the truth was above the divisive denominationalism that scored the town.

Young Harriet Hanson, the traditionally trained daughter of a Universalist and a Quaker, was perhaps better situated to question than those whose families were not divided in belief. Like many other mill boys and girls, Harriet was naturally attracted to the new sects that stressed the Father's love. She was also attracted to the Episcopal Sunday school, "because their little girls were not afraid of the devil, were allowed to dance, and had so much nicer books in their Sunday-school library."[12] From that library she borrowed and enjoyed *Little Henry and His Bearer*, and *The Lady of the Manor*, identifying with the beautiful Estelle and her romantic milieu. By contrast, the little "orthodox" Congregationalist girls were not allowed to read stories, even religious ones, and one of Harriet's friends took her to task for buying a copy of Scott's *Redgauntlet* because it was a *novel*.[13]

Nevertheless, the power of Evangelical Congregationalism was strong. In 1840, when Harriet was fifteen, a religious revival took place in Lowell. At the prayer meetings held in the houses of her young friends after school, many "experienced religion." Harriet sometimes attended these meetings. One starlit night as she walked home from a Congregational prayer meeting, an older girl asked her whether she was happy: "Do you love Jesus?" "Do you want to be saved?" "Why yes," Harriet answered. "Then you have experienced religion . . . you are converted."[14] Startled, but unable to deny that something had happened, Harriet went home in an "exalted state of feeling."

Doubting, however, the conversion to the church, Harriet called it an "awakening" instead. She felt she had been converted "*from* nothing *to* nothing," but caught up as a convert, she was asked to relate her "experience" in prayer meeting. She was subsequently put on probation for admission to the church. Harriet told her mother, although she had been cautioned to keep the matter secret. Her mother replied she should go ahead with it "if you think it will make you any happier. . . . I do not believe you will be satisfied."[15]

Harriet was sprinkled and baptized into the church, along with many other little girls. But she had not been instructed in Gospel principles, nor had she ever seen the Articles of Belief, to which she was required to subscribe. Even as she was pledging support to the Articles, she realized that she could not accept them. Her major stumbling block was "We believe . . . that at the day of judgment the state of all will be unalterably fixed, and that the punishment of the wicked and the happiness of the righteous will be endless." According to this belief, Harriet alone in her family would be saved. Her mother, an unbeliever, and her little brother who had drowned in the Merrimack would be punished and lost forever. The same instincts that had led her mother toward Universalism caused Harriet to question the reality of eternal punishment. Could a loving and compassionate Father cause fallen innocents to suffer? The classic conflict between the goodness of God and the evils of the world tormented her. The more she thought, the less she believed, and she went to church no more.[16]

The Universalists urged her to join their society. As a lapsed Congregationalist, Harriet would have been a plum. She did have sympathies for the group, but she was hesitant about joining a second church and "fearful of subscribing to a belief whose mysteries [she] could neither understand nor explain."[17]

Certainly, many had fallen away from the church in the past and would continue to do so. The Congregational minister then put the standard procedure into effect by appointing a committee of three, including a deacon, to labor with Harriet. While Harriet and her mother sat at their sewing, the three questioned the girl about her duty as a church member and argued in favor of the Articles of Belief. Harriet sat with downcast eyes, unable to answer, but her mother, who had had some experience in religious disputes, "gave text for text." Harriet "trembled at her boldness" and thought that "she had the best of it." The committee threatened Harriet with excommunication if she did not attend their church meetings and fulfill her covenant to the church. But she mustered up her courage and with shaking voice said, "I do not believe; I cannot go to your church, even if you do excommunicate me."[18]

Perhaps the matter might have ended after the interviews, but in the spirit of the times the holy war had to continue. Harriet's Universalist friends urged her to take action against the threat of excommunication and publicize the reasons for her rift with the Congregationalists. She was to write a letter explaining her theological position, arguing against the Articles of Belief and giving her reasons for nonattendance. The letter, which was published in a Lowell newspaper on July 30, 1842, closes with a

request to her "brothers and sisters" to "erase [her] name" from
the church books rather than follow the "usual course, common
in cases similar to [her] own, to excommunicate the heretic."[19]
The letter was mostly written by Harriet's older brother, John,
who was soon to become a Universalist minister. He used his
sister's case to strike a zealous blow for his chosen faith; John was
an impetuous eighteen-year-old, and his behavior promised a
career similar to some other contentious Universalist divines. In
this way Harriet's case became part of the propaganda war between the opposing sects. Her arguments against the Articles
made excellent publicity for the Universalists and embarrassed
the Congregationalists, who were forced into further action.

> The church book for November 21, 1842, reads: *Whereas*, it appears
> that Miss Harriet Hanson has violated her covenant with this church,—
> first, by repeated and regular absence from the ordinances of the gospel,
> second, by embracing sentiments deemed by this church heretical; and
> *whereas*, measures have been taken to reclaim her, but ineffectual; there-
> fore,
> Voted, that we withdraw our fellowship from the said Miss Hanson
> until she shall give satisfactory evidence of repentance.[20]

At seventeen years of age, Harriet Hanson was thereby excommunicated from the church of her ancestors, for, as she said, "no
fault, no sin, no crime, but simply because [she] could not subscribe conscientiously to doctrines which [she] did not com-
prehend."[21] Actually Harriet was excommunicated because her
newspaper challenge embarrassed the church. She did not live up
to her committments and the church was justified in removing
her.

Her situation after her excommunication was a difficult one.
Girls who could tolerate Baptists and Catholics had a harder time
with a "heretic" and a "child of perdition." Harriet's ostracism
and consequent loneliness served to strengthen her as a person, a
free thinker, and a partisan for justice, but she nonetheless felt
isolation and disgrace. Understandably, she developed a distaste
for religious reading and stayed away from the Bible. She felt
justified in her defiance when the deacon who had visited her and
who was also the overseer in the mill room where she worked
offended some of the operatives by his "familiar manner." Har-

riet called him to her drawing-in frame and remarked that he did not set the example of good works that he had preached to her. Silenced by this criticism, he walked away, and soon after dismissed the reproachful Harriet from his room with an honorable discharge.[22]

Organized religion was now closed to Harriet, but she remained a believer. She moved toward the position Lucy Larcom later outlined, becoming a "creedless Christian." She concentrated, as Lucy was to suggest, on the blue sky beyond the decaying branches of the mighty tree.

🙘🙘🙘

In 1845 John Wesley Hanson, Harriet's older brother, arrived in Wentworth, New Hampshire, to begin his pastoral duties as a Universalist minister. He was twenty-one, a bright and articulate young man, with high ambitions for his future in the church. He had been clerk to the agent in the Tremont Corporation, but with commendable zeal, he had cut himself off from life in the mills and entered an area that promised him some professional standing.

John had attended grammar schools in Boston and Lowell and Lowell High School until he was fourteen. While working as an accountant in the mills he studied Latin, Greek, German, and theology, preparing for the ministry under local Universalist ministers, along with eight or ten other young men.[23] John delivered his first sermon in Methuen in 1843 and preached several times in Lowell before he left for New Hampshire.

At this pastorate in Wentworth, John found the people to be good when "their feelings [were] enlisted," but "many, too many, [were] 'twice dead and plucked up by the roots.'" He felt, however, that he was making some progress, because some of the ninety families in his circuit who had not been to services in eight months promised to attend regularly.

Soon after he arrived John was unexpectedly called to officiate at the funeral of a seventy-five-year-old man who had died a "confirmed Universalist, and in the full triumph of the gospel." The public services, held in a schoolhouse, attracted a large crowd of people of every faith. John's extemporaneous sermon "succeeded beyond [his] best expectation"[24] The young minister foresaw continued success: a field of his own to cultivate and harvest, and adulation from the community at large.

John arranged to have his mother move up from Lowell to keep house for him and enjoy the country life; he was determined to provide well for her. "She must be happy," he wrote to his sister, Harriet, "and I hope will spend her days pleasantly and happily, here, or in a similar place until she goes home to the Fathers. I hope she will not be obliged to work too hard. We shall help her as much as possible, and make her toils light."[25] They settled into a good house with enough land to grow a crop that would supplement John's modest ministerial earnings.

Harriet, now twenty, came to Wentworth for a summer vacation, as mill girls whose families had farms often did. She climbed mountains with the village girls, picked fruit and vegetables, and got healthy and brown. The family unit was complete when nineteen-year-old Benjamin Piper Browne Hanson, their one remaining brother, appeared in Wentworth. Tired of his job in Claremont, New Hampshire, about fifty miles away, Ben had walked over to move in with the family. He could work the land, chop wood, milk the cow, and in the winter learn a trade. For some reason, John's ambitions for this brother were considerably less than for himself and Harriet, who, he hoped, might come back to live with the group until she was married. Less than a month after assuming his new responsibilities, the young minister was master of a house and gathering his family about him.[26] He wrote to Harriet to say, "You, mother and Ella [his intended,] [are] the Sacred Trinity of my Heart! We four can live and love together. May the hour when we shall all dwell together in unity soon arrive."[27] Curiously, Benjamin Piper Browne Hanson who was on the scene, was omitted from the sacred grouping, but he was allowed to share the homestead.

One evening the poetic young parson finished his Sunday labors and, content with his life, pulled up a chair to rest in his sitting room. Under the shadows of a lilac bush, with a book for a desk, he described the scene: "The air is weal with the melody of feathered Songsters. The wood-pigeon is warbling from the rock maple grove on the river bank, and the robin is changing his vesper-hymns. Great bands of frogs are singing in concert, and thousands of busy, brown bees are sounding their low bugles as they hasten to their distant cells."[28] All of nature was orchestrated for his pleasure.

A few months later, however, his feelings about Wentworth and the ministry there had changed. Despite his effective beginning, John's efforts at rousing the people to more religious feeling had been unsuccessful, and he began to consider the Wentworth situation hopeless. The twenty members in town attended, but "they say, that a minister always has good houses for a little while, but that at last, they fall away," and no one can keep a large congregation. The field now promised little harvest, and he began to consider other options: "If experience proves that I cannot have good houses, and do some good, then I go."[29]

To improve his time and his finances, John opened a school, which "prospered finely." He taught forty children five days a week. The local people, who thought an idea could not be put into the head unless it was driven in through the stern, marveled that Hanson did not find it necessary to punish his pupils. But the church work remained discouraging. "Oh dear Harriet of a stormy day here audiences are small enough. Not enough to swear by."[30] He saw the people as a "set of confirmed heathen."[31] By spring he had decided to leave.

In June of 1846 John traveled to New York, where he married Eliza R. Holbrook, a Lowell mill girl he had known for five years. They honeymooned at the state convention of ministers and then went on to his new assignment in Danvers, New Mills. "Wentworth," he had written, "is not the place *exactly* for her, or you, or I to live."[32] The people in Danvers seemed to be likable and faithful, and had newly papered the church in a "superior" manner.[33]

But less than six months later John was discontented with Danvers and the Universalist Church in general. Fearing that his motives for entering the ministry had been romantic and false, he bought some law volumes in order to prepare himself as a lawyer. He planned to leave the church as soon as he could honorably do so with the prospect of making a living.

The "crosses and miserable trials" of a minister's life had become unbearable. John felt "trammelled in thought and deed" by the church: he had to "sit all the day long as it were silent, while all around me great truths are advanced by others." Moved to join in, the young minister had to pull back, for "custom says, these themes are not adapted to the Pulpit." He was sick of making formal calls, preparing sermons, saying set prayers, and, worst of all, attending funerals.[34] In Lowell he had delighted in combating other denominations, winning new souls to his side, but in Wentworth and Danvers he had found apathy. Universalism now seemed an old institution, suited to those who dwelt in the past.

Less than two years after John's promising advent into the ministry he was ready to quit. By September of 1848 he had left Danvers and the church to make his living elsewhere. Casting about for a profession that would involve him in current ideas, he decided to begin a newspaper in Lowell.

༄ ༄ ༄

Harriet, meanwhile, had become involved with another Lowell newspaper editor, William Stevens Robinson. The two became friends and then started to keep company. The first time he "waited on" Harriet at home, another girl referred to him as "Your Mr. Robinson." "Yes, said I, *My* Mr. Robinson!" Harriet did not know why she said it at the time, but apparently she had made her mind up to a union very early on.[35] She would visit William at the newspaper office, down by the depot; through the round window she could see the red-cheeked editor in his shirt sleeves reading the daily papers. They spent many evenings together standing on the central bridge in Lowell, talking and watching the water.[36]

Robinson was a man who loved well enough but was not likely to do anything foolish about it. Gentle and humorous, he went through life in good spirits. A charming valentine he sent to his intended shows his style of lovemaking. These fresh little verses transcend the stock sentiments.

> I can't forget! I can't forget!
> The lovely, gentle Harriet,
> Whose first glance filled my soul with love,
> As pure as Seraphs know above.
>
> I can't forget! I can't forget!
> Her lovely form and Eyes of jet,

Those eyes which caused me first to feel
The pangs which she alone can heal.

I can't forget! I can't forget!
That oft one thought of Harriet,
Has chased my sorrow far away,
And turned my midnight into day.

Do not forget! Do not forget!
That I most truly love you yet.
But one kind smile on me bestow,
To light me thro' this world of woe.

> Ever thine
> My Valentine.[37]

Harriet and William became engaged. Robinson's prospects were good. He was the influential acting editor of a leading newspaper. His debts were paid.[38] He planned to settle in Lowell, where his wife would be a respected matron with an astral lamp of her own. But inflamed by antislavery feeling, he soon quit the Lowell *Courier* and entered the service of the Free-Soil and, later, the Republican Party. He moved to Boston and took over the editorship of a temporary campaign paper, the Boston *Daily Whig*, to work against Zachary Taylor and Millard Fillmore, running for President and Vice President of the United States.

Harriet and William were married after the election of 1848, at his brother Jeremiah's house, in Salem, Massachusetts—neither Harriet's nor William's mother had a house in which they could be married.

Although the wedding had been delayed, in the end it may have been hastened by family circumstances. By September of 1848 Harriet's brother John found himself in desperate straits: his newspaper did not pay and the family circle he had carefully drawn around him had fragmented. His wife, Ella, was living in Maine with relatives. Their daughter, Flory, had died, which devastated both parents. John's mother, Mrs. Hanson, whom he had pledged to care for, was now living with a "Mrs. G.," whose child she had nursed through his last illness. Guilt-ridden for lapsing in his duty, John tried to explain his mother's condition to

Harriet without letting himself look bad for shirking his responsibility:

> The old cough she has had so long is rather bad at present. . . . She is not well, though I do not think her sick. But she must not work and (out of gratitude for what she has done for them) they will not suffer her to. Still, she ought to have a *Home*;—a place where she could be with those who love her and whom she loves.

He regretted leaving Danvers. "I wish you was so situated," he hinted to Harriet, "that you could give her [a home] *at present* for I know that by and by *I can*.[39]

This plea tapped Harriet's basic strength, and two months later, despite Robinson's precarious financial situation, William and Harriet were married. Harriet then had her mother come live with her, and although John later requested that she go to him, Mrs. Hanson stayed with Harriet for the rest of her life. Harriet took the burden upon herself. She became stronger as the men around her showed weakness.

John went on to recover his spirits and his direction. He took on a church assignment at Norridgewock, Maine, where he prized the same conditions he had scorned at Danvers—a small congregation of hospitable and kind people, a low salary, and a large house. He eventually left the pastoral life again, devoting himself this time to editorial work for Universalist publications and to scholarly research.[40] He found himself a place in the church where he could lead the life he wished. He ended up spending almost sixty years in the service of the church he had been eager to abandon in his youth.

෴෴෴

The Hansons were a religious family. All members believed in a Creator and found truth in the Bible. Yet their religious vacillations during the decade of the 1840s were dramatic and profound. In all cases their wanderings took them away from organized authoritarian religion toward a freer, more humanistic belief. Painful wrenchings marked the entrance to each new stage; real suffering was involved as commitments were made and broken. But the pain faded as these individuals moved further from the discipline of the church. When Harriet confessed

to William the story of her excommunication as the greatest of
her shortcomings, he laughed heartily and ridiculed the whole
affair. As if the episode had been a good joke, he would say to his
gentlemen friends, "Did you know my wife had been excommunicated from the church?"[41]

V

William S. Robinson
The Making of an Idealist

ᗡI snuff up the east wind, like the jackasses, & grow fat on it.
—*William Robinson to his mother, 11 February 1845*

William Stevens Robinson sprang from a family similar to Harriet Jane Hanson's. His ancestors were longtime Yankees and hardworking artisans. By William's generation, all pretensions to prosperity and social leadership had been outgrown, and the family lived close to the bone. Robinson accepted his family's reduced fortunes with equanimity. While his wife fiercely accorded to her faceless ancestors every small accolade that could be collected about them, Robinson laughed. He cared more for his descendants than for his ancestors.

No thanks to Robinson, eight generations of Cogswells and Robinsons were searched out and well documented. In the mid-1700s the families had intermarried; William Robinson's two grandfathers each married the other's sister, giving his parents a common ancestry and making them double cousins. Of William's family Harriet concluded that they "esteemed truth and duty above the things of this world; and, though they were people of what was then called good condition, I do not find a wealthy person among them after 1734. At the time of [William's] birth, in 1818, the wheel of the family fortune had reached the lowest point in its descent."[1]

Jeremiah Robinson, William's great-grandfather, lived in Littleton, Massachusetts, and supported his fourteen children as a doctor. His son Jeremiah, the shoemaker, married Susannah Cogswell in 1767, and from this union sprang William's father, another William Robinson. Born in Concord, Massachusetts, April 21, 1776, he married his cousin Martha Cogswell on November 4, 1804. William, Sr., died in 1837, a the age of sixty-one, leaving Martha a widow for twenty years. Their six children all lived to maturity, although only three of them reproduced. William Stevens was the baby of this family, arriving thirteen years after his eldest brother, Elbridge Gerry, who was born in 1805 and followed by Susan Cogswell, Benjamin Franklin, Jeremiah Albert, and Lucy Call. The double names as well as the inclusion of famous names may have indicated a new public consciousness.[2] If, however, the senior William Robinson was striving toward higher status, he was not successful. A poor man, he made hats with his father-in-law for a living; his wife trimmed them.

The Robinsons and the Cogswells had moved to Concord in time for the stirring Revolutionary activities. Lieutenant Colonel John Robinson, the brother of one of William's grandfathers and grandmothers, came over from Westford, Massachusetts, on the 19th of April, 1775, to serve with the minutemen under Colonel William Prescott.[3] That same day one of William's grandmothers buried the church's communion silver in a soap barrel to protect it and confronted two British soldiers with a rifle; in true motherly fashion, she fed the boys, but she would not let them into the house.[4] William's maternal grandfather, Emerson Cogswell, Jr., served as a second lieutenant in the Concord company, putting in some three months of service. William's forebears, in sum, had considerable Revolutionary activity to their credit even if they were not as dramatically involved as Harriet's grandfather Seth Ingersoll Browne.

On the Cogswell side, John, clothier, begat William, who begat William, who begat Emerson Cogswell, tanner. Emerson married Mary Pecker, daughter of Bridget and James Pecker, a wharfinger in Boston. Pecker was the one wealthy branch on the family tree.[5] A half of his considerable property was eventually settled on each of his two daughters, but what became of the inherited wealth is a question; Mary and Emerson Cogswell showed no signs of prosperity. Mary and her sister, Susannah, lived as widows to a great age, Susannah keeping a "pastry school" and Mary teaching a dame's school attended by her grandchildren.[6]

Emerson Cogswell, Jr., the son of Mary Pecker and Emerson Cogswell the tanner, was one of William Robinson's more colorful and documented ancestors. An officer in the Concord militia, he was a member of Concord's Committee of Public Safety, which after the Revolutionary War continued as the "Social Circle."[7] Meetings were held even after the group had dwindled to only Cogswell and a Mr. Fay, who whiled away pleasant evenings with sumptuous feasts, singing, and stories. All women were rigorously excluded from the festivities.

Before Cogswell died, in 1808, the club was revived when a group of notable citizens was invested into its ranks. Dr. Ezra Ripley, Ralph Waldo Emerson's minister grandfather, was one of the leaders of the new group. In 1871 the Circle was still going strong, with an elected membership of twenty-five, who met weekly at different members' houses for nine months of the year. It was for a meeting of this group that William Robinson prepared a sketch of his grandfather Emerson Cogswell, honored founder of the club, and read it to the assembled members.[8]

The dignified Emerson Cogswell was always referred to as "Leftenant Cogsdill," the accepted pronunciation of those words. He wore smallclothes, after the old fashion, and was "portly, not to say fat; so that his wife was obliged to buckle his shoes."

Cogswell began the family tradition of free thinking in religious matters. He fell out with Dr. Ripley, finally refusing to go hear him preach at all. But he continued to read his Bible "diligently, and perhaps ostentatiously," as the people passed by on their way to meeting, and apparently he remained on good personal terms with the minister; when Cogswell died, of consumption, Dr. Ripley attended the funeral and said that Mr. Cogswell was a good man if ever there was one.

Cogswell lived to be sixty-four, and during his lifetime had three wives, among them Eunice Robinson, William Robinson's grandmother, and fourteen children. The only public office

Cogswell held in Concord was that of hogreeve—in charge of impounding stray hogs—to which he was elected at the time of his third marriage, in 1794. It was considered a good joke to put the village's most recently married man into this office.

Cogswell's hat-making enterprise took him to Canada sometime after 1790 in order to learn how to make napped hats, the first in the area. He failed in business, however, because he had bound himself for the debts of a Mr. Brown, who defaulted and fled to the South. Cogswell and Captain Safford, of Beverly, Massachusetts, pursued Brown on horseback for many months and then found him, but they could get no money from him; all they got was title to a poor piece of land. When the avenging pair finally returned on Sunday in January 1800, an attachment had been put on Cogswell's property and the doors had been closed. Cogswell threw open his doors, for which, the next day, he was hauled off to jail. Captain Safford settled the debt for his friend with "buckets of specie" and took over the Cogswell property. The Cogswells were then allowed to live on in their old home, paying rent to the Safford family. William Stevens Robinson was born there, in the comfortable old-fashioned house with a big elm tree planted by his grandfather. But the family no longer owned the land they lived on.[9]

The statistics of past family life make grim reading when unaccompained by personal material. Harriet's ancestors, fleshed out with the carefully culled and preserved anecdotes, take on a character that seemed equal to the vicissitudes of their bleak economic lives. Emerson Cogswell also rose above the unfortunate aspects of his life. If he dissented from the local minister, still he maintained a well-thumbed Bible and kept the minister's respect. If he failed in business and lost his land, he made a manly effort, throwing open his doors in defiance of authority. If he was elected to no higher position than hogreeve, he founded a social club still in operation almost a century later. The man was more important than his net worth would indicate.

As in Harriet's background, there were no ministers, no university graduates, no high town officers, no people of note or consequence among William's forebears. Five generations of honest tanners, shoemakers, and hatters made up the Robinson-

Cogswell family. Yet collateral lines of the same family produced a Ralph Waldo Emerson, and William Stevens Robinson was, in his way, as remarkable as that distant cousin.

Robinson's grandfathers had made hats and shoes. His father continued in the hat business, not self-employed, as his father-in-law had been, but as a worker for Comfort Foster, who had a shop on the main street, and for others. William used to go to and fro across the Common with a dozen or so hats strung over his shoulder, taking them home for his mother to trim.

The independent farmers and artisans of the past had become workers in other men's shops. The land owners were now landless. At this inauspicious point in the history of his family, on December 7, 1818, William Stevens Robinson was born.

A Concord friend first remembered Willie Robinson at two years of age, when he came into her house with his mother, holding fast to her dress. He went everywhere with his mother until he was a big boy, "preferring her company to the rude plays and games of his schoolmates." He was rather frail and no one thought he would live to be a man.[10]

Robinson was a bookish boy, small for his age, who frequented the town's public library and read all the books that came his way. Neighbors remembered him sitting across the door sill of the old family house on nice afternoons with a big book in his lap. The other boys would be off in the woods or swimming in Walden Pond. When he wanted company Willie took his books to a neighboring shoemaker's shop and read to the men as they worked at their lasts.[11] He shared a great deal of Cooper and Scott in that way.

The family worshiped at the Unitarian Church, with the good shepherd Dr. Ezra Ripley as their pastor. Ripley taught children everyday manners, as well as obedience to Christian duty. One November day young Willie Robinson and his brother Jerry brought the minister a gift Thanksgiving turkey from their parents. When Ripley opened the door, the boys thrust the fat bird at him and began to run away. The minister scolded them for their lack of manners:

"Let me show you the proper way to deliver a gift,"
he said, stepping out of the door so he could hand
the turkey in through the doorway.
"My mother sends her compliments," he said, in high
falsetto, "and wishes you a happy Thanksgiving."
Willie solemnly took the turkey and gravely replied,
"Thank you, boys, and now if you will go to the kitchen,
Madame Ripley will give you some cookies."[12]

Willie's quick wit bespoke a bright mind. He did well at the town school, a little brick building where boys and girls together studied Latin and parsed Pope's "An Essay on Man." The grander Concord Academy, or the "Catermy," as Willie and his friends called it, had been established to educate the children of more prosperous families than the Robinsons.[13]

The school available to William seemed to fulfill his needs. He was taught Latin grammar, English composition, and the rule of three with great diligence. Small classes were drawn from the larger registration for specialized studies, and so he recited his Latin in a group of three and Greek in a group of two. When he was fifteen he recited in the first class in reading, in which the teacher commented on his "good emphasis and tone." The next year he stood first of seven in his parsing class and first of six in astronomy. He maintained his primary position the next year as the first student in the parsing class and the first of thirty in composition.[14]

A teacher encouraged Willie to enter Harvard, saying he could work his way through, waiting on tables or cleaning. But his father opposed the idea in a striking statement of out-at-the-elbows pride: "He shall never take a broom there: if he can't get a living without *rubbing against* that college, he may beg."[15] College had never been part of the picture for Robinson men, and Harvard may have been particularly threatening. To acquire an education by demeaning labor seemed a step down rather than up. So this promising student who excelled in academic subjects left school on July 18, 1835, at the age of sixteen, not even staying for the final examination a month later.

Willie did not regret leaving school. He cheerfully told his brother that if he intended to be governor of the state or a

Congressman he should certainly go to college, but that a man could be President of the United States without a diploma. In any case, he did not expect to be any of those great characters but rather planned to learn a trade as soon as he could determine which one.[16] Serious and hard-working but not particularly ambitious, bright and articulate but not eager for company, an excellent student who showed no real desire to go to college, a precocious wit who did not mind having his jokes attributed to others, Robinson was an unusual variation on the American success pattern. His gifts were sufficient to propel him to a high place, and enough powerful men respected him and urged him on that he might have risen higher. But he always drew back from the public role, preferring to make his contributions anonymously or in minor positions.

In August of 1835, a month out of school, the young Robinson went to work for Mr. G. F. Bemis, the editor of the Concord *Gazette*. "I know he wants an apprentice and perhaps he would as leif have me as any one else," William had written to his father.[17] The boy learned the practical side of the business so thoroughly that later on he was able to set his flaming editorials in type as he composed them.

William lived at home while he learned his trade at the *Gazette*. His strict mother now managed the household, as his father had begun to fail; the rest of the family had dispersed. His sister Susan was often away caring for an infirm relative. His brother Elbridge was editing the Norfolk *Advertiser* in Dedham, Massachusetts. His brother Jeremiah was in Lowell, learning the dentist's trade— soon to settle in Salem, Massachusetts, living above his office on Court Street. His brother Benjamin Franklin sold his printing business in Cleveland, Ohio, to become a deputy sheriff and constable. Willie's favorite sister, Lucy, kept a school in Marlborough, Massachusetts. She married and then died young.

Concord had not yet become an intellectual center when Ralph Waldo Emerson abandoned his Boston pulpit in 1834 and went to live there permanently. Dr. Ezra Ripley, Emerson's grandfather, monopolized the spiritual interests of Concord's Unitarians, but Universalism was being preached increasingly, and the Robinsons listened with interest. They had great respect for the

Universalist ministers John Murray and Walter Balfour; Robinson's father, at least, had gone to hear them preach. The family subscribed to *The Trumpet*, the Universalist paper, and soon went wholly over to that belief.[18]

William Robinson, though not particularly religious by nature, enjoyed church services and on occasion went to two funerals in one day in order to hear sermons by both Dr. Ripley and the Reverend Ralph Waldo Emerson. Emerson had not yet delivered his shattering Divinity School Address, of 1838, nor dropped the clerical title from his name, but when he did so, he deeply impressed the country boy. Robinson said later that it was impossible to "estimate the incalculable effect [the address] had upon the minds of the young men of his time."[19] Robinson read the transcendentalist publication *The Dial* faithfully from its first publication, in 1840, and studied the works of the transcendentalists Emerson, Margaret Fuller, Theodore Parker, and others as they undermined the authority of the traditional New England religion. After Emerson published his first book, in 1836, Dr. Ripley's sermons and the teachings of Universalism had less influence on the young mind. William became a "creedless Christian" and no dogmas ever directed his life again. He followed his new teacher, Emerson, who said, "faith makes us, and not we it; and faith makes its own forms."[20]

☙☙☙

In September of 1837, having learned the newspaper trade faster than most apprentices, William went to Dedham, Massachusetts, to work at the case for his brother Elbridge Gerry Robinson, thirteen years older, who published the Norfolk (Massachusetts) *Advertiser*. William lived with the family and was paid $2 a week. A contemporary described him at that time as a "fresh, red-cheecked, prepossessing youth, with a taste for books, and a capacity for the debating society."[21] Elbridge, who resembled William physically and mentally, guided the boy's reading. Both Robinsons were fatalistic rather than optimistic, and took life very easily. Elbridge knew the value of a laugh, saying that it was "worth a hundred groans in any market."[22]

The *Advertiser* was a strong temperance paper that also covered other reform issues and welcomed contributions from high-minded young writers. William became acquainted with several of these writers, who were later to be close colleagues on political matters, among them C. C. Hazewell, E. L. Pierce, F. W. Bird, Seth Webb, Jr., and S. B. Noyes. But the shy young Robinson, small for his age and quiet, did not attract a great deal of attention from his elders.

In June of 1838 William published his first long article, a rather heavy-handed discussion of "The Miseries of a Near-sighted Man." Among other misadventures, the hero invites a young lady to accompany him for a buggy ride, and as he busses her discovers, to his horror, that she is black; this suggests that Robinson's antislavery sentiments, so strong within the next few years, were still undeveloped.[23] A similar piece of literature was his proposed *"Wonderful Providence* exemplified in the remarkable & hairbreadth escapes of W. S. Robinson from the meshes and toils which beset him in common with all the sons of Adam," complete with engravings.[24] Otherwise Robinson's work was primarily setting type, with the occasional opportunity to write up steamboat disasters, which he ironically noted was "extremely cool and refreshing" work in the hot summer weather.[25]

William's mind filled with politics and he became an ardent Whig. "We have beaten the Locofocos [Democrats] handsomely," he delightedly crowed to his mother in 1838. In his spare time he enrolled in a singing school, along with seventy or eighty other scholars. He expected to be a "tremendous fellow on the bass," and thought that this activity just might lead to some connection with a member of the fair sex. "I say mother, don't you think its about time for me to be doing something in that line?" he wrote, and answered himself, "'Get out you dog! time enough these three years.'"[26]

He found Dedham boring and wanted to go back to Concord. "I *stay* here yet—and make myself contented as I can," he wrote his sister Lucy, "but after all, Dedham is a miserable dull hole, and I am sorry that I left Concord to come here. Old Concord, after all, is the King of towns—don't you think so?"[27] William was particularly eager to visit his mother, who had lived alone since his father's death, in December of 1837.

In January 1839 Robinson did return to Concord to take over the *Yeoman's Gazette*, a Whig paper that was squarely "anti-masonry, anti-Van Buren, anti-Locofoco, and [for] the dissemination of Whig principles."[28] The *Gazette*, then without an editor, was made over to Robinson by Daniel Shattuck, Nathan Brooks, and other young Whigs who were determined to have a good local Whig voice. No money appears to have changed hands; Robinson was to finance the paper by advertising and job work. He changed the paper's name to *The Republican*, declaring in the prospectus that it would be "devoted, as its name imports, to the support of sound *republican principles*, to the diffusion of truths, to the exposure of abuses, to the fair and candid discussion of public measures and public men."[29]

In the first issue of *The Republican* Robinson's editorial concerned the election to Congress of Nathan Brooks, a close friend and backer of the paper, as well as an abolitionist Whig. Brooks's Locofoco opponent was William Parmenter. William Robinson proclaimed in a style that was to become characteristic of his political writing:

The real question which you are called upon to decide is this: Will Mr. Brooks truly and faithfully represent your views on the subject of slavery? Will he act and vote as you wish? Do you in all sincerity and fairness believe that he is the friend of justice, liberty, and equal rights; that he is an enemy to slavery, and in favor of its immediate abolition? The times are critical. . . . And will not the people, who have the remedy in their own hands, redress their own wrongs, and right themselves through the ballot-box? To the polls, then! and, regardless of minor differences and small sacrifices, strike for liberty, rebuke corruption, thrust all unfaithful servants into outer darkness, and raise honest men to places of honor and trust.[30]

The high moral tone, the rhetorical questions, the simplification of issues, the tenor of his arguments, the partial repetition of political catchwords—all characterize much of the political writing that Robinson would go on to produce. His easy dramatic style often relied on images and emotions rather than argument. Robinson reported that he was "brim full of politics & [had] little time for any thing else,"[31] but he did include literary matter in his newspaper, publishing Emerson and Hawthorne in the 1830s.

The Republican was a spirited sheet, but it did not flourish. Robinson reported in April 1839 that business was tolerably good, but not so good as a month earlier. A competitor, also feeling the pinch, had "*enlarged*" his paper "*smaller.*"[32] Robinson had to set his thoughts in type and print them, as well as trim lamps, sweep up, and write and read dunning letters, while his competitor sat all day in an armchair snipping selections from "the choicest Locofoco [Democratic] literature." "Reader, you see our relative situations," editor Robinson explained to his public. "He flourishes 'like a green bay-tree.' We must leave off this scribbling, and go to sticking type, or 'The Republican' won't be out today."[33]

Robinson might have been bitter enough, having discovered that he was writing for fun, not profit, but he took things with his usual equanimity. He sold the paper to William Schouler, of West Cambridge, for "not half enough to pay its debts." In his last editorial he announced that he was leaving as he had come, with less than a dollar of ready money:

To our readers we wish every blessing. May they have full purses and content hearts!—not so contented that they will not make an effort to better their condition, and free themselves from the prejudices and bigotry of the age; but so contented that they may not be always grumbling with their lot, and finding fault with the Disposer of it.

He even wished well to his competitor in everything but his Locofocoisms. "He is not half so bad a fellow as we have represented him to be."[34]

The Republican was removed to Lowell, where it was absorbed by the Lowell *Journal and Courier*, William Schouler's newspaper. Robinson went to Lowell with Schouler in 1842 to become assistant editor. There he was soon caught up in the politics of the bustling factory town, broadening his views to national politics, when Schouler sent him to Washington as a correspondent.

Upon his arrival in the capital, the slavery issue immediately involved Robinson. He owed his seat in the press section of the House to the ill luck of his colleague the Rev. Charles T. Torrey, on whose person the notes of an antislavery convention had been discovered, for which he was clapped into jail as an incendiary abolitionist.[35] Robinson was moved to defend Torrey in print and to question the quality of government practiced in the House. "The speeches were filled with abuse and blackguardism." Quarreling, whispering, laughing prevailed. "Members rise with professions of patriotism and love of country, and revile their opponents by the hour together. . . . Truth, honor and their country, may go to the bugs if they stand in the way of their party." Robinson claimed that better debate could be heard in a country lyceum than in Washington.[36]

Many antislavery people had been converted to the cause while residing in the South. Robinson did not record any visits to slave auctions, lashings in the fields, or other haunting injustices. He had no black friends. His disgust with slavery, rather, was intellectual. The subjection of one person to another converted him to abolitionism; he sensed if the system were to continue that free white men might eventually be bought and controlled.[37]

But immersed as he was in politics, the country boy still yearned for his rural home. He confided to his friend Henry Fuller that he rather hoped that Schouler would think his correspondence "poor stuff" and call him back to Massachusetts. "Just suggest it to him, will you?" Robinson asked his friend.[38] Here again was the strange diffidence so central to Robinson's character. Vexed and sore over the injustices of Congress, he was still eager to give up the fight and return to his country life.

William's wish was soon granted. The Washington correspondence was discontinued and he returned to his job in Lowell. His political efforts were aimed at uniting the Whigs behind Henry Clay. When some abolitionists founded the Liberty Party, in 1840, Robinson opposed them, thoroughly believing at this time that the Whigs could and would abolish slavery. He favored reform from within the party, thinking that it would be a mistake to bolt to the Liberty Party. "The Whigs have gone uniformly for the slave; and theirs is the only party which goes to work constitutionally and practically to bring about good results."[39] He developed some dissatisfaction when at the Middlesex County Whig convention nothing was said about slavery.

By March of 1844 Robinson's support of the candidate Clay was rational but not wholehearted. He asked his nephew to send him some election songs about Clay, as "Mr. Schouler would be in an exstasy to hear them. He is a straight-out Whig. . . . He swallows rather more than I can." Robinson now supported Clay mostly because Van Buren's restoration would be the "direst evil."[40]

Robinson's first act of insubordination to the Whig Party came in 1845, when he opposed the annexation of Texas. The dependence of Nathan Appleton and other "Cotton Whigs" on Southern cotton for the Lowell mills had persuaded them to support the South in extending slavery westward, and Robinson wrote a "slashing and crushing editorial" denouncing this wicked weakness.[41] An anti-Texas convention was held in Concord in September of 1845, and strong resolutions were passed.

The war with Mexico that followed from the annexation aroused the spirit of Northern politicians. On September 23, 1846, at the Whig convention held in Faneuil Hall in Boston, Stephen C. Phillips, Charles Allen, and Charles Sumner proclaimed the division of the Whig Party, the divorce between "Conscience" and "Cotton." Robinson acted as secretary at this convention and also wrote up the proceedings for the *The Journal and Courier*.[42] Dissatisfaction and distrust between the two Whig factions steadily grew until the formation of the Free-Soil Party, in 1848.

✸✸✸

The Robinsons were respectable, hard-working, small-business men. William threatened that tradition. In his generation the family had little enough money, and his siblings moved from town to town in an effort to earn a livelihood. For William higher education had been dismissed in favor of a steady trade. But he succeeded in making that trade as unsteady as possible. He threw over his regular employment in Dedham to take on a newspaper unlikely to pay him well and which was bound to fail because of his strong identification with a minority political group and his undiplomatic pronouncements. And the editorial quality suffered because of his lack of capital and help.

Robinson had a good base working with Schouler, the opportunity to travel to Washington and to write influential editorials in a paper with a significant circulation. But in September of 1844, back in Massachusetts, where he wanted to be, he casually threw over that job, too. Mr. Schouler had asked him to collect bills, and Robinson felt that dunning was beneath him.[43] Now on the edge of destitution, he was wholly unconcerned. He planned to stay around Lowell to follow local politics until the Massachusetts legislature adjourned. Then he would find something else.[44]

Robinson found an interim job in Manchester, New Hampshire, editing *The American*, a Whig paper, until election time. After the election he was able to report that the Locofocos had been beaten handsomely and that this pleasant result was "mainly attributed to my coming here! I think the Whigs of the Union had better get me to go about reforming the politics of Locofoco states!"[45] But he was out of a job again; he looked for work and could not find it. He considered going West, but even if he had had the money, he would not have gone; Massachusetts politics were too important to him. He had no overcoat, but he claimed to have gotten used to the cold: "I snuff up the east wind, like the jackasses, and grow fat on it."[46]

Robinson's mother may have resented this unwillingness to settle down, marry, and work for a steady wage. William had been her baby, her devoted son, perhaps her favorite, and he seemed uninterested in curbing his selfish desires. He had no home for her to go to, and though generous when he had money, he was too often broke. His lighthearted improvidence may well have been the cause for difficulties that later developed between them.

Robinson returned to the Lowell *Journal and Courier*. Whether he compromised his stand and collected debts for his boss is unrecorded, but probably he did not. He sat in the office on his damaged three-legged stool, pegging away at editorials designed to crush the slave interests. He became increasingly outspoken, daring to point out to Charles Sumner his political duty. He urged others like Sumner to jump into the fray:

Let not this class of men complain of the meanness of politics, while they sit quietly in their offices, and do nothing to ennoble it; and let them not complain of bad measures until they have done something besides vote against their adoption.[47]

He took charge of *The Journal and Courier* while Schouler traveled to Europe, and anonymously published some strong antislavery articles with which Schouler would not have agreed.

Robinson got little credit for his own productions. As he wrote to a friend who had urged him to speak out for his rights, "I lack the quality commonly and expressively called brass, assurance, impudence, confidence, boldness, or—what you will." Few people knew he was the editor. He was so modest, unassuming, full of jokes and of "the most imperturable good-nature."[48] His own wife was to admit that he was the sort most people would pass by without noticing; he had no presence or manner. But those who came to know him found he did "open well."

Robinson's reticence may be partly accounted for by his modest physical demeanor. He was used to fading into the crowd. The sunny disposition could well have been a defensive posture that had developed from his inability to play any other role successfully.

His social position also limited his possibilities. In democratic America, social differences were all the more powerful because they were not institutionalized and their existence was denied. Robinson's family, however honest and hard-working, was not much, and he did not try to transcend them by dissociating himself or by getting a college education, or even by doing well. He accepted as a rule, much more than his wife ever would, that people moved in fixed social spheres.

Back at *The Journal and Courier*, Robinson "stumbled" upon the young woman who would "answer [his] purpose."[49] He engaged himself to Harriet Jane Hanson, who aspired to make her way with the pen. The match seemed a propitious one. They might have been quickly and quietly married if politics had not interfered.

Robinson's refusal to temper his strong editorials led to differences with the Conscience Whigs, the group that had backed him. Robinson could not support the slaveholding Zachary Taylor as the Whig nominee for President, and he would not keep quiet on the subject. This strong stand alienated the moderates of Lowell, who depended on slave-produced cotton and who looked to Daniel Webster, the leader of the Massachusetts Whigs, to guide them through political difficulties by his compromises. One Conscience Whig wrote, "I read your leaders of Monday with great interest, but with some degree of misgiving, and Wednesday with unqualified approbation. The Webster article has a good deal in it that may be justified on the ground that it is *God's Truth* but I was sorry you happened to say it just now."[50] On June 12, 1848, Robinson—absolutely refusing to be silent for political reasons, needing to spread "God's Truth" without hindrances—left *The Journal and Courier*. The marriage, which Harriet might have hoped was the most important thing to him, was postponed while Robinson fought the good fight against Taylor as editor of the Boston *Daily Republican*—and lost.

After the election Robinson again put his mind to the wedding. He wrote his mother that he planned to be married sometime around Thanksgiving, probably at his brother Jeremiah's house, in Salem.[51] William and Harriet published the banns, secured a room to live in in a boarding house on Boston's Hayward Place, and made plans for a simple family ceremony. "You will of course go down to Salem before that time—shall you not?" Robinson asked his mother.[52] But his mother did not come. Discontented with William's choice or his lack of support, or generally perverse because of her old age, Mrs. Robinson did not travel the thirty-odd miles from Concord to Salem to attend the marriage of her son.

The wedding took place on Thanksgiving, the 30th of November, 1848, at five in the afternoon. Elbridge's family, Jeremiah's family, and Harriet's mother were present as the Rev. B. F. Bowles performed the ceremony; he later said he had never done a better job. The bride, in her white dress with a white satin sash and her laced bronze slippers, remembered nothing of the ceremony but the pattern of the carpet at her feet.[53] At seven the bridal pair set off for their new home.

A few days later William sent his mother a cool report:

I hope & dont doubt, that we shall live happily together. . . . We wished you had been there—but you wouldn't come. Hatty will help take care of me now, mother—you have done it all along & I hope I shall never be ungrateful for your goodness, in bringing me up, till 30 years old—& bringing me up well, I think. You wont care any the less for me & I know I shall not, for you.[54]

The little bride, touchingly deferential to her rather hostile mother-in-law, wrote a few days later:

I wanted to write . . . to let you know that I was not unmindful nor forgetful of you though we are separated and so little acquainted. I hope too by this means to be remembered by you kindly as I always hope to be.[55]

So began a marriage with lofty hopes and modest promise, the union of two extraordinary individuals who nourished each other's needs and were the richer for sharing their lives.

VI

Married Life

Introduced Hattie to Mr. Bowles as the man who married her father and mother. She turned quickly to him and said, "Thank you." It amused us. Another good thing I remembered. Some one asked her how her father was at home whether he unbended there and how he appeared in the "bosom of his family." She turned towards me and said, "There is the bosom, you can enquire there."

—*HHR Diary, 30 May 1871*

One of Harriet Hanson's relatives disparaged the choice of William Robinson for a husband. His party was not likely to last long and then where would Harriet be?[1] The relative was right in assuming that William's connections with institutions would be brief and that the family would know hard times. His tenure as the editor of the Boston *Daily Republican*, a Free-Soil and antislavery paper, was short. In February 1849 Henry Wilson informed him that he had hired a new man for the office and that Robinson's salary would be reduced from $20 to $15 a week. No hard feelings were involved, but "much complaint [had] been made . . . about the paper since the election." Robinson was to feel free to leave at any time after a few days' notice. Chagrined and insulted by the demotion, Robinson left the paper the same day.[2]

Now there were two out of a job. Harriet did not record her alarm at being cast adrift in the world. Her jocular brother John commented that as Willie was not then doing anything, he had at last entered that profession "for which nature intended him!" John suggested that Robinson begin a new Free-Soil newspaper in Lowell—if he could do so without incurring any risk to himself. "Make those rich old cocks fork over. They can, they ought,—and I believe they will."[3] It is interesting to remember that John himself had recently gotten into financial difficulties editing a paper in Lowell.

Charles F. Adams and other Free-Soil leaders regretted that Robinson had been dismissed so summarily, and there was considerable opinion that something should be done for him. J. G. Abbott and John W. Graves, an overseer on the Lawrence Corporation, along with some others, raised a sinking fund of $500 for the publication of a new newspaper. Robinson added a few hundred dollars of his own, and preparations for the publication of the Lowell *American* began.

Robinson was welcomed back to Lowell by his old pro-Taylor friends, who liked him though he now stood on the wrong side in politics. He was back where Whiggery was strong and cotton was king. An unidentified newspaper colleague observed that while Robinson was "unquestionably the ablest political editor we have ever had in Lowell," the Free-Soil ground "is just now pretty well covered by the Boston *Republican* and consequently establishing a new paper must be the work of time, patience and perseverance."[4] *The American* competed directly with two papers—*The Daily Republican* and the old Lowell *Journal and Courier*—that Robinson previously edited. Practical minds would have assessed the situation and seen that success was unlikely.

While Robinson was editing *The American*, the family was on short rations. Harriet later figured that during the years of its publication the family spent an average of $400 a year.[5] But she denied that she suffered from privation. She admired Robinson's indifference to luxuries and tried to be like him, as his willing "younger companion" and student. It was in those years of self-denial, she later recounted, that her husband tried to teach her the "real meaning and duty of life,—that it was not to live for ourselves alone, or for those we love, but to forget ourselves, to aim at a higher life, and to do some one thing to make the world better, wiser, and happier for our having lived in it."[6] Harriet's high-minded reading of Robinson's activities gave her own hardships meaning, but did not describe his. He was driven by need to expose sham rather than to sacrifice.

The lack of money closely circumscribed the Robinsons' family life. Harriet and her mother managed on two calico dresses each a year. The editor bought no clothes. As there was nothing to wear, there was no churchgoing. They did not water the baby's milk or burn the chamber doors for firewood, but they thought twice before spending a penny.

Harriet's mother, Harriet Hanson, helped the family live decently on the edge of poverty. She did all the cooking and assisted with the children and the cleaning, labor that was as uncomplaining as it was unrewarded. Harriet's eagerness to have her mother back from a visit was practical as well as loving—"You can't think how much I want to see you, mother. I shall be glad when you come home. I really dont know how to get along without you."[7] William said that Mrs. Hanson was "good enough to redeem the sins of a whole generation of mothers-in-law,"[8] a comment that acknowledges the expected difficulties with mothers-in-law as well as Mrs. Hanson's martyr status.

The unrestricted society of her mother was not necessarily the company a young wife would choose, and Harriet frequently lost patience with her. "Mother and I," she noted, "with whom I am mostly with—don't have many subjects in common—of interest I don't suppose we have ever found each other out yet."[9]

On December 4, 1850, a little over two years after the Robinsons' wedding, Harriet gave birth to her first child, who was named Harriette Lucy, after her mother, her grandmother, and William's late sister. Perhaps the fancy French spelling of the daughter's name—which Harriet occasionally used for herself—indicated some ambitious hopes for the infant. The baby came "gently and deliberately" into life. "It's a girl!" William was told. "What's a girl?" quoth he, half awake.[10] After assuring himself that all was well, he described Hattie's advent to his mother:

I know you have been waiting anxiously to hear we get along, & will be glad to know that [Harriet] got along pretty well. The baby—a girl—was born about one o'clock this Wednesday morning. It is hearty & healthy & weighs, we judge, about eight pounds.[11]

A couple of days later William had overcome the trauma of childbirth and regained his characteristic tone. "You may brag on the baby as much as you please. It is a nice one."[12]

The baby delighted her parents, who reported that she was "as fat as butter and so cunning and pretty. . . . You would almost eat her up."[13] They were always finding some new wonder in her. This love for their daughter was unfeigned and poetic. When Hattie was fourteen months old Harriet wrote of her, "Dear little creature how pleasant it seems to have her round she fills a large place in our home and hearts, even her little *shoes* when she is asleep are full of interest, and when she wakes she is our life. Dear little Hatty."[14]

So valued was little Hattie Robinson that her family sacrificed to buy her a treasure, a silver spoon. Judge Ebenezer Rockwood Hoar, an old Concord friend, had given the Robinsons a dollar each New Year's Day to buy a turkey. Harriet had thriftily put by 1851's dollar, and with 1852's dollar, and sixty-two cents saved up, she bought the spoon and had it marked "Harriette Lucy 1852." The spoon was to be "hers forever, if she is spared to us."[15] So the household scraping by on $400 a year spent a considerable sum for an extravagant item, a silver spoon for a little girl.

Despite her pride in motherhood, some ambivalence crept into Harriet's comments. One day she stayed away longer on a shopping expedition than she had planned and the baby was crying hard when she got home. Harriet "soon gagged her," but she "felt condemned ever since for staying so long." Hattie was "very good indeed, scarcely any trouble, yet she is a *baby* and the best of them are a great deal of trouble, or care."[16] This language contrasts with her usual loving words.

Harriet weaned her baby at fourteen months. A natural trepidation, combined with the warnings of well-meaning relatives, indicated the seriousness with which Harriet contemplated this breaking of the last physical bond between mother and child; she feared the baby would become ill. The event thus took on a ritualistic importance beyond its physical aspects, but in fact the weaning went very smoothly.[17]

By January 1852 Harriet was pregnant again, and on September 11, 1852, at 3:30 a.m., Elizabeth Osborne, a "*peart* and bright

& strong" baby and the easiest birth of all, was born.[18] Lizzie was named for her mother's childhood friend, a fragile girl who had worked in the mills and died young. This was the only time Harriet and William departed from using family names for their children.

For Harriet the years in Lowell as a married woman (1849 to 1854) were a period of limited access to the world. Her life was circumscribed by her husband, children, and mother. She scarcely mentioned her friends who still worked in the mills—two exceptions being Harriot Curtis, a Lowell *Offering* editor, and Lizzie Clemence, a recently married mill girl like herself.

Harriet showed little interest in making new friends. As she did not go to church meetings, she had few opportunities to meet housewives like herself, and she neither entertained nor received invitations to other homes. She dismissed the overtures of her landlady, Mrs. Morrill, and was glad to move to a house on a more secluded street, distant from disagreeable neighbors[19] (it was in this brown cottage on Abbott Street that Lizzie was born). When a neighbor shoveled away a new snowfall on the Robinsons' walk, Harriet was surprised and pleased; apparently such neighborliness was uncommon.[20]

During the evenings William read to Harriet from serious books sent to the newspaper for review, while she sewed and mended. This "companionship of a mind more mature, wiser, and less prone to unrealities than [her] own," she wrote, continued her education, and gave her the "leisure to read good books . . . in the quiet of [her] own secluded home."[21] With her determined optimism Harriet remembered, when recalling those days, that she was "young and full of hope and light of heart and busy with [her] babies." She wondered why she had ever grown ambitious and worldly.[22]

If Harriet had few friends, she did have her larger family. She and William often visited William's brother Jeremiah in Salem until he moved west to Cleveland, where his brother Franklin had already settled. Mother Robinson, reconciled to the Robinsons' marriage, made the rounds from Concord to Salem; to Lowell, to see William and Harriet; and to Dedham, to see Elbridge. Elbridge died during this period, in 1854, but his widow, Martha, and children, Mary and Nathaniel, remained part of the family circle. Such visiting, along with mutual help, kept the Robinsons close.

The Hanson relatives also formed a network by regular visiting. When Harriet's younger brother, Ben, turned up after three years, he had improved in looks and ambition, and was keeping school and studying law. He married a local beauty named Angelia Gould. This early promise ebbed away, however, and when he later resigned from the army, the family realized that his "want of *force*" would doom him to subsistence living.[23]

Brother John, the Universalist minister, was now comfortably settled in Gardiner, Maine, as pastor in a handsome church with a bell and two clocks. He worked hard, later serving as chaplain and historian for the Massachusetts Sixth Regiment during the Civil War and then moving on to Dubuque and Chicago, where he was involved in Universalist publishing.[24] Mother Hanson, who was so much a part of the Robinson family, began her regular annual long visits to see these sons, visits that shaped the year for Harriet, for then she was obliged to keep house alone.[25]

While Harriet was occupied with her babies, William worked hopefully at his paper; by November of 1849 the thrice-weekly *American* had more than 500 subscribers.[26] In 1851 he decided to extend his sphere of influence and succeeded in being elected to the Massachusetts House of Representatives. Now holding two jobs, he spent a good portion of the next two years commuting to Boston. As William departed for the legislature, Harriet recognized an upsurge in family fortunes. She began a journal and persuaded William to write in it:

I am glad on many accounts that I am chosen—sorry on but a few. I love my home & do not like to be away from it. But I shall get a little money and much knowledge, and shall extend my acquaintance & by that means, I hope, my facilities for getting along in the world.[27]

Harriet was more lyrical:

My ambition for him is great, though not so great as my love, but being tied to me will not earn him bread, or fame, or a knowledge of the world, or of himself which is greater than all. Oh my Willie I would have you honored in the world as much as I honor you, and no weakness of mine should ever clog your footsteps for an instant.[28]

These two comments describe the relationship between William and Harriet during most of their marriage. He was fond and warm, she fiercely proud and ambitious for him. Her diary references to him seem to be universally positive: "(Dear good and true husband) I love and honor him more every day." "After three years of marriage my heart still leaps when I hear his step, and is the happier for his coming." "My darling and I sit here in the parlor together with baby asleep in his cradle, all the rest are abed, we want no other company. He is a good hubby to me." After a session of the legislature closed she wrote, "I feel as if I had a companion once more. I find little real companionship without him." William was less effusive: "I know she loves me well, & she deserves all the love I can give her."[29]

William coped with the hard business of two jobs, rising at half past six to catch the railroad cars for Boston. It would be eight before he got home to Lowell, and although Harriet helped with the editing, he would have two or three hours of work still to do on the paper.[30] He carried this double load for two terms.

Robinson's efforts to gain political influence and establish an antislavery newspaper in Lowell were both eventually unsuccessful. The paper never paid its way, and Robinson was caught between trying to pay his bills and trying to collect what he was owed. "We *really need* all that is due us, and *must have it*, or we cannot pay our debts,"[31] he repeatedly published in his paper. Finally, exhausted by business worries and overwork, he fell ill with typhoid fever and did not leave his room for eleven weeks. A hired friend put out the paper during Robinson's illness, and after he recovered he ran a few more numbers, but *The American* was finally discontinued.

Robinson published the Lowell *American* for a total of four years and seven months. For his years of labor he had little to show but an increased reputation as an impractical idealist and some fat debts. Harriet conceded "In a pecuniary sense it was a failure, but in no other."[32]

❧❧❧

When *The American* failed, the Robinsons shook the dust of the ungrateful Lowell from their feet and moved to Concord. They lived there from August of 1854 to the fall of 1857. Robinson said that anything, "however feeble and uninteresting, that had the name of Concord upon it, would always be interesting" to him.[33] But it was filial responsibility, not love of home, that drew him back. His mother was old and unwell, and since Elbridge's death and Jeremiah's move westward, Willie was all she had.

After the demise of *The American*, Robinson became the assistant editor of the Boston *Commonwealth*, a daily Free-Soil paper that had resulted from the merger of three newspapers, including the old Boston *Daily Republican*, which Robinson had edited. In 1854 *The Commonwealth* changed hands and was renamed *The Telegraph*. After the change Robinson remained assistant editor and writer and then came briefly into the editorship, before his outspoken editorials against slavery, and particularly the Fugitive Slave Law, caused his demotion back to writer. Nevertheless, throughout the Concord period William was employed at a steady wage and the family welcomed comparative prosperity.

Life in Concord promised pleasant social experiences. Harriet recorded that she had been to eight dances in the winter of 1854. The family rented a pew and went to the Unitarian meeting on Sunday. They attended lectures, had callers, and made visits. The fine free library of Concord provided books and they read a good deal.[34]

Robinson commuted daily to Boston on the Fitchburg railroad, which since 1844 had been transporting Irish laborers, lyceum speakers, and commuters between the city and the small market town of Concord to the west. By the 1850s Concord had become a center for progressive thought, and Robinson, to some extent, moved among the literary leaders. Hawthorne had already departed for Liverpool as American consul, appointed by his old friend President Franklin Pierce, but the Alcotts and Channings were acquaintances of William's and Harriet's, and the Robinsons revered Ralph Waldo Emerson.

They knew the Thoreaus well, for they rented their house from John Thoreau, father of Henry David, who came to work the land. The younger Thoreau was often seen walking across the sunny meadows, and sometimes he called on the Robinsons. Sitting with his head bent over, he could carry on the conversa-

tion all by himself, outtalking people even in their areas of expertise.

Harriet did not have a great deal of respect for this loquacious
neighbor. She questioned the economics of *Walden*, convinced
along with other incredulous townsfolk that Mrs. Thoreau had
regularly supplied her son's larder. Harriet resented Thoreau's
shambling, casual way, and thought he should have done more
with his talents and education. She found the family eccentric
rather than admirable.[35] When the Robinsons bought a plot in
Sleepy Hollow Cemetery, Harriet noted with pride that it was
next to the Hawthornes' but for one, that unidentified "one"
being the Thoreaus'.[36] She recorded that Thoreau was "considered to resemble Mr. Emerson but I do not think he does. Mr. E.
is a god by the side of him."[37]

Of Emerson she later gushed, "He is most a divine man, besides
being so great a genius, there never was a better husband, father,
or family man, no doubt, besides being a most excellent towns-
man and public spirited withal."[38] One of Harriet's first published
articles was a worshipful tribute to Concord's great man in the
form of a review of a biography by Oliver Wendell Holmes for
The North American Review. (The $7 fee brought her great plea-
sure.)

Mr. Holmes's book may be delightful reading to some persons, but many
of its details are too trivial to suit the taste of such a devout admirer of Mr.
Emerson's genius as your correspondent. . . . It pains me to read that
"Master Ralph Waldo used to sit on a brick wall, longing for pears which
belonged to his neighbor" and that he was once "carried in his night-
gown to a neighboring house." But if these little details of a hero's life are
painful to read, what shall be said of the story of Emerson as a perpetual
devourer of that New England conglomerate, pie? Yet Mr. Holmes tells
us that Mr. Emerson was a "hopelessly confirmed pieeater"; that he ate it
for breakfast, when "morning opes with haste her lids," on his journeys,
and perhaps even for luncheon, when he was writing those great
thoughts of which your critic so justly speaks. Shall a god eat pie? I do not
like to have my illusions dispelled in this way. I like to think of Emerson
and the other great writers as I know them through their books, and
prefer to form my own estimate of their characters. I deplore this literary
hash, and I desire in future to take my gods "clear," neither seasoned by
weak praise nor warmed over to suit the popular taste.[39]

Harriet Robinson's friends in Concord were drawn from William's old acquaintances: Sarah and Nathan Stow, a lawyer and legislator; Mary Merrick Brooks, leader of the Concord Anti-Slavery Society, and her husband, Judge Nathan Brooks, a founder of Concord Academy; Dr. Josiah Bartlett, the abolitionist physician;[40] Ephraim Bull, cultivator of the Concord grape, and his family. All these were longtime friends. Judge E. R. Hoar continued to buy the Robinsons an annual New Year's turkey. Cousin Anna Cudworth and friend Lizzie Clemence, of Lowell, came to visit. Harriet revived her distant friendship with Lucy Larcom, and they were close for many years.

Harriet Robinson had now been married for almost six years. She had grown stout but looked better, some said, than when she was slimmer. She had learned to make bread and was not above the petty cares of housekeeping. She did some reading, though was no "blue stocking." She considered herself to have come a long way from the "sentimental and misanthropic young person who used to write 'such stuff.' "[41]

On October 6, 1854, "after 25 hours illnes," a third child was born to Harriet and William. Young William Elbridge was named after his father and his late uncle. Harriet recorded some illuminating facts about this confinement.

"I took ether, but did not escape the *finale* nature was stronger than ether." She carried out the cold-water treatment (hydropathy) "daily and freely" and was attended by a cold-water nurse. On the fifth day after the birth she walked out in the garden. "I was never as well nor so free from sick days and nights as at this time, no long wearisome confinement no fever, no medicine, not even *castor oil*, all to be attributed to the free and faithful use of *cold water*."[42]

In the early days of her marriage Harriet had fastened on two popular medical systems—homeopathy and hydropathy. Both have since been challenged and are no longer in the medical mainstream, though advocates for each can still be found. For Harriet they represented practical and humane approaches to illness, as opposed to the standard practices of nineteenth-century doctors, who commonly bled, vomited, and purged patients in an effort to rid them of poisons and relieve the pressure in their sick bodies. In a simplistic way these traditional practitioners were styled as "allopaths," or doctors who tried to cure disease by producing conditions incompatible with the disease and so forcing it out. In February 1858 Harriet declared that she was and had "long been sick of allopathy in all its forms," and that for a year or two she had given her allegiance to homeopathy.[43]

Homeopathic doctors prescribed minute doses of drugs or benign substances in an effort to cure diseases by producing similar pathologic effects upon the body. If the drugs were stronger than the symptoms, the disease would be destroyed.[44] Homeopathy filtered down to middle-class people, who learned to practice the system at home. Supplied with a book of directions and a box of phials of globules and powders, mothers treated their little ones with harmless medicine and hoped for the best.

With book and box Harriet dosed her family as the situation dictated. She used homeopathic medicine on her mother's boils[45] and later on her baby Willie's "milk-crust." When Willie's head did not heal she went to her family friend Dr. Bartlett, who treated the sores with salve, saying that a spoonful of cold water was as valuable as homeopathy. "He goes too far," opined the convert.[46] When little Willie was so sick she did not "dare to trust" herself she called in a homeopathic doctor, as she did when Lizzie came down with typhoid.[47] The children recovered nicely.

One literate homeopathic doctor encouraged the use of cold water—"There can be nothing better"—adding that ice could be used with perfect safety.[48] Harriet had always had a great deal of faith in cold water, and perhaps because of this connection with homeopathy, she became a disciple of hydropathy, the popular system in which all ills were treated with baths, wet compresses, or drinks. Hydropathy was the principle behind the water cures and spas to which the well-to-do withdrew, for social as well as medicinal purposes. Harriet adapted the cure to her own needs. She herself took no medicine except cold water. She applied cold water locally on whoever in the family was ailing and required all members to take cold baths daily.[49] Mrs. Hanson, who *hated* the bath, almost cried when her daughter forced her into the tub.[50] Harriet retained her faith in the curative powers of cold water throughout her life, wrapping herself in a wet sheet when sick until she got up a good sweat. She also advocated several other cures: "Sleep is my medicine. & fresh air day and night."[51] She kept on hand "Neutralizing Powder and composition tea," two old herbal Thomsonian remedies,[52] and worked out other variations on an eclectic medical system that suited her taste. "I have faith in anything that will cure—whatever 'pathy' it is of."[53]

In her care of the sick and infirm, Harriet found her mother-in-law, Martha Robinson, old, tired, and cross, her chief burden. Mrs. Robinson lived in a furnished room most of the time, but in the winter she moved in with her son William, at which time she mistreated the children. She was not happy with anything but reminiscences of the distant past and what was forgotten by everyone else. When Martha Harriet Robinson, Jeremiah's daughter, announced her coming marriage, her grandmother became very angry; she thought the girl a "fool," and declared that she would write her no more letters.[54] Perhaps Mother Robinson thought Martha Harriet should remain single for the sake of her grandmother's correspondence. The incident may help to explain Mrs. Robinson's strange behavior concerning William and Harriet's marriage. She wanted the past to remain as it was; William would always be her baby and Harriet was an interloper. Mrs. Robinson was not well when she came to stay with William and Harriet in the late fall of 1856, and she died soon after her arrival, at the age of seventy-three. She had been a widow for twenty years.[55]

❧❧❧

With the advent of young William Elbridge the Robinsons had every reason to be proud of their growing family. Harriet counted her blessings, thankful for Hattie, a large, stout girl of four with dark hair and eyes, for Lizzie, who was straight and slim with large eyes and lighter hair, and for blue-eyed, hairless Willie.

Needless to say, however, Harriet's cares had also multiplied with these beloved additions. Moreover, despite her friendships, Harriet found Concord dull, "like the sleeping town in the fairy book where the very flies slept on the wall."[56] She seldom met anyone on her walks, and she was scornful of many Concord women, who were too "tender" to walk a mile.[57] Harriet, by

contrast, was healthy and blooming; a Concord friend commented that she knew of no one who looked as healthy and well as
Harriet did. (Harriet told her, of course, that she owed it all to
cold water.)[58]

The Robinsons had also grown dissatisfied with their Concord
house. They decided to move. William wanted to be nearer Boston, and Harriet wanted to be out of Concord:

It is a dull old place. It is a narrow old place. It is a set old place. It is a
snobbish old place. It is an old place full of Antideluvian people and
manners. It is a sleepy old place. The women are all sick. the leaves never
shake on the trees and the children never cry in the streets. It is full of
graveyards, and winters are endless. The women never go out, and the
streets are full of stagnation. It was so still that walking up and down its
street filled me with horror. I used to feel that I must jump up and *holler*,
or do something desperate to make a stir. A good place to be born and
buried. but a terrible, wearing place for one to *live*.[59]

William had been turned down for membership in the Social
Circle, the club founded by his grandfather,[60] and perhaps this
and similar slights persuaded Harriet that they would never rise
to the top of the heap, however unworthy the heap might be.

A political friend, John Quincy Adams Griffin, a lawyer and
later a state representative, urged them to settle in Malden, Massachusetts. There the Robinsons hoped to make friends with
people different from those in Concord. "A strange place, but
near Boston, and we like. It certainly costs less to live and we enjoy
more."[61]

Malden, just five miles north of Boston across the Mystic River,
boasted beautiful woody heights and rocky glens. It had been cut
off from the metropolis by two toll bridges, but when in 1845 the
Boston & Maine Railroad ran through the town, providing easy
transit to the city, industry and commuters moved in. The tolls
went down and eventually were ended. A line of omnibuses that
crossed the river via ferry also increased access to Boston. The
population had risen rapidly just before the Robinsons arrived, in
1857.[62]

William Robinson at this time was editing and writing for the
Boston *Telegraph*, fervently opposing Know-Nothingism. When
in 1855 the "enemy" was elected——the stockholders of the pa-

per deemed it wise to depose the editor, although they continued to publish his articles. Robinson was then available in 1857 when Samuel Bowles, editor of the Springfield (Massachusetts) *Republican*, attempted to consolidate three papers—the Boston *Traveller*, *The Telegraph* and *The Atlas*. Robinson was engaged as a writer for this new *Traveller*, but the consolidation lasted only a few weeks. *The Traveller* returned to itself, *The Telegraph* and *The Atlas* were no more, and Robinson was again out of a job.[63] With the Know-Nothing American Party dominating state politics, Robinson's articles could find no home. He was told that his writing would "kill any daily in Boston."[64]

In 1856 Robinson had begun his weekly "Warrington" letters for the Springfield *Republican*, a paper strong enough to deal in controversy. Rather than censoring Robinson, *The Republican* ran opposing editorials. The paper paid him $2 a letter. The next year he began writing weekly letters for the New York *Tribune*.[65]

Robinson regretted being out of work, his wife recorded, less because of the money he was not earning than because he was obliged to sit idle when he was eager to write. He thought the public could not "afford that I should be silent."[66]

Harriet Robinson got tired of the struggle. "Out of work," was a hard thing for a woman to hear from her husband when they had just moved to a new town and had three small children.[67] "Sometimes I feel as if he need not work so hard and would earn more, if he were not so scrupulous—so rabid," she lamented.[68] Times were hard then and she "almost gave it up though [she] did not tell William that it was no use standing out and being so much in advance of the majority of the people."[69] This was the only time that Harriet was tempted to give up the struggle.

How interesting that the outspoken Harriet, who bridled at having herself and her children sacrificed to Massachusetts politics, said nothing about it! The Robinsons' marital relationship did not allow her to question her husband's decisions. Even when the decisions cut across her interests she had to affirm that they were right.[70] She was only grateful that the "odour of a shuffling politician hangs not on his garments."[71]

Robinson turned his hand to odd jobs but found no relief. Then a tempting offer came his way: $25 a week for a staff position on the New York *Tribune*, a stable, prestigious newspaper. His friends saw the New York offer as a great chance for him; but he turned it down. The necessary divorce from Massachusetts politics and the grim prospect of big-city public schools for his children dissuaded him. To his wife, who had urged acceptance, he said, "Don't hanker after the loaves and fishes."[72] Neither poverty nor prosperity, not the well-meant wishes of his friends and wife, not the hunger of his children could move him.

The situation was pretty desperate. Money was so short and the Ferry Street house so damp that the family was constantly ill. At this point, on May 4, 1859, Harriet gave birth to a "man child."[73] The baby was named Edward Warrington, the Warrington part after his father's *nom de plume*, and called Warrie.

Later that year five-year-old Willie grew sick. Harriet nursed him and sent for the homeopathic doctor to treat him. But the ministrations proved unsuccessful. The promising child died. The diagnosis was typhoid fever, caught from their damp, unhealthy cellar.[74] The family was devastated. Already weakened by their financial trials and steady illness, they felt they could not bear this loss. William then "first knew grief, and felt its heaviness upon him."[75] Harriet felt rage, fury that she had been deceived by homeopathy. Her boy had been sacrificed to ignorance. She burned her book and threw the box of pellets into the sea.[76]

Willie's death caused the family to reconsider religion. Days were spent in vain speculation. "O my bright faced boy, my sunny-eyed boy where is he?"[77] mourned Harriet. The Robinsons could find no comfort for their loss , and William wrote: "What is called the consolation of religion in time of sorrow is but another name for insensibility. Infidels and philosophers put religionists to shame at such times."[78] The family was forced to believe in resurrection and an afterlife, since they could not face the thought of Willie's being nowhere, and death lost its terror for Harriet. It seemed a little thing to die herself, for Willie had already done so.[79]

Lucy Larcom offered her sympathy in a letter that could only torture the distracted mother:

I have often thought when with you, what a terrible thing it would be if some such blow should fall upon you; your happiness always seemed to

me so wholly centered in your little family circle. I hoped you might
never be called to suffer this; but the wise and good Father above knows
just what his children need.[80]

The idea that the Father had taken her son to teach her a lesson
was unacceptable theology to Harriet.

Five years after Willie's death, Harriet was still mourning for
him, still searching for answers. She reported how her neighbor,
Frank Converse, a bank president and church deacon, had been
reconciled to the loss of *his* son, a promising young man who had
been shot by a bank robber. Converse knew several young men
who at that time were "serious" about religion and if the death of
his son could be the means of bringing even one of them to
"repentence" (i.e., joining the Baptist Church), then the father
would be satisfied. Meanwhile, the Converse family were not
permitted to show their anguish or even feel it, as "Church
etiquette forbids it."

Rachel *would not* be comforted, because they were not. But this Baptist's
mother is reconciled. *God!* How is it with a heart untrammelled by
creeds? Never forgetting, always yearning, constantly missing one dear
face, *never, never* reconciled, nor *comforted—because "they are not."*[81]

Although Harriet could find no comfort in creedal religion,
she could not give it up, either. Her diary notes indicated that she
went to church meetings about two-thirds of the time. In Concord, where the family had rented part of a Unitarian-church
pew, the Robinsons had condescended to attend, if not to praise.
"Went to meeting and endured another of Mr. [Barzillai] Frost's
sermons. It is a mystery how he can *always* be so dull, 'He never
deviates into' brilliancy."[82]

In Malden the family shopped around for churches and found
much to criticize in both high and low congregations. Of a Unitarian picnic held at Walden Pond, largely attended by ministers
and their wives, Harriet wrote, "The 'prunes and prism' 'how is
your mother—and family' sort of woman was very predominent."
There was "much speaking, all from men, which consisted of self
glorification and begging for money. They took the credit of all
the reforms of the age and laid it at the door of unitarianism."[83]
The family was as disgusted with this performance as they were
with spiritualist meetings.

Harriet Robinson dismissed spiritualism, with its trances and extramortal intercourse, as superstition, though many respected people—including her friend Lucy Larcom—practiced table tipping and interpreted messages from the dead. Harriet attended some meetings where spritualists attempted to commune with spirits, but she does not record any efforts to reach her own dead. She objected to the people involved: At one "Spiritual" meeting she found "A coarse woman medium . . . pawing the air and giving vent in a loud voice to all sorts of common-place stuff, while most of the audience gaped with open mouths and dilated eyes, narrow foreheads and credulous faces." This medium called herself Blue Belle—"Cabbage or sunflower would have been more appropriate."[84] Harriet never saw "such a collection of oddities & *individuals*." Almost every face "lacked something, or had too much of one thing. Such vapid faces, such watery eyed people. All with that far away look. It seemed as if with the sound of a trumpet, ignorance & superstition had gathered from all the hidden corners of the earth. . . . *Spiritual!* Phoo. they smelt of the earth earthy. Cat like & rat like. Rabit like & wombat like."[85]

Such scorn carried over to most of the church meetings the Robinsons attended. In a Methodist church they "were rewarded by having bombshells of emptiness *shot* at us."[86] Harriet complained of the Universalist preacher Mr. Powers, " 'Oh Lawks' I never heard such a washy mess, and looking around at the people—I thought it a shame that they should have no better *bread* offered them."[87] Harriet remained cool when the feminist Mary Livermore preached for the Universalists: "People liked her, and many women wept at her affecting stories. Began to rain."[88] A "chippy, orthodox sermon" was so dry she wondered what sin the parents had committed that should "entail such drought of soul" upon the congregation.[89] At a Methodist meeting a man "preached of another world through his nose."[90] When the Dows, neighbors of the Robinsons, joined the Congregational Church, Harriet prophesied it would put an end to their spiritual growth, "as well put a rock in their heads."[91] The Robinsons could only conclude to stay home; from time to time Harriet noted that none of the family went to church, as there was no attraction there. "The *Lord* is *not* there."[92] When Wilbur Haven, a friend and the founder of the local Methodist Sunday school, taxed Harriet with staying at home from meeting so long that he feared she was backsliding, she told him she had nothing to backslide *from*.[93]

Yet of the Robinsons Harriet was the most faithful church attender. Daughter Hattie noted that her "irreligious lazy family" had stayed home from church again. "The fact is when mother is not able to go no one goes and she is not well."[94] Harriet, ambivalent and indecisive, stood between the belief of the past and the religious unconcern of her family.

Rare positive comments on religious meetings were awarded to the Methodist minister G. G. Jones, who preached sermons of unusual practicality. When he dealt with the "sensible text" "Your Garments are Moth Eaten," Harriet thought that the mouths of the congregation "gaped with interest rather than with snores."[95] A later sermon on John the Baptist led Jones to preach against gluttony and self-indulgence: "Good," said Harriet. "I believe in preaching against individual sins. Though he hit my besetting one still will I praise him."[96]

It was in the Bible that Harriet found the religious consolation she had been seeking. The diction in her commentary reflects a peace and assurance in reading Scripture, in marked contrast to the carping comments about church services. After reading the Old Testament she was "filled with the wisdom of its teachings, [I] feel larger and better for the reading." Without the help of creeds she could find the "whole duty of man" laid out there. The teachings of Christ, even though lacking in divinity in her eyes, remained central. She made her religious connection directly with the Scriptures, bypassing any organized churches, and from that position she considered herself a "believer." Without being what could be called religious, she could see "how God has led me from childhood through poverty and a troubled youth—to ease and prosperity."[97]

Harriet Robinson maintained this peace with the Gospel throughout her middle years. As her feminism developed, she might have been expected to have difficulty with women's secondary treatment in the Bible; Elizabeth Cady Stanton, whom she greatly admired, attacked the Bible as being a major justification of female oppression. But Harriet had no such difficulty. Having come into harmony with the Scriptures, she interpreted them to encompass her feminism:

But what I see in the meaning of the Trinity is this. God (male and female) said "let us (male and female) create man in our image after our likeness" and so "God created man in his own image (male and female) male and female created he them." And God (they) being love as the expression of his (their) love created the son. who was always and ever shall be the image of his father (and mother) God. And this is the Trinity. God the father, God the mother, who is the holy spirit of productive love. and the son. Three in one. A perfect family. An example to all the families of the earth. Father & mother, child, & children. Neither greater than the other, but a perfect Trinity of Love. The male, the female, both one in God, and the perfect Child made after the image of God the father and the mother. There is nothing mysterious in this to me.[98]

Striving to understand one of the more basic Christian doctrines, Harriet remade the Trinity into the image of her own happy family.

๛๛๛

The Robinsons' pressing financial needs of five years abated in 1862 when Robinson was elected clerk of the Massachusetts House of Representatives. As early as 1856[99] he had been putting himself into candidacy for the clerkships of the house and senate, but had always been defeated. By the early sixties he was suddenly on the right side in politics, with the Republicans in ascendancy and the nation fighting a war he had advocated. His political colleagues considered that he had earned this modest perquisite and voted him into office. Now the pressures that had held William down through the years of trouble and loss were removed, and the family was overjoyed. In this sudden accession of comparative plenty—$1,600 a year—the parents saw the chance to pay off their debts and educate their children.[100]

The eleven-year period from 1862 to 1873 was a golden age for the Robinsons. The clerkship provided a modest stable base salary, and Harriet's careful huswifery made life comfortable. Robinson worked hard at the fussy duties of clerk and wrote political pieces on the side. He was in the center of political life without having to take a leadership role. It was the life Harriet had been hoping for.

The children—Hattie, solemn and mature, Lizzie, slight and

elusive, and Warrie, the precious, pampered remaining son—could grow up in a stable environment. Warrie's monthly "wheezes," caused by asthma, required his mother's constant care. She rocked him in his cradle, telling him stories.[101] These attentions encouraged both his sickliness and a precocity, but they served to keep him alive. His pert and fresh comments were made much of. "Warrie, won't you ever be a good boy?" "I don't know, perhaps I shall once in a while."[102] Harriet could not be angry with him, whereas such behavior would not have been countenanced in her daughters. When Harriet asked Warrie if he would like a little brother or sister, which would mean relinquishing his large cradle, he was loud with his "No! . . . I don't want one, if there is one comes, I will *jam* it round as bad as I do the cat."[103]

Warrie slept in his parents' room until he was eight years old, when he was banished to a little attic bedroom. The wrench was painful for Harriet, who felt "sad at night to feel that he had left [her] side forever. . . . No longer to reach for his little warm hand in the night."[104] This sensual talk indicates a prolonged closeness of mother and child that might be considered unhealthy if physical sickness had not been involved.

Certainly Harriet's close relationship with Warrie must have affected the Robinsons' marital practices, a subject on which Harriet was entirely silent. There were no children after Warrie, although Harriet thought there might have been.

For the month after Warrie's bed was moved, Harriet thought she was pregnant. She wrote of a "private matter" that she could not explain in her diary. She consulted a female doctor, who decided her case other than she had hoped, resulting in "a severe disappointment."[105] The next day she put "out of my sight" her baby things and labeled them in her heart "a dead hope." She wrote several letters of "restitution" to clear up earlier announcements of an expected child. Harriet was forty-two at this time, and the end of her childbearing years was in sight.[106] Hattie remembered her mother crying when she found out that her supposed fifth child "wasn't one after all."[107]

The incident is illuminating, because it is evidence that Harriet and William were carrying on their marital relationship even though their small son slept next to them. The time lapse indicates that Warrie was moved because Harriet thought that she was pregnant rather than that she became pregnant after he was moved. Yet despite such apparent openness in the presence of her child, Harriet was too inhibited to write candidly of pregnancy in her diary.

Though she longed for more children, Harriet showed some impatience with the ones she had. Even to her "partial eyes," Hattie and Lizzie showed no "traces of genius."[108] When the attractive Mary Ellen Bull was visiting from Concord, Harriet asked her diary, "Shall I ever have so pretty a daughter?" (Later, repenting her harsh judgment, she put "yes 2 of them" in the margin by the entry.)[109] Hattie's development, especially her size, seems to have been a particular concern of her mother's: "Hattie is almost as tall as I am and larger than I ever was at her age, and almost as odd." Hattie at fifteen was "very large and forward and womanly."[110]

Harriet had fought for and prized two years of high school for herself, so that it is curious that the education of her daughters was sporadic and haphazard; there were more options and fewer satisfactory results. Admission to Malden High School was by competition. Hattie was admitted and worked her way up from fifth to first in her class, receiving such praise as "She presses right on" and "Few excell her."[111] Lizzie, after four attempts at the examination and tutoring in public and private schools, was also finally admitted. Neither girl graduated.[112] Both girls took the year 1867–68 off to learn housekeeping. Hattie also helped her father at the state house.[113] The next fall Hattie began her studies at the progressive Mrs. Handy's secondary school, at 20 Essex Street in Boston.

Mrs. Handy's school featured the great abolitionist Theodore D. Weld, who taught philosophy, literature, and geography, and his wife, Angelina Grimké Weld, who taught ancient and modern history. The curriculum also included geology, chemistry, astronomy, Latin, French, and German. May Alcott (sister of Louisa May) taught drawing. Mrs. Caroline M. Severance taught practical ethics. The tuition ranged from $150 to $200 a year. Mrs. Handy stressed physical culture and required a bloomer suit for the gym class.[114] Hattie was horrified: "I *cried*," she said, "but got used to it! Perhaps if my legs hadn't been so big it might have seemed less drastic!!."[115]

Nonetheless, Hattie liked the new school and did well there. She read Shakespeare and played Henry V and Richard III quite successfully. When Dr. Handy cut open the leg of a live frog to show its circulation, Hattie found it "wonderful." Her spelling was so good that she graduated out of that class; "Oh my! Ain't I smart?"[116] There was, however, no talk of college for Hattie.

In 1871 Hattie became her father's official assistant clerk in the House of Representatives, the first woman to hold such an office.[117] When the session was over she went back to "Mr. Weld's" school, where by then her brother and sister were also enrolled. Meanwhile, Mrs. Handy had turned the school over to a Dr. Hosmer, who soon failed, and the promising school broke up in 1871.[118] Warrie went back to the town school and at the age of thirteen was admitted to the high school, where he stood eighty-third in a class of 101.[119]

Harriet Robinson seems to have been a more apt and ambitious pupil than any of her children. Although Hattie had been first in her high-school class, none of the three was a brilliant student, and all preferred other activities. Moreover, the Malden schools lacked the promise that the old Lowell high school had held for their mother. And shopping around for better schools and spending money on their education failed to inspire the scholars. In contrast to her own experience, when Harriet wrote of her daughters' future, education was not the key: "Our daughters all life is before them. They are full of promise. Words cannot tell how much we count on and think of them." Of the nonintellectual Warrie, painful reality was gradually accepted: "Warrie is yet young—and gives signs of many good qualities. Let him be an honest and virtuous man—whether brilliant or not."[120]

Their children's spotty schooling notwithstanding, the horizons of the Robinsons were expanding in scope and variety. Though financial improvement had been by no means steady or sure, in the 1860s they found themselves in a comfortable social position. Their circle of friends divided into several groups. The old Lowell people Harriet still saw consisted of Harriot Curtis,

Lucy Larcom, and occasionally Lizzie Clemence's mother and children, after Lizzie's death. The Concord people came to visit and Harriet stayed with them while visiting and replanting Willie's grave; of these their closest friends seemed to be Nathan and Sarah Stow, Ephraim Bull and his family, and Mrs. Brooks, with whom Harriet liked to rendezvous in Boston for a day of shopping. A third group was made up of workaday journalists—editors and columnists like William; these included Frank Sanborn, James Redpath, and C. C. Hazewell—they had an in-group camaraderie. Another set of friends, William's but not his wife's, were the politicians he met with. Harriet did not like many of these "cronies" and hardly any of the cronies' wives.[121] A few, however, included Harriet in their friendship with William—Frank W. Bird, the papermaker from Walpole; the Bottumes, he a representative from Melrose; and John Quincy Adams Griffin, a lawyer. The final group of friends was made up of Malden neighbors, many of whom remain fairly anonymous in Harriet's diary references to them. These were people who came over to the Robinsons' to play croquet in the evening, were visited when sick, and were invited to occasional parties. Wilbur Haven and his wife and elder brother, Gilbert Haven—a vigorously integrationist Methodist bishop—became the Robinsons' closest intellectual friends in Malden. Bishop Haven, who seemed too liberal to most of his other friends, often discussed religion with the Robinsons, who, needless to say, stood to the left of him.

By 1872 the Robinsons were comparatively prosperous, well known and respected, and hopeful for the future. Their circle had steadily widened, and the world they occupied, with its network of family and friends, seemed likely to open further.

Housekeeping

🐛 *A good poor man's wife*

—HHR Diary, 10 October 1864

Harriet Robinson was grateful to be married and the mistress of her own house. She spoke in euphoric terms of her married life. "I had a good visit but I was *so* glad to get home. Truly her home is a womans world."[1] Harriet's mother had lacked such a home for most of her life. Despite Harriet's early literary ambitions, she chose marriage and thought it essential for the realization of a woman's potential. She did not hesitate to tell the single Lucy Larcom, who was reveling in her freedom, that she was "an undeveloped person, on account of her single state." "Women pay a price for development," she said later, "but it pays in the end to be married. You can't be developed in all sides without being married."[2]

Though Harriet continually defended this decision, it cost her some pain. In 1860, when she had been married for twelve years, she wrote a poem which testified that she had not given up her poetic aspirations, and told only too clearly of her conscious self-sacrifice in marriage. A sensitive husband would recognize this tribute as a backhanded compliment.

My Choice—to W.S.R. in 1860

In shady paths, serene, content I grew,
Nor knew for me what gifts fair life enclosed;

When sudden,—with her gilded lyre held forth,
Came Poesy—bright maid, who smiling said;
"Take me, dear child, take me and Heaven espouse"
I struck the lyre, and knew ambition's joys,—
The praise of men, and all the world's applause.
Then love,—with soft beseeching arms appeared,
And said with low-drooped eyes; "Come thou to me!"
In doubt I stayed, in sorrowing tears, I moaned.
But god-like still he waited long and sought.
Till I, forgetting men's applause, my dreams
of high renown, with cries to him I fled.
And now, serene, content, with him I roam
In sunlit paths. Nor care what life contains.
Since love I keep, which holds embraces all.[3]

The poem may have been meant as a compliment, its title indicating that she had exercised a preference in her own life, and leading as it does, to the sweet, fatalistic resignation at the conclusion. But within its scope Harriet makes clear that her "Choice" was a bad bargain. The "bright maid" with "her gilded lyre" who brought her "ambition's joys,—/The praise of men, and all the world's applause" (a rather inflated remembrance for a woman who had published half a dozen poems in local periodicals) obviously had more to offer than Love, who waited out her reluctance with his "soft beseeching arms" and "low-drooped eyes."

1860 was a time of financial hardship and grief for her son Willie, who had died the year before. Harriet kept no daily diaries for three years after that loss. This pseudo-positive poem, with its self-pitying wife, was probably an effort to work out her feelings; she made no apparent effort to have it published. The poem indicates that Harriet's sunny enthusiasm about married life sometimes failed her.

More often, however, Harriet willingly and happily plied her trade of housewife with increasing skill and confidence. She believed that it took "a woman of Genius" to do housework, and that cooking was "one of the fine arts."[4] Her industry and ingenuity provided her family with a higher standard of living than they would have been able otherwise to afford, and she prided herself on being a "good poor man's wife."[5] Her diary notes describe some of the housekeeping practices that allowed them to live pleasantly within their means, and also make it possible to reconstruct the Robinsons' rising standard of living.

The Robinsons' first home was a room in a Boston boarding house at 18 Hayward Place, off Washington Street.[6] Having lived in boarding houses for some time, neither Harriet nor William had accumulated much in the way of personal goods. They might have rented a furnished dwelling, but instead they "prettily furnished" it themselves with a "wedding outfit," which cost the considerable sum of $245.72, as documented below.[7]

Wedding Outfit of W. S. and Harriet H. Robinson, 30 Nov., 1848

book case	22.00	girandole	14.00
clothes rack and		candles	.83
folding board	4.25	fire set	2.25
easy chair	26.00	spittoon	1.00
carpet	39.24	chamber set	2.67
backing	1.50	2 pails	.50
sofa	28.00	hod	1.00
bedstead	28.00	brushes	1.25
matress	16.00	broom	.25
pillows, bolster	5.00	hand brush	.25
p. leaf mattress	4.50	stew pan	.62
sofa lamp	2.17	dust pan	.17
bed lamp	.20	flat iron	.75
lamp glass	.70	waiter	.62
table	28.00		
mirror	13.00		$245.72

This "outfit," which would furnish a good-sized bed-sitting room or a living room with a sleeping alcove, included enough modest purchases to make it quite complete. Cooking items were not necessary, because the Robinsons ate downstairs in the common dining room. The bookcase—significantly listed first by this literate couple—the easy chair, the carpet, sofa, bedstead, and table were all pieces of substantial quality and cost. A thirteen-dollar mirror and a fourteen-dollar girandole, or ornamental branched candleholder, were luxurious additions, indicating some ambition beyond the utilitarian. The Robinsons apparently sent their washing out.

Within a few months William changed jobs and the couple's income was cut by more than half. Robinson earned $20 a week in Boston, but then in Lowell they managed on $400 a year, which covered rent, fuel, clothes, and food for the growing family. The pretty furniture was packed off to 29 Chapel Street, at the corner of Lowell's Elm Street, where Mr. Morrill charged the Robinsons $84 a year in rent.[8] The family later moved to a brown cottage on Abbott Street, owned by Watson Woodman, where the rent was $85 a year.[9]

William wrote his mother requesting any old furniture that she could spare, and Mrs. Robinson responded generously with a wagonload of things, some of which had belonged to her late daughter Lucy Robinson Green. Harriet was delighted to have her house filled with comfortable furniture, and sent her mother-in-law a grateful and deferential letter.

Ever since you sent to us so many things I have wanted to tell you how much we thank you, and how much help they have been to us towards housekeeping. I have found a great many things I wanted but should have tried to have done without if you had not sent them—yet I could not help thinking that you had sent many things which you perhaps needed, or could have made use of. I am sure I should be very selfish could I take comfort with any thing I thought you had robbed yourself of.

Having duly recorded her appreciation, Harriet went on to describe the home in which she obviously took great pleasure.

We have not got settled yet, though nearly so. The clock was put up to day, and is ticking merrily away behind me. The two best tables are in the sitting rooms, I am writing on one of them. The three rocking chairs and four of those cane seated ones are here also, I thought I would put two of them [in] one of the chambers:—but you must come and see how we have got things arranged: we have a very pretty, snug house, and hope to make a happy home for you whenever you come. I think you would like here, at any rate we should try to have you. . . . I shall try to take care of [the furniture] and keep [it] as nice as you could wish, for I do not forget that most of [the things] were Lucy's and though I never knew her, yet I know what a mothers feelings would be in my own case.[10]

Harriet and William's furniture had been increased by three rocking chairs, at least four straight chairs, and a clock, all items they had lacked before, as well as another two tables. They could now arrange chairs around a table for dining and fill out a sitting room. Little else could be afforded, although Harriet was in the market for an old-fashioned armchair if she could find one for 75¢.[11]

When the family then moved to Concord, in 1854, to care for Mrs. Robinson, William was again regularly employed, receiving $20 a week. Even as they paid off their burden of debts from *The American*, the family's standard of living began to inch up.

Once settled in Concord, Harriet took a rare trip into Boston and bought herself $40 worth of new parlor furniture, including five chairs, a whatnot, and a small table.[12] Later she bought another $60 worth. William's reaction to the new furniture was "What a pity it is for people to work so hard for a few stuffed wooden things to set up in a room to be looked at! What does it all amount to? There is no happiness in it, nor no good, either."[13]

Within two years Robinson's income had risen to about $30 a week, produced by his salary and fees for extra writings. When Harriet totted up her household expenses for 1856 she found she had spent $1,000, a marked advance from the $400 of the few years previous. "Too much, we must not spend so much this year. Tho' I dont know as we could spend less," recorded the ambivalent Harriet.[14] Even silver spoons and a silver-plated cake basket took their places in the modest household. But despite the increased spending, the family still paid off their debts and saved money.[15]

A beautiful garden grew up around every house William and Harriet inhabited. Neither of their famlies had been dependent on the soil for several generations, but planting a garden had a regular place on Harriet's yearly calendar. In Concord she grew her own lettuce and tomatoes, and with the help of Ephraim Bull, she added the more permanent rhubarb and grapes. Flowers were included, and years later, when she returned to visit her old houses in Concord and Lowell, a favorite pastime was to hunt for the descendants of the flowers she had planted.[16]

The Robinson's increasing prosperity allowed Harriet to hire servants. Her experience with domestics must have repeated that of countless other thrifty American housewives. She and her mother had always done the housekeeping, but in 1855 Harriet first hired a "help" while Mother Hanson was in Maine for a long visit to Ben and Ange. She chose Mary Sweeny, a good-natured red-headed girl who came to her well recommended. Harriet found Mary willing, kind to the children, and skilled at washing and ironing William's shirts. No difficulties with Mary were recorded. But when Mother Hanson came home after two and a half months away, Mary was sent off. Harriet said that she and her mother preferred to do their own work alone, "until we are better off at least, pecuniarily."[17]

After that when Mrs. Hanson was away, Harriet handled everything herself. "I get pretty tired," she said, "but I like to be alone and had rather do it than to have any one else here but mother. Wm. helps me some."[18] Privacy and finances governed this decision, for Harriet had not been displeased with the virtuous Mary. Mary's Irishness was not an issue either, though this rather sinister comment was recorded when Mary brought her brother to America: "So another one is added to the Irish population they increase like a swarm of flies, but they are thrifty in their way and industrious and can live on nothing and are, I think, bound to inherit the earth. It is singular, they have a foothold in every house."[19]

When the family first moved to Malden, in 1859, William's unemployment precluded much thought of servants. Harriet's accumulated experience in housekeeping had made her a more exacting mistress when improved fortunes did allow for help. In December of 1863 she hired Dora Stockwell, a native New Englander, whom her employer first pitied and then became impatient with. "She is a *slouch* Poor white trash." Unfortunate Dora was "about as fit to be in a decent house, as a bull to be in a china shop," and Harriet packed her off. Less than a week later Harriet noted that the next girl had also turned out badly: "She seemed to have all the faults, and none of the virtues of help."[20] Harriet did her own work until the following week, when Bridget arrived.

Bridget promised satisfaction. After four days of employment, Harriet could say, "Bridget does my work nicely so I have plenty of Leisure to 'see to things.' . . . It seems good not to have to work all the time. I shall not do it again till I am obliged to."[21] Yet after a month or so of this pleasant leisure, the mistress again began to voice her discontent. Bridget was dishonest.

Bridget skimmed the milk thin, drew the tea strong, and filled it with water, modest enough sins. She denied everything. Harriet warned Bridget that her work was unsatisfactory and complained that she was obliged to take on girls without sufficient character recommendations. (William commented from the sidelines that perhaps recommendations for mistresses should be required, as well.) Bridget was dismissed within a week. Harriet continued to seek a saint who would do housework, contending that the price of an honest woman was above that of a virtuous one.[22]

Harriet's displeasure led to a growing use of anti-Irish invective. The Irish Bridget, for instance, used the "weapon of degraded races pretty freely—Deceit." Harriet was heartily "sick of *Irish*—the kind we have here." After Bridget's departure, Harriet tried to get a black servant, her intolerance not extending to that group of helpers. She applied through the wife of a black minister who kept an agency for working girls. None was available.[23]

Julia, another Irish girl, who "quite whitened out" the laundry, became Harriet's "help." She worked for a month before her mistress began describing her as "under our feet" and "cross," and a "nuisance generally." When Harriet complained, Julia retaliated with a strike and a demand for $2 a week, twice what her mistress was willing to pay her. The defiant Julia then announced her intention to leave that evening. "Then 'go,'" quoth the proud mistress; "I cant stop to talk to you now." The girl stayed on, meek and docile, but her days were numbered.[24]

Unable to live with servant girls, Harriet determined to make do without them. "By a bold, coup de état, I informed [Julia] that her services were no longer needed, that I had concluded to do my own work—in other words that I was sick of her and help in general, and had rather live in peace and alone if I did have to work. I then went through the ceremony of washing my hands of

Harriet Jane Hanson at eighteen, about 1843.

By courtesy of the Trustees of the Boston Public Library.

Harriet Hanson Robinson at twenty-eight, about 1853.

By courtesy of the Trustees of the Boston Public Library.

The Robinson children about 1871. Left to right: *Elizabeth Osborne (Lizzie) about nineteen, Edward Warrington (Warrie) about twelve, and Harriette Lucy (Hattie) about twenty-one.*

Courtesy of the Schlesinger Library, Radcliffe College.

William Stevens Robinson at forty-eight, about 1866. This engraving was used as the frontispiece of "Warrington" *Pen-Portraits (1877).*

Courtesy of Zivan Simonian.

The Robinson House at 35 Lincoln Street (earlier 9 Lincoln Street) in Malden, Massachusetts.

Courtesy of the Schlesinger Library, Radcliffe College.

This picture dates from about 1881, at which time it was pasted into Hattie Shattuck's Scrapbook, vol. 104. She wrote the following comments under the picture:

Bought by W.S.R. in 1866
Many improvements made both before & after his death.
Bay window built on by HHR to enlarge her sleeping room.
Two other front windows up-stairs & one side are windows of Sidney's and my room.
Other side window Lizzie's room.
Warrie slept in attic until Grandma's death, when he moved into room over the L, behind the trellis.
Parlor below my room, sitting room under Lizzie's room, kitchen behind. Our sleeping-room on side of house not visible.
A happy home if ever there was one in the world.
[Later]
Before my marriage I shared the side room with Lizzie.
Mother & father's room was in front where I afterward, with Sidney, lived. Father died in that room. Grandma died in the east room over the kitchen. I boarded at home after marriage in 1878 . . . .
Came back here on Dec. 1st 1892 to stay.
Sold to E.R.A. [Elizabeth Robinson Abbott] after mother's death 1911.
New house built by ERA in 1920 beside this on south.

Harriette Lucy (Hattie) Robinson, a wedding portrait from about 1877. She was married to Sidney Doane Shattuck in 1878 at the age of twenty-eight.

Courtesy of the Schlesinger Library, Radcliffe College.

Harriet Hanson Robinson at about sixty, about 1885. This engraving was published in the third volume of the History of Woman Suffrage *by Elizabeth Cady Stanton, et al., accompanying the article on Massachusetts written by Harriet Robinson.*

Courtesy of Zivan Simonian.

Harriet Hanson Robinson at sixty-eight, about 1893.

By courtesy of the Trustees of the Boston Public Library.

the Tribe called 'Paddy' and mentally painted on my door posts, until we are all lazier than we are now, 'No Irish need apply.' "[25]

Having hired and dismissed several "helps" in three months, Harriet convinced herself that the daughters of Erin, lacking the niceness and efficiency necessary for housework, were a poor bargain. Thousands of other American housewives of moderate means who hoped to escape some of their drudgery came to the same rude awakening. Harriet was impatient at the girls' inability to carry out her demands, yet she was unwilling to take on the missionary labor of teaching them. The servant problem was a major difficulty of the women's sphere, unsatisfactory to mistress and maid alike.

In the 1860s a series of articles entitled "The House and Home Papers," written by Harriet Beecher Stowe under the masculine guise "Christopher Crowfield," was published in *The Atlantic Monthly*. Crowfield, the cultivated master of a middle-class home, discoursed in a learned and pompous manner on the merits of wallpaper, fashionable dress, architecture, and so on. Each article was framed by a domestic scene wherein his wife, an admirable housekeeper, and his fashionable daughters commented on his theories. Much of the series was later incorporated into *The American Woman's Home*, the encyclopedic work on domestic science by Mrs. Stowe and her sister Catharine Beecher.

Harriet read these articles and commented on the sixth of the series, "The Lady Who Does Her Own Work," published in June 1864. The article justified a servantless household, saying that only in America was it possible to find a class of women "of education, cultivation, and refinement" who would be recognized as ladies in any circle though doing their own work. In a sense it was nobler to do housework than to hire to have it done. At the very least it was respectable.

A lady could do her own work because of wise early training. Mothers must instill proper skills in their daugthters, even those girls who might marry very well—such mistresses would then never be helpless against the demands of their servants. As Stowe said, "She who can at once put her own trained hand to the machine in any spot where a hand is needed never comes to be the slave of a coarse, vulgar Irishwoman."[26] The recommended course was to train the daughters of the house as if they were respected household helpers.

Harriet took this advice to heart, hiring Hattie and Lizzie to set tables and wash dishes for 25¢ each week. Harriet was to cook, happy enough to get the dinner on in peace. The girls worked willingly, preparing themselves to be, like their mother, "good poor men's wifes."[27]

To say that Harriet did her own work after firing her maids is not to say that she was without help. Apart from her daughters' and Mrs. Hanson's assistance, Harriet regularly hired women to come in during the day to help with the washing, ironing, and housecleaning. Mrs. Curley and Mrs. Ivory, married women of limited means, each worked one day or so a week. Harriet readied things and worked beside them. "Doing her own work" meant that a housewife supervised its completion, rather than doing it all personally.

Each spring Harriet religiously cleaned her house from attic to cellar, from floor to ceiling. She took pleasure in this cleansing ritual, extending her household sphere to the limits of her home. She stirred up the "dust and dry bones" in the attic and set the woodshed to rights, where she had four maids' worth of "dirt to clean up."[28] During this busy time she would have a woman in to work daily.

It took Harriet a full month or more each spring to put her house in order. Washing windows, arranging drawers, sweeping, and dusting were relatively simple tasks, amounting to two or three days' work in each room. It was the carpets that constituted the major chore. Every year each carpet had to be taken up, cleaned, mended, dyed, if necessary, and nailed back down. Each room was disrupted in turn as its floor was bared. Twenty years into her marriage Harriet was still using her wedding carpet in the parlor, but most floors were covered with rag carpets, which wore badly in some spots. Darning was necessary, and often a carpet required "remaking," cutting out the bad spots and putting it back together in a new way. This "terrible job" made Harriet wish to be rich enough so she could rip up the old rags and sell them or give them away.[29]

Gradually Harriet was able to replace the rag carpets in her house, putting a straw carpet down in the sitting room for the first time in 1866.[30] The next year she replaced her parlor carpet with a bright new one, bought for $66. A couple of years later the combined library and dining room were carpeted with a green-and oak-colored floor covering, costing $1.62 a yard; the rug was nothing expensive, but plain and neat. This major housecleaning took place in the spring; a more modest effort set the house to rights in September.

May and June were devoted primarily to sewing. Harriet kept herself and two growing daughters fashionable, and also sewed for her mother and for Warrie, until he reached adolescence. She bought her first sewing machine in 1859[31] and later a new Singer, in 1871, for which she paid $100, less a $20 trade-in.[32] When Harriet wrote that she had bought a new dress, she meant that she had bought the yardage and trimmings to make it. She hired the local dressmaker to come over by the day and work with her cutting out the desired dresses and sewing them. The dressmaker also helped Harriet recut in more stylish modes her old dresses, some of which were remade almost every year. Harriet recorded that the dressmaker came in for eight days in 1867, fifteen times in 1868, and six times in 1869, figures that may err on the low side. Again, Harriet did her own work, but with a considerable amount of hired help.

Although spring was the major time of sewing, Harriet sewed throughout the year. She could finish up a dress in two or three days, even though fashion required "27 [or 34] mortal buttonholes" down the front. She ingeniously remade old clothes, particularly during the Civil War. She dyed tassels to put on "Hattie's 'opera cape' made out of Warrie's pink flannel baby cloak." Lizzie's hooded red opera cape was cut down from an old dress and dyed. Harriet cut down William's suit for Warrie and even had her old cloak taken to the tailor to be remade as a dress coat for her husband. Her black alpaca dress, remade for at least a third time in 1866, looked "finely," with points before and behind, a trailing shirt bound with velvet, the waist and sleeves trimmed with velvet and lace—very fancy and stylish.[33]

Harriet rightly took pride in her ability to keep her family well dressed for a modest sum; photographs show them fashionably and attractively attired. Harriet described one set of her daughters' outfits: "Hattie all in white,—with Salmon colored ribbons & flowers & gloves. Did [Lizzie] in Pink muslin and white & lavender flowers & gloves. Hat's hair was done up in heavy braids with two long curls behind and fuzzed low on her forehead. Lizzie was done in rolls high on her head and short curls in front below her hat, almost every one turned to look at them as they passed along. I write this for future reading—so that I may remember just how they looked at 16 & 18 years of age."[34] Their outfits represented planning, ingenuity, imitation, eking out, and labor—all of the economic virtues. Clothing her family was work of value and significance, even if Harriet did have to say so herself.

Sewing prepared the family for the long summer vacation. From 1860 until 1873 the Robinsons spent about a month each year at the Ocean House in Manomet, a small watering place near Plymouth, Massachusetts. The big frame house, owned and managed for two generations by the Holmes family, could accommodate fifty or sixty guests. The Robinsons were introduced to the place by F. W. Bird, who liked to do some political planning there.

Days at Manomet were passed in walking on the beach—often to "Mother's Rock," named and christened by Harriet with red paint—bowling on the green, fishing and boating, bathing in the ocean, reading, and writing letters. Innumerable games of euchre, whist, croquet, and bezique were played with old and new friends. The women tatted, embroidered, and crocheted, though Harriet preferred not to lift a needle while there. Excursions were taken, by buggy, train, and boat.

William and Harriet led out in social activities, sparking the dinner conversation and organizing charades and tableaux, using props brought from Malden in their three stuffed trunks. In the evenings they joined in the singing and parlor games. One year Harriet and several others wrote chapters of a novel to be read as an evening entertainment. An acquaintance considered the Robinsons among the most attractive aspects of the resort.[35]

The month at the sea over, the annual round continued as Harriet happily returned to her closed-up house. She opened the windows and blinds. She wound and set the clock, made a fire, "brought water in the pump," called the cat, and sent William to bring her mother home from her sisters' house in Waltham. The next day she went after a washerwoman to do up the accumulated fifty pairs of dirty stockings. Mrs. Ivory scrubbed for eight hours, leaving three tubs of wet clothes in the clean kitchen.[36] The family was back in residence.

ⓜⓜⓜ

In 1866 the Robinsons' landlord, Mr. Amerigi, offered to sell them the house they were living in, on Lincoln Street. William preferred to pay $50 more in rent each year rather than be encumbered with a house, but the landlord urged him to reconsider, offering the place to him for $3,600, $400 less than he would charge other buyers; Amerigi thought the house was worth at least another thousand. On June 18 Robinson decided to buy the place, and on June 29 he exchanged $3,600 for the deed.[37]

Apparently Robinson had $2,600 in savings, and he went to his friend Henry L. Pierce, a rich lawyer and political friend, and signed a note for the other $1,000. No banks were involved in the transaction. The Robinsons paid off the note two years later.[38]

William's clerkship in the state house paid $1,600 in 1862. Then for two years he did without an assistant and was paid $2,000 annually. In 1864 he was raised to $2,400, and later to $2,500. In the early 1870s Harriet reported that he was making $3,000 a year for his work during the legislative session. To his wife's surprise, William had turned out to be a good provider, after all.[39]

Some of their money they put back into the house. The simple two-storied frame dwelling was painted white with green blinds. Built in the mid nineteenth century, it still stands, at 35 Lincoln Street, a quiet residential neighborhood in Malden. The interior has since been extensively remodeled, but in Harriet's day the little house was divided into many small rooms. The ground floor had four public rooms, the parlor and the library at the front and the dining room and sitting room behind them. The kitchen was at the back. On the second floor Harriet and William shared the front bedroom, Lizzie and Hattie shared the bedroom on one side, and the spare chamber was on the other. Grandma Hanson occupied the bedroom over the kitchen until her death, in 1881, when Warrie moved down from the attic. It was, Hattie later recalled, "A happy home if ever there was one in the world."[40] The house became the Robinson symbol for stability and remained in the family for three generations.

Even before buying the house, they began to refurbish it. The walls of the sitting room and dining rooms were re-covered, so that the "dowdy paper no longer [swore]" at the rest of the place. Harriet had carpenters apply weather stripping and fix up a "soft water arrangement," to catch the rain. Mr. Page repapered the front entry in plain lilac with a crimson-and-gold border, the spare chamber in green with small figures, and Warrie's small new room—recently partitioned from the attic—in a "cunning little red dot," all for $31.83. The next year the carpenters were in again to build steps and a bulkhead for the new cellar they had dug. A sliding panel was installed to pass food from the kitchen to the dining room. The old icebox was "grained over" (painted to resemble wood grain). The next year an arch was cut between the sitting room and the library, making one larger room. New bookcases were built to house the Robinsons' sixteen hundred volumes. A furnace was installed, with registers throughout the house, at a cost of $270, including carpentering. The parlor mantel was moved to the dining room and a new one built in the parlor to accommodate a large clock. The dining room was repainted. Some men came in to "grain" the kitchen and the sitting room.[41]

In 1870 the sanitary facilities were brought indoors when an addition was built to the house. "I ought to have hung out a flag to denote the demolishment of my ancient landmarks," Harriet noted, as the privy was dismantled. The new room was accompanied by two drains—"for I am a believer in good drainage"—and a new cesspool, eight feet square, "which I hope not to hear from for twenty years." This addition cost about $400.[42] The house was always being improved rather than just maintained; Harriet generously expended money on it.

All these improvements were accomplished by outside workmen. There is no word of William's lifting a finger toward household maintenance or of Harriet's doing anything but supervising. At one time she noted six men busy about the place, putting in a new pump, building a chicken coop, and working in the garden. Another time seven workers were on the premises: two painters, two plasterers, a butcher, a milkman, and a fish boy.[43] Again the picture of Harriet is of an executive rather than a solitary toiler. She hired her work done rather than doing it herself.

When Mr. Amerigi visited the house in 1873, seven years after the Robinsons had bought it, he said it was now worth $11,000. They had paid $3,600 for it and put $3,000 into it—by contrast, their friends the Havens had built a house costing them $15,000.[44] The Robinsons had done up their simple house nicely, but it remained a modest dwelling.

While the house was gotten in order Harriet also worked over the large yard. She commissioned a neighbor to make her a croquet set and brought a favorite Manomet activity to Malden. During the good weather she had at least one man in almost daily to spade, plant, fertilize, gravel the walks, or whitewash the fences and shed. The big garden produced twenty-five quarts of strawberries by early July, and two bushels of peas at a picking. Harriet had infected cherry trees taken out, planted peach trees, and cultivated beds of rhubarb and asparagus. She tried horticulture experiments with grapes and currants. William said the backyard looked like the Garden of Eden; "I hope he thinks I am the Eve," Harriet noted, twenty years after their marriage.[45] She had created the ideal garden/farm, the rural life her family had not known for generations.

Harriet's indoor gardening was also impressive. She had petunias and morning glories growing all over the parlor; five kinds of petunias bloomed at once and ivy went all around the room. Verbenas, nasturtiums, and mignonettes hung in pots and bloomed in the windows. Mrs. Haven was "in extacies" over Harriet's elegant plants.[46]

Harriet got the "hen fever" and had a coop built to house eight hens and a rooster. Soon the coop was enlarged to accommodate thirty hens, and the whole project paid for itself in eight months. The next year the family began selling eggs. Some of the egg money was turned over to Mother Hanson, who after a lifetime of hard work was elated to have a bank book and an account of $25.[47]

Harriet's diary notes reveal some of her shopping habits. She bought flour by the barrel once or twice a year. Butter she bought by the forty-pound tub and used a lot of it. Sugar was expensive during the war, so she bought it by the pound every month or so. Fish and produce were purchased from vendors. She bought lard and salt pork in bulk—thirty pounds of lard and fifty-five pounds of pork—and tried them out herself. The next day's labors cubing the lard, cooking it down, and squeezing the globules blistered her hands, but she was through with the job for the year. One year she went to Boston to market, where she bought eighty-eight pounds of beef, sixty-three pounds of leaf lard, seventy-four pounds of pork to salt, and a ham; she would need more ham and beef, but she had her year's supply of pork and lard.[48]

Harriet also ordered food in bulk from her brother Ben in Maine. One fall Ben sent down seven barrels of potatoes, two of apples ("Mostly rotten, some villain swindled Ben"), one of barley (for the hens), four chickens, a goose, and a quarter of beef, as well as some pork.

In 1867 Harriet began to preserve tomatoes in tins noting that previously her tomatoes had always fermented, no matter how much sugar she added. The next year she put up fifty-one tins of tomatoes, made jelly from twenty pounds of grapes, and "did up quinces and sweet apples." She canned another fifty-two quarts of tomatoes the following year, as well as a bushel of peaches.[49] Her larder and cellar were so well stocked that even though she did not produce all she needed, she had a good supply of most of the things she used. She was as self-sufficient as farm wives of the past.

Harriet frequently shopped in Boston, meeting her old Concord friend Mrs. Brooks for a day at the stores. She bought dress goods, crockery, and some food there, her transportation simplified by the season ticket on the railway, which she commenced using in 1864.[50] She went "downtown" to Malden to shop less often than to Boston, usually going to Malden, with Warrie in tow, simply to meet William at the train station. The station was a short two blocks from the Robinson house, and the train itself roared through a gully at the back of their property. They could sometimes see family members returning south on the train by looking through a hole in the back fence.

The family was not always delighted with Harriet's purchases. After a trip to Boston on which she had bought French cambric for a new dress, she recorded the following reactions:

> GRANDMA: "*That* your new dress?" (contemptuous)
> HATTIE and LIZZIE: "It looks like house paper."
> WARRIE: "Phoo!"
> GRANDMA: "If I had the whole of Boston to *range* in I would get something prettier than that."

William, however, always liked her things—"He is a man of taste."[51]

In 1867 Harriet shopped in Boston at least ten times, in 1868 twenty-five times, in 1869 twenty-seven times, in 1870 twenty-five times, and in 1871 twenty-five times. All these were specific shopping expeditions, other Boston trips being frequently made for cultural and social events. "I enjoy this running into Boston,—it refreshes both body and soul, and relieves the monotony of every day life," she wrote.[52]

The diaries record the Robinsons' steady stream of visits also to Waltham, Salem, Winchendon, Maine, and farther afield. And such a relentless stream of reciprocal visitors settled in on the Robinsons that it would seem that entertaining was Harriet's favorite activity. Generally she enjoyed it, but sometimes she preferred to be alone. The "gabblers" would pour their "wishy, washy flood" over the hostess, who could not escape them to pursue her cultural activities; she grew bored with "no French, no reading, no nothing."[53] But welcoming relatives was accepted as a standard responsibility of the housewife, so though Harriet enjoyed only certain of the guests, she continued to entertain the others just as often.

Harriet gave parties in Malden. For a large group—forty guests—Harriet scheduled charades, "dumb orator," games, and readings before serving refreshments. The "tea fight," however, was more characteristic of her evening entertainments. This was when six or eight couples were invited in for lively conversation and a tasty meal.[54]

Young people were also entertained. Hattie and Lizzie had a party for sixty friends when they were in their early teens. All but one had a good time, it was noted. The house was readied by hanging six new pictures, putting up a bracket for wax flowers, and making bouquets and "eatables," which included the following items.[55]

2# candy
2# conversation lozenges
4 sheets of sponge cake
1 loaf of Concord cake (which was not needed)
chocolate drops
2 loaves Dover cake (not needed)
2# lemon tarts
a measure of Charlotte cake (not needed)
10 quarts of ice cream
5 dozen cocoa nut cakes
butter and biscuits made with four quarts of flour
ten quarts of pop corn
water
flowers (50¢)

All in all a rather sumptuous feast for $20.

Harriet was competent, maybe even inspired, in her job as housewife. She had mastered her calling and could not help thinking well of herself. Her diaries are peppered with positive comments about her successes. She considered herself as handy in the house as anyone, smugly noting that it was her "misfortune" that she could do "almost everything after some sort." Had she married a rich man, a "good poor man's wife" would have been lost in her.[56]

Harriet never questioned her ability to do the job, but sometimes she wondered whether the job was worth doing; she always decided that it was. "Busy at cooking and other thankless jobs— thankless I say, because there is so little to show really as the results of such labor—yet, I must confess that healthy and well kept bodies are a great deal." "A woman with both hands full of *mended* stockings ought to find admittance among the just sooner than one with palms and roses."[57] Houseworkers deserved more credit than they received.

The high standard of living Harriet had set for the family required what seemed like a lot of work. She therefore tried to use her mind to save her body. "I think of every way whereby a woman can get along easier and I dont see any, while people eat three meals a day. or have to get four, as we do."[58] She recognized that few amenities were required in order to live, but to live comfortably required great effort.

How hard did Harriet actually work? Raising children on limited funds is always difficult, but, as Harriet said, she had been young and enthusiastic when she did that. She had had the help of her industrious mother even when she could not get on well with live-in maids. And she freely hired help for her heavy work and any specific tasks that needed doing. Though she was always on call, her major duties were managerial rather than manual. The work she did she chose to do. She had abundant time for reading and social events and probably worked no harder than in the early factory days.

As the years went on Harriet acknowledged that she was not as elastic as she used to be, that sometimes—dared she admit it?—the work began to seem like drudgery. William, who had never required hard labor of her, gave her the interest on his $1,000 bond to pay for her sewing and buy her a month of rest.[59]

Although Harriet wrote less about housekeeping as the children matured, she never disavowed her identity as a housewife or demeaned her homely activities. Even after her life was centered on other interests she enjoyed escaping back into domesticity. "Attended to household affairs pretty well after this weeks dissipating, with Shakespeare and the Odyssey, and it was quite refreshing to make baked bread, cook roast beef, macarroni etc and darn my stockings."[60]

VIII

Politics

A lymphatic, shut-in man, smiling only round the mouth, which is carefully covered with hair to hide the smile; short, thick-set, with his head not unlike that of Irving's great Dutch governor, which Nature made so perfect, that she could find no neck to match, and so set it directly on his shoulders; high forehead; slightly bald; thin hair; ruddy of face; and the keenest political writer in America.

—*Bishop Gilbert Haven, describing William Robinson,*
"Warrington" Pen-Portraits

William Robinson generally occupied an adversary role in politics. Belligerence and disgust were the attitudes he most easily assumed, and ridicule was a favorite weapon. No one was above criticism; his darts fell on the just and the unjust. Once, when he "broke out with his accustomed objurgations levelled at several very worthy and excellent men," George Frisbie Hoar, a political friend and ally, baited him with, "William, it is fortunate you did not live in the Revolutionary time. How you would have hated General Washington." Robinson agreed. Washington was "an old humbug, wasn't he?"[1] Only anonymous underdogs, the fugitive slaves and poor workingmen for whom he felt compassion, were safe from his pen.

When Robinson entered politics in earnest, in the late 1840s, he defined himself against the Whigs, whose reliance on Southern cotton caused them to waffle on slavery. His early membership in the Free-Soil Party and the sacrifice of his job with the Lowell

Journal and Courier in order to speak out against slavery were typical. He needed to precede the crowd and liked to take outrageous stands. For a short while in the early fifties he helped hold together a shaky coalition of Free-Soilers and Democrats, and went to the Massachusetts house for two terms as a representative from Lowell. There he supported measures—the ten-hour labor law and the secret ballot—that favored workingmen. Neither measure had any success, however; he failed to persuade even the members of the committee he chaired on the merits of the ten-hour law.

Robinson next took on the Know-Nothing Party, vehemently opposing that vigorous, though short-lived, nativist phenomenon. "Steal, steal, steal," was the watchword of the Know-Nothing state government, according to Robinson.[2] He continued to deplore slavery and call for war with the South until no newpaper but the Springfield (Massachusetts) *Republican* would publish him. Samuel Bowles, *The Republican*'s publisher—who sympathized with some of Robinson's views—prided himself on allowing his correspondents to form their own judgments and express them.[3] To William, John Brown, whose armed opposition to law and order had earned him a death sentence, was a hero: "To break a law is not necessarily to commit a crime," Robinson insisted.[4] Harriet saw her husband very much in the light of John Brown, the willing martyr for the good cause. And she saw herself in the position of John Brown's wife, a woman who could be proud of poverty occasioned by a noble sacrifice.[5]

Only during and after the Civil War, when public opinion had caught up with Robinson's foresighted urgings, did he become respectable. He had always believed that the people were to be trusted, that their basic instincts were good, and that it was his duty to help show them the right way.[6] During the war he could voice the righteous patriotism that perfectly suited the public mood. "We shall have no freedom, no peace, no commerce, no national life, which is exempt from panic and peril, so long as slavery dominates over us. We have risen against it. . . . If ever there was a holy war, this is the one."[7] On the wave of this popularity, the gadfly became a part of the political establishment.

William Robinson's activities as a politician took three major forms: his clerkship of the Massachusetts House of Representatives, his weekly "Warrington" letters in *The Republican*, and his membership in the politically influential Bird Club. When Lincoln was elected, bringing the Republican Party into power, Robinson was told that he might have almost any political office that he asked for. Robinson declined the offer, refusing, according to his wife, to hold any office to which he had not been elected by the people.[8] He finally accepted, in 1862, Governor John A. Andrew's nomination of him for the clerkship of the Massachusetts house, a position he had sought unsuccessfully several times before. This job required annual election by the members of the house and paid $1,600 a year. A steady income, even one so modest as this, meant a great improvement in family fortunes. Harriet had never seen her husband so elated as after that first election.[9]

As clerk William occupied an essential and central position, but also an inconspicuous one: just the sort of place where he was most comfortable. He sat at the front, but to the side. He was involved, but silent. He performed his duties meticulously and was always ready to draft a bill or report if such was needed. He had clerked for a number of political conventions and his knowledge of parliamentary law was equaled by few. These years of experience in the house led to the one real book he managed to write, *"Warrington's" Manual*, on parliamentary procedure.

This little book, small in size and running less than a hundred pages, shows Robinson's mastery of the subject and his quick, clear judgments on procedure, as well as impatience at considering exceptions and leading along the uninitiated. His personality never intrudes in this tight volume, as it did in his newspaper columns, and there are no charming asides. Writing the book apparently brought him little pleasure. All parliamentary law, he later said, could be reduced to a single rule: "Never put an ass in the chair."[10] The sales were modest. This impatience with the tools of his trade indicates that Robinson was actually more interested in the political milieu of the house than the clerkship itself.

Each year, as he came up for reelection, William prepared the family for his likely defeat. Instead, for eleven years—from 1862 to 1873—he held the office, kept up with politics, and did the literary chores his conscience allowed for the Republican Party. Several times he was unanimously reelected. A newspaper as far away as Detroit commented on this remarkable popularity for a sturdy radical Republican. The writer in the unidentified paper praised Robinson as a practical printer, a "brilliant newspaper writer," and one who had earned his "foremost position by labor and perseverance."[11]

If Robinson was fairly inconspicuous as a person on the Boston scene—where politicians strutted and fretted—his reputation as a columnist was considerably larger. The persona he projected as a writer had always been larger than his physical one, and as the Springfield *Republican* had a statewide and even national circulation, his voice was heard. A friend of the Robinsons' visiting in Lawrence, Kansas, in 1858, reported on a fellow traveler's reading *The Republican*. This traveler took the paper, he said, to find out what "that fellow 'Warrington' has to say." He didn't agree half the time, "but I can't get along without reading it."[12] Robinson first began his "Warrington" letters in 1856, taking the pseudonym from the character in Thackeray's novel *The History of Pendennis*. The "strong thoughts, the curt periods, the sense, the satire, and the scholarship" of George Warrington appealed to Robinson, as much as the fact that he "wrote for his bread."[13]

This writing was easy for Robinson who sat in the evenings at the big family table, where his wife and mother-in-law were mending and his children doing their lessons.[14] He would scribble furiously and then read the best parts aloud, laughing at his own wit. His mind was full and he had only to "draw the cork" and let his letters flow. He thought that with some practice anyone with a clear mind could write.[15]

Robinson's weekly letters also appeared in the New York *Tribune*, from 1857 to 1861 and at intervals afterwards until 1869, and he wrote articles for *The Daily Evening Traveller* (1857); the Fitchburg *Reveille* (1857–58); the Worcester *Transcript*, in which he styled himself "Boythorn," (1857–60); and *The Daily Atlas*

(1860–61). He contributed occasional pieces to *Zion's Herald*; *The Congregationalist*; the Hartford *Press*, in which he called himself "Kremlin," (1865); *The Commonwealth* (1862–76); and the Boston *Journal* (1870–72). He edited the campaign newspapers entitled *The Straight Republican* (1857), *The Tocsin* (1861, 1862), and *The Reveille* (1870), as well as guest-editing for a season in 1868 the Hartford *Courant* and the Concord (New Hampshire) *Monitor*.

Although his writing was often in demand, Robinson's earnings were not excessive. In 1856 he was paid $2 apiece for the Springfield *Republican* letters, and in 1861 $4 apiece. In 1865 he received $7 a letter, and in 1867 $10. After 1870 *The Republican* paid him $12 for each.[16] When William was making $7 a letter, the New York *Tribune* offered him $10, and he yielded to lucre for a year, for the benefit of his children's education, but felt disloyal to his abandoned flock in Massachusetts; he returned to *The Republican* when that paper met the raise. In 1864 he had two offers to edit newpapers; one of them, the Rochester, New York, paper, suggested the high salary of $2,500 a year. Harriet told her daughters she felt quite rich and noted, "We should really begin to think that father was somebody." Hattie, the loyal daughter, countered, "I *always* thought he was."[17]

Robinson was not unique as a passionate man of letters who lived by his wits. Among his friends were several other journalists, moving from one occupation to another to make a living from their pens. James Redpath had emigrated from Scotland at the age of nineteen and soon went to work for Horace Greeley on the New York *Tribune*, where he wrote from 1852 to 1882. An energetic abolitionist and general reformer, he was "always seething with ardor in some cause or other" and "scornful of compromise," much like Robinson. Redpath moved on to establish a lecture booking agency and edit *The North American Review*.[18] Frank Sanborn, who had graduated from Harvard in 1855, began as a schoolmaster in Concord, where he became a disciple of Parker and Emerson. Like Robinson he supported John Brown and became a Free-Soiler and editor of the Boston *Commonwealth* before he moved on to the Springfield *Republican* as editor and columnist. Sanborn later served as secretary of the state board of charities, and wrote and edited books about the Concord men of letters.[19] Though more successful financially than Robinson, these two men had similarly patchy literary careers.

Robinson turned out his weekly "Warrington" letters with comments on Massachusetts politics and the war, support of woman suffrage, and portraits of the statesmen, politicians, and newsmen he had known and observed. His deep immersion in the state's political situation from the age of sixteen gave him familiarity with the local scene. He exposed foolishness, ridiculing it whenever he found it. He championed the poor and underprivileged, particularly the workingman and the fugitive slave, and like a ragged and slightly malevolent pied piper, he attempted to lead his sluggish readers to some ideal land of true democracy. Brilliant and irresponsible, he followed his own elusive sense of right rather than any party loyalty.

Robinson's third sphere of political influence was as a member of the Bird Club. This unofficial organization, which for years met without an officer, a record, a treasury, a committee, or even an established membership, was named after its central figure, Francis W. Bird, the "Sage of Walpole" and a radical politician.[20] Bird was a paper manufacturer who favored free trade, a vegetarian noted for his sumptuous dinners, and a thoroughly honest man, who exercised considerable political skill behind the scenes. Harriet thought Bird "a wonder . . . so original and so deep."[21] He occupied the place where Harriet would have liked to see her husband, and indeed was William's political patron to the extent that he had one.

The Bird Club had begun informally in the old Free-Soil days as a regular Saturday-afternoon dinner. Among the early and constant members were John A. Andrew, James W. Stone, Henry L. Pierce, Robinson, and Bird. Those attending paid a dollar each for the dinner Bird had ordered for them. The fee later climbed to two dollars and the site of the meeting place changed several times, coming to rest in the Parker House. Charles Sumner, Henry Wilson, Governor Claflin, Ben Butler, and Samuel Gridley Howe, among many other "equally pronounced radical Republicans," joined the group.[22] No formal speech making took place, but a regular aggregation of such potent personalities could not help but influence affairs.

Bird's affiliative nature gathered friends about him, and always
there was political activity. He took people shooting in the Adi-
rondacks; he introduced the Robinsons and others to Manomet
for seaside holidays. It was in Manomet in 1860 that the vacationing pols got word that Know-Nothing Governor Nathaniel P.
Banks had accepted a post in the West and would not be running
for reelection. Bird thereupon conferred with Robinson, Pierce,
and Judge Adin Thayer and decided that they should hurry
home to work at securing the nomination for their friend John A.
Andrew. It was this concentrated effort that helped to make
Andrew the next governor.[23] Robinson was willing to wager that
Bird combined, better than any other man, political foresight and
practical organizational wisdom, and thought that his influence
upon politicians and other public men had been greater than that
of any other individual of his time.[24]

Robinson's connection with Bird, Pierce, and Wilson—all men
of wealth, power, and presence—legitimized his role in public
life. He was a Bird Club member for about thirty years, the club's
most active period, before it devolved into a monthly social occasion. This club, his writing for newspapers, and his annual Janu-
ary-to-adjournment stint at the state house gave Robinson a central role in politics during his prime years.

Robinson found it tame to be on the winning side. Moreover,
he was disillusioned with Lincoln even before the President's
second election, calling him a "clog and brake on the wheels of
progress," because of his hesitant action on slavery. William deplored the greed of those profiting by the Civil War, and particularly the "tendency toward personal government, instead of a
government of politics."[25] By the early 1870s he thought that the
Republican Party was corrupt. "The Republican *party* as an organization professing to have certain principles of administration, is
dead," he stated in 1875.[26] Robinson considered approaching the
Democrats or working toward a realignment that would unite
like-minded members of both major parties, but he did not do
so.[27] Francis Bird did bolt from the Republicans, running for
Massachusetts governor as a candidate for the Democratic and
Independent Republican parties in 1872 and becoming a Demo-

crat "of the old school" in 1874.[28] While this general disillusion was setting in, William enjoyed one last long intraparty battle with his old colleague Ben (General Benjamin Franklin) Butler.[29]

Robinson and Butler had much in common—a poor New England boyhood and early political experience in Lowell, Massachusetts, where both championed the mill worker and were elected to the state house in 1850. But there the resemblance ended. Unlike Robinson, Butler managed to attend college (what has come to be Colby College, in Maine) and to be admitted to the bar. In contrast to William's Spartan adult life, Butler earned huge fees and amassed—by good means and bad—an estate valued at over $7 million. While Robinson was a Free-Soiler, Butler was a Hunker Democrat, preferring not to interfere with slavery, an institution that he thought would probably be outgrown. (Butler did later become a favorite of the Negroes, once even earning the introduction to a black audience that though his face was white, his heart was black.)[30] While Robinson had a modest public demeanor, Butler—no larger nor better-looking, and cock-eyed to boot—was a fabulous dramatic speaker, whose power could sway a crowd.

Butler had volunteered to serve in the Union army, and had distinguished himself as military governor of New Orleans while disgracing himself in combat. Grant had relieved him of his command, and the two were not overfond of each other. But resilient and opportunistic, Butler soon popped up as President Grant's dispenser of Massachusetts patronage. He built himself a powerful machine and was elected to the U.S. House of Representatives first from Essex County and later from Middlesex County.

Butler was a demagogue, a man with vast lower-class support and fancy personal tastes. He delighted in the conflict that surrounded him, egotistically sure of his ability to win. He was unmatched as a rough-and-tumble political fighter. Respectable citizens stood aghast at his antics. No serious wrongdoing was ever proved against him, but he was tainted by continual rumors, and wherever he was, there was disreputable trade. A man of enormous natural gifts, Butler had many fans and possessed qualities that would make him a leader in any cause he might espouse. On the other hand, Butler seemed lacking in some of the basic rigors of honesty. He himself admitted that he "never knew what true happiness was until [he] lost [his] character."[31] Clearly, Butler was an opponent Warrington could enjoy chewing on.

Butler sought the office of governor of Massachusetts seven times, achieving it finally in 1883. During Butler's first two attempts, in 1871 and 1873, Robinson had led out against him. In return Butler attacked Robinson, among others, in his nightly speeches, charging that the clerk unfairly received his fat annual salary of $3,000, and that he employed his daughter as his assistant.[32] Warrington countered in daily pieces with his usual scorn, arguing ironically that Massachusetts was better off with Butler in Washington. He admitted Butler was a demagogue: " 'Well, everybody knew that.'—'He was a blackguard.'—'Of course he was.'—'He was a scamp and a disorganizer generally.' I could not deny it. But still I insisted, that, if Essex County wanted him [to represent it in Congress], it ought to be allowed to take him."[33]

Robinson published a piece in *The Atlantic Monthly* deploring Butler's tendency to personal government and relating in some detail Butler's angry encounter with Massachusetts's two Republican Senators, Charles Sumner and Henry Wilson, who had been persuaded to oppose publicly his nomination.[34] Feelings ran high at the Republican Convention and not only was Butler soundly defeated, but he also pledged himself to support the Republican candidate, Washburn. Warrington was widely congratulated for his part in the defeat, having been one of the "first to take hold of Ben, and the last to let go."[35]

In 1872 William Robinson joined a convention of liberals of all parties at Cincinnati to nominate a third-party candidate for President. He had been thinking of such a new organization, uniting Westerners and Free-Soil Republican types, since 1852.[36] Robinson had no confidence in the incumbent President Grant, but his enthusiasm for Horace Greeley, who was nominated at Cincinnati, was hardly greater. William's attendance at the convention jeopardized his status as a Republican and consequently his employment, for the house clerkship was in the gift of the party in power. At the last, however, he went back to the Republicans, voted for Grant, and was returned to his own office, with only eleven dissenting votes.

Butler did not make a run for the governorship in 1872, being occupied with his Congressional race. Robinson was informed that, among other activities, Butler was working to take away the clerkship. Disinclined to rally his friends or make any effort in his own behalf, he responded, "If Butler's gang can defeat me, let them do so. I will not stoop to mix in their dirty work for twenty clerkships."[37] When the legislature of 1873 first met and balloted for officers, Mr. Robinson stood at his desk to hear the results of the election. He had lost by 107 votes. He was stunned, as were his friends.

Because William believed in public fights, he had made no effort to defend himself against a secret attack. Harriet claimed he was the victim of a *"stab in the dark,"*[38] castigating Butler for his vindictiveness. Quite possibly, some legislators were taking revenge on the clerk for his threatened defection of the preceding year. In any case, this "undeserved affront" was keenly felt, especially as it came when Robinson's "health was impaired" by years of hard service in the Republican Party. Badly hurt by the defeat, Robinson did not "whine, put finger in the eye, and sob," but "bore his defeat manfully." His friends at the state house, out of fear for their own jobs, stopped talking to him.[39] The insider was suddenly invisible.

Butler, on the other hand, was entitled to strike back. Robinson's attacks against him were not necessarily well reasoned or fair. Butler could claim the support of many good men, including William's friend Gilbert Haven, who had once dramatically stated, pointing to Robinson's dwelling, "There in that little house burns the only light in this State that Ben Butler is afraid of."[40] Frank Bird, albeit unenthusiastically, also supported Butler![41] Robinson had taken on a heroic but unpopular cause, and had been swept aside.

Robinson had not intended a fight to the death. He wrote with a vitriolic pen, but bore no ill will to those he attacked. Newspaper invective was a competitive sport for him. He had been spoiling for some contention for some time and had fastened on Butler. The Republican Party was too tame, too successful, too unani-

mous, and William was "dying for someone to tread on [his] tail
. . . so he could fight them."[42] But it was to be a war of words. To
cut off his purse strings seemed unfair.

Both Robinson and Butler were Republicans, so the former
was in no position to scream for party support. He had refused to
try to rally his friends, and he was somewhat tainted for mixing in
with the new liberal party. Still, the defeat was a bitter blow. He
went to bed "to think it out"; he said he had been on a ten-years'
cruise and had gotten a "hole stove in his bottom and must lay up
for repairs."[43] He then pulled himself together and went back to
ill-paying odd jobs.

In 1873 Butler sought the governorship again. Robinson's
attacks this time centered on Butler's successful efforts to pass a
bill raising the salaries of national leaders in the executive, legislative, and judicial branches. Robinson wrote a pamphlet detailing
this activity, called *The Salary Grab*.[44] It has since been pointed out
that Butler, with his fabulous wealth, cared little for the $2,000
annual raise voted in for Congressmen. What he wanted was the
President's favor for the $25,000 raise afforded the chief execu-
tive, a measure that was obscured in the fuss about raises. Butler's
consummate skill in shepherding the bill through a Congress
unwilling to appear greedy was very impressive. By contrast,
Robinson's pamphlet—which dealt only with the surface workings of the measure, failed to treat Butler's cultivation of the
President, and went too far in its accusations—seemed inept. One
of Butler's biographers takes Robinson to task for charging that
Butler authored the bill, an incorrect assertion.[45] Actually, Butler
came closer to defending himself against Robinson's charges than
against anyone else's, acknowledging them and answering them,
when he ordinarily ignored criticism. Harriet claimed that William was approached by Butler forces who promised him security
in exchange for silence,[46] a temptation that only speeded the flow
of Robinson's attacking words. Thanks in part to this attack,
Butler was again defeated at the convention for the Republican
nomination, by the same margin as two years before. Having
spent his all in the effort to stop an immensely powerful adversary, Robinson then dropped out of the fight.

Few contemporaries saw this fight as a personal match between Butler and Robinson, as Harriet did. George Frisbie Hoar, who opposed Butler in public debate and resigned his post as head of Harvard's alumni association rather than meet Butler officially as governor, saw himself in the prime contender's role.[47] In Butler's own massive *Autobiography*, admittedly apologetic and selective, Robinson figures only as an inflammatory "Irishman" from the Lowell period; he is not even mentioned in connection with the gubernatorial contests.[48] Robinson wagered and lost all in a game in which he was not recognized as a player.

Harriet was on the whole glad to have William out of the state house, to have him free of that "abominable air," to resume his noble employment as journalist. "If we are poorer we can live, if richer how much the better."[49] She urged him to write his books. *"Warrington's" Manual* was completed in the fall of 1875, and Robinson anticipated a book on woman suffrage and a biography of Charles Sumner, whom he had always respected. Harriet wanted him to collect his Warrington letters, but, diffident as ever, he refused, saying there were "too many books already."[50] Robinson's friends urged him to run for the clerkship again, but he would not, and clearly he was not up to it. His political life was drawing to a close.

Friends took the occasion of the Robinson's silver wedding anniversary, in 1873, to honor them and to present Robinson with a gift of $5,000. Henry L. Pierce, who had financed the Malden house, led the list, with $1,000. At the celebration Frank Sanborn, a fellow journalist, called Warrington a soldier "working in the trenches and fighting on the ramparts of journalism, more for others than for himself." He said that Robinson had volunteered for "the most conspicuous service, and had drawn on himself the fire of the other side, while many a more selfish man would have kept in the ranks." Sanborn stressed Robinson's loyalty, although he acknowledged that there was scarcely a man who had subscribed to this testimonial "who had [not] smarted under [his] criticism, or, at least encountered his reproof."[51]

Harriet thought a sea voyage might be the thing for the drooping warrior, and, leaving the girls in Malden, Harriet, William,

and Warrie set off for Liverpool and a European journey in
1874.[52] The sea voyage did little to restore William, and he wan-
dered through Europe, lagging behind his determined wife and
young son. They traveled to London and Paris, through Italy and
to Carlsbad, in Bohemia, for the waters, to Switzerland and
Germany and back to London. Harriet was delighted to see the
places she had read about, though she often preferred her imag-
inings to the disappointing realities, such as the streets of London
swarming with filthy and hungry human beings.[53] William would
have preferred to remain at home. His mind was on Massachusetts politics and he wanted to be back there writing it out.
After eight months abroad the Robinsons returned to Malden,
William's health no better for the trip. He resumed his writing for
The Republican and for the Boston *Daily News*.[54]

Butler continued to try for the Massachusetts governorship
and in 1883 was finally elected for a single term. As the only
Democrat (he had changed parties) in a government dominated
by Republicans, he was prevented from taking much decisive
action. Robinson's fear that Butler's election would incur the risk
of "permanent and incurable rottenness"[55] seems not to have
been realized, possibly because of his relatively powerless position. Perhaps the greatest irony is that when, in his bids for the
governorship in 1882 and 83, Butler spoke out for woman suffrage, he was supported by Harriet Hanson Robinson.[56] Harriet
saw Butler as her husband's most deadly foe, yet she could support him for office.

In January of 1875, at the age of fifty-six, Robinson took to his
bed. The news of his deteriorating condition spread, and his
friend and fellow writer James Redpath wrote him a handsome
eulogy. Robinson rallied, but the paper had already set the piece
in type, so it was run as a tribute. Robinson sat up in bed and read
his proposed obituary by Redpath—who, by the way, had been a
primary journalistic opponent in the Butler battle.[57] Redpath's
piece stressed Robinson's courage in the face of poverty. He was
the "bravest public man in New England," a man of convictions
and fortitude; "without the breastwork of an assured social position or an independent fortune, and without a band of devoted
followers pledged and proud to fight his battles, he was as brave

in the advocacy of his views, and as independent in his criticisms of politicians, as Wendell Phillips, or Gerritt Smith, or Gen. Butler." When a man was as poor as Robinson and had a family dependent on him, and his position was under the control of politicians, he needed "the heart of a hero to criticize without fear and without concealment, and without equivocation in sense of phrase, the errors of the party, and the motives of the leaders." Robinson had the pluck. He was a "rough, brave, and honest warrior."[58]

Frank Bird suggested that Robinson follow the water cure at a Northampton, Massachusetts, resort, kept by Dr. Denniton. He duly went off, though an unwilling exile, preferring to stay at home with family and friends. At the resort, amid the unhappy company of terminal cancer patients, weary housewives, and the insane, Robinson thought about politics. He regretted that after he had been ousted from the house he had not "fought" his way back. "Had I not better plunge into politics, and write again, and so plunge out of myself?"[59] Having broken with the Republicans, he wished the Democrats would elect him, so that he could be useful again; he was no good at anything else. "They knocked me out of my 'sphere,' " he wrote to Frank Bird, "and I fear I made a mistake in not immediately fighting to get back. Is it too late now? God knows, if there ever was a man of small ambition, and apt for usefulness, it is your servant and friend."[60] No one took his hopes of reentering the political procession seriously. He had stepped out of the line three years before and the hole had closed, leaving no place for him.

Disillusioned with Dr. Denniton, who hoped to keep him there as long as possible, Robinson packed his bags and went home to die. "Can it be," he said, looking around the books in his library, "that I am to leave all this work undone?"[61]

The sturdy warrior retreated from the rebelliousness that had characterized so much of his life. His burdens, cares, and ambitions fell away from him, and he became as gentle and sweet as a child. At the same time, a belief in the immortality of the soul grew up in the old agnostic, and he perceived that this world and the next were as close as his joined hands. In his mind he walked daily by a hedge looking for a gate to go through. During his last weeks he felt the veil of flesh grow thin and transparent, and his chamber was thronged with spiritual visitors, "apparitions and ghosts," none of whom he recognized. He felt his family and friends must live some distance away, "on the other side of the hedge," and that he would see them later.[62]

One bleak morning, March 11, 1876, William Stevens Robinson died quietly in his sleep, holding his wife's hand. Harriet went in to Hattie's room and told her that "Papa is gone." Hattie dressed and went for the Noyes family, close neighbors, who came and closed William's eyes and stayed awhile. Harriet "sat crouched before the stove saying nothing."[63]

The Survivors

⤙ *Bye and bye after you have done drudging you shall be an author. You have escaped immortality, being switched off the celestial railroad on to a side track, leading to an old coal yard. You shall be paid for it someday. If not here, hereafter. Luther promised his dog that in the resurrection he should have a golden tail. You shall have a harp for music, or a pencil for painting and or a chisel for sculpture—and I will be your delighted proof reader and critic— and take the money for your golden books. Seriously.*

—William Robinson to HHR, 1868

⤙ *As I stood by my graves in Concord, I said, "My youth was buried in Willie's grave." "My best friend lies in my mother's grave." "But my life was buried in my husband's grave."*

—HHR Diary, 20 September 1899

⤙ *"I am going to leave you to make the struggle all over again." And I have made it.*

—William Robinson quoted in HHR Diary, 12 March 1904

William Robinson died in March of 1876. By June of the following year the book *"Warrington" Pen-Portraits*, with a long biographical introduction by Harriet Robinson, had been published, and Harriet was on the road as a book peddler, making the necessary money to pay the printing costs. Harriet's urges for power, barely disguised in her introduction, led her to complete the book and market it in such a dramatic fashion. She hoped to build a place for herself on her dead husband's career. Unlike the other widows in the family, she refused to take a dependent role.

This project had been begun during William's illness, and was to have been his next book. Harriet had cut out and pasted all the Warrington letters into scrapbooks, rereading them and marking those worthy of preservation. "How much you have written and how much good you have done and how hard you have worked," she exulted, encouraging the weary man.[1] Harriet wanted the book to be "bright and sketchy," in order to sell well, but the money was secondary to her major purpose: "Above all I want your fame assured before we 'go hence.'"[2]

Harriet now saw herself as carrying on her husband's work,[3] and her diligence and daring in defense of his good name outstripped anything he had done. The widow risked her future bread by this venture. In her determination to place the book, she waited on the politically powerful of the state, enlisting their interest and aid. With an influential patron heading the subscription list in each town, she called on newsmen and politicians, and in face-to-face confrontations attempted to sell them copies of the book.

The tough-minded, clear-spoken Harriet Robinson was not above a little fawning when it suited her purpose. To her Lowell patron, a Mr. Knapp, she wrote fluttery, affected phrases designed to arouse his paternal concern. In Worcester, she told Knapp, she was "engaged in that vocation, with about the same success as that I was so fortunate to meet in Lowell." She would always recall with pleasure the kindness of those who did "so much to 'abnegate the asperities' of book peddling."[4]

To the family she was more frank. She left Lowell, she told them, pretty miserable with fatigue and worry, but by the time she had been in Worcester a few days she was fairly sure of paying the $1,200 she owed, and "a fig for the other three [$300] say I." Even from the road she continued to run her household, sending minute instructions about ordering coal, mailing books, and saving every scrap of business paper for her later perusal.[5]

Old friend Samuel Bowles, of the Springfield *Republican*, discouraged Harriet's coming to his town, saying that Warrington had been forgotten. But Harriet refused to believe it, and sent for another influential name to head the local list. Bowles would be all right when he saw "what a determined 'critter'" she could be.[6] And so he was, kindly entertaining her and taking her out one evening.[7]

Once, while she was waiting for a horsecar somewhere out in the country, she "sat down on a lonely stump and cried." Then she got up and sold four books that afternoon. Every book was sold "with a struggle and a sigh," but she put on a brave face. In Dalton, Massachusetts, Mr. Crane of the Crane Paper Company lent Harriet an open-seated wagon with two horses and a driver, so that she could peddle in style. "No one could say 'no' when they saw me," she rejoiced, risen to her proper place at last. "I know the value of horseflesh now."[8] She hoped to sell 900 books, which would give her enough for the bill and a little over. Then she would come home and pay off the debt in person.[9] After two difficult months on the road, Harriet returned home triumphant.

"Warrington" Pen-Portraits is a substantial book, of which Harriet could be proud. The text runs close to 600 long pages, about two-thirds of which are selections from Warrington, divided by topic and identified by date and newspaper (the other third being Harriet's introduction). Many of these entries are brief biographies of contemporary political figures—hence the title—who are sketched with broad, frank statements. Cogent and pithy, the letters are accessible and entertaining to today's reader. The whole was fully indexed by Hattie, making it a valuable reference work. Harriet's 180-page introduction, with its wealth of information and its unquestioned devotion to the subject, is a complex pen portrait in itself.

Harriet's strategy was to tell the truth about her husband's characteristics, but to redefine the categories of success and goodness so that they applied to him. Though she clearly imputed heroic qualities to her husband, she avoided sentiment and spoke in the specific detail that strengthened her case. This description of Robinson illustrates many of her devices. He was remembered as a

> modest, unassuming person, full of jokes and stories, and of the most imperturable good-nature. He was short of stature, had a rosy complexion and blue eyes, and was a man most people would pass by unobserved. There are people, who, by the mere arrogance of their *personnel*, their bodily presence, delude you into the fancy that you have met a god. This sort of person is often disappointing: on further acquaintance, the soul you expected to find seems to melt away, and your god turns out a thing of brass and clay. There are others who do not impress you at first, but surprise you continually with new developments of character. They "open well:" they never disappoint you. Mr. Robinson was of this sort. He did not impress strangers. His unpretending manners deceived those who desired favors from his pen. He listened deferentially and silently to all that was said to him on such occasions, and sometimes gave the impression that he was convinced. The pen then became his interpreter; and the meaning of that was always understood. He had a hatred of pretenders and shams.[10]

That Robinson was unobtrusive and childlike in appearance, Harriet did not deny. Yet with all his drawbacks, he was the superior of the two types she described. The flashy alternatives, who by their "mere arrogance" "delude" you into thinking that you have "met a god," proved "disappointing." Unobtrusiveness and modesty were here equated with goodness.

Harriet steadily hinted that she had a better candidate for "a god" than the people of "bodily presence." She told the story of a crusader fighting the forces of evil that surrounded him. He battled against Locofocoism, Hunkerism, Know-Nothingism, Gardnerism. He was anticoalition, antislavery, anti-Butler. He was only briefly on the popular side. Instead of reading this story as a failure, which could easily be done, Harriet extended her Christian images to those of divine mission and martyrdom.

Robinson was the suffering servant wringing redemption and fame out of the gloom.[11] He was the sorrowing father trusting the people who steadily disappointed him.[12] He was the party regular who refused to play politics, almost forcing his own people to sacrifice him. His fight with Benjamin Butler was his "crowning glory."[13] He called his *Republican* letters his sermons, and the readership his parish.[14] The ninth chapter of the book, which tells of his failing health and death, is entitled "The Successful Man"!

Warrington's quoted comments contrast wonderfully with his wife's exalted prose. The modest William Robinson maintained that "a history of my life cannot be long or very interesting,"[15] and that "though I have little learning, I have less house; and my land is nothing."[16] Again he fit the Christian pattern as the greatest who was contented to be least.

Harriet used his modesty in building up her myth, but the actual situation must have been very frustrating to her. She had a husband who refused to seek the power and fame she yearned for. In her supportive and secondary position, as his wife, she was forced to ascribe to him her own drives. Power exercised with divine righteousness was what she claimed for her late husband. She proclaimed that his "obscure pen" had become "a power to be felt all over the state."[17] The key to her husband's character was "never to refrain from speaking 'God's truth' at the right time."[18]

Robinson functioned as the wise judge even before his crucifixion. At the height of his career, when he held the modest office of clerk of the House of Representatives, Harriet made the most she could of his influence.

These were "Warrington's" times of power. It is not too much to say, that, during the years of his clerkship, few men could have held high public office in Massachusetts without his advice or suggestion, such was the controlling influence of his pen. . . . His was the power behind the throne,—sometimes the veto power,—ever exercised unselfishly for the good of the people. It is difficult to estimate his influence upon his time.[19]

He had "power," "controlling influence," "power behind the throne," "veto power," power, the ultimate goal. Notice, however, that he was still the power in disguise. His influence was hidden and still "difficult to estimate." In order to make Robinson the power Harriet wanted to represent him as, he must be other than he appeared to be.

Harriet's assessment of Warrington was difficult to challenge. Her forthright, intense assertions defied dispute. She was in deadly earnest; besides, the man had passed on.

Most local critics were inclined to be kindly to one of their craft, recently deceased. "The wit, the sagacity, the broad humor and strong sense—above all, the dauntless independence of the man,—these all shine forth on nearly every page," sang out the New Bedford (Massachusetts) *Evening Standard*. The Taunton (Massachusetts) *Republican* found the book "The most acceptable volume of the year to those interested in political or literary matters." "Mr. Robinson was, without exception, the most able and brilliant newspaper writer of his day and generation in Massachusetts," stated the Boston *Herald*.

Harriet also came in for some measured praise. The Boston *Globe* found her introduction "Such a record of patient and careful work as is encouraging to read." The Boston *Advertiser* thought she had "written with entire simplicity and with literary skill by no means to be despised." Good friend Bishop Gilbert Haven wrote in *Zion's Herald*, "The genius of America has found a fitting chronicler. His wife has gotten up one of the choicest volumes of the year. . . . One will find few books of such sparkle as this."

The reviewers at some distance from Massachusetts were more objective and critical. The New York *Nation* in June of 1877 pronounced that "A more careful, or perhaps we should say a less partial, editing of the "Warrington" papers would have ommitted much that is now irrelevant to anything, much that is mere repetition, and some things that are calculated to make the judicious grieve." The New Haven *Review* bluntly allowed, "This book will have no permanent value. And there is too much of it. It tells the war and anti-slavery history, at least, one time too many. But it is brightly written and is the life of a noble man who fell, from bloodless wounds after a great battle, wherein his plume was always far in front."[20] The shortcomings of the book justify this criticism, but the reviewers were wrong in their final assessment. Harriet's anthology is often quoted, and Robinson's work might easily have been forgotten without her labors.

𝒞𝒷.𝒞𝒷.𝒞𝒷

Three generations of women lived in the Lincoln Street house in Malden, with Harriet as the leader. When William died, in 1876, the family consisted of Harriet, then fifty-one, her mother, aged eighty-one, Hattie, twenty-six, Lizzie, twenty-four, and the single male member, young Warrie, aged seventeen. The house remained a refuge, which Harriet intended to keep always so that family members would have a place to return to. As it was, not one of them had yet left. For herself the house was a place where she could "hide her tired head and be at peace,"[21] a place to serve as protection from the world.

Mother Hanson, so helpful and loyal, still "frisked around here like a young girl." Harriet treated her like a daughter, sometimes losing patience and speaking sharply to her. Then Harriet ate the "bread of repentence," resolved to do better, and repeated the offense.[22] Harriet recognized that she would never be "half as good and useful" when she was old. She was "too uneasy and aspiring."[23]

Sometime in her last decade—she was to die in 1881—Mrs. Hanson lost her sight. Hattie used to read to her, later regretting that she had not done more of it—"I was a selfish unthinking witch, not to!"[24] But Gram kept her hands busy, always earning her keep with some worthwhile enterprise. She braided rugs and mats, cheerfully dictating to Warrie her own sad self-evaluation: "Old women are useful as long as rags are plenty."[25]

Mrs. Hanson lived to be almost eighty-six years old, finally slowing down and dying of paralysis. Harriet wrote her a handsome obituary, which noted that she had survived her husband by fifty years and which read in part, "She was resolute and liberal minded and of a singularly unselfish disposition. . . . She was a strong advocate of woman suffrage and registered as a voter at the school committee election in Malden."[26] Harriet had reason to feel satisfied with the way she had cared for her mother, even though it was not the way she would choose to be cared for herself.

Hattie and Lizzie, twenty-seven and twenty-five at the time their mother came home from the peddling trip, were both still at home. Someone once called them the two prettiest girls in Malden. Hattie thought the description applied to Lizzie, but not to her: "Too fat and serious, and sarcastic."[27] Hattie was realistically hard on herself. Her pictures show her to be short and rounded, with abundant dark hair and big dark eyes. She might have been a romantic figure, soulful and curvy, but for her steady gaze and grim expression.

More than the others, Hattie was the heir of her parents. She was a great deal like her father, and Harriet thought Hattie might have made the mark her father had if she had been a boy, for "she has more heat with her coolness than he ever had."[28] She always spoke to the point; if anything, Hattie was too abrupt and direct.[29]

In 1870 Hattie dramatized Dickens's novel *Our Mutual Friend* and played in it for the benefit of the woman-suffrage association, making $70.[30] Her group of friends got up two dramatic societies and performed several spectaculars in public.[31] She also studied singing for several years in the hope of an operatic career.

No true fond lover had come along to make her completely happy. She once became involved in a triangular homosexual relationship with a girl named Emma Foster. Hattie, just twenty-one at the time, had a crush on a pretty girl named Lou Hunt. Emma Foster then attached herself to Hattie and won her over. Hattie recorded that she had "a strange love affair with a girl friend—very passionate . . . and I all the time labored under strong excitement."[32] Emma flirted both with Hattie and with Lou, treating them badly and then making up. Hattie was pretty miserable through the year. In retrospect, she found the whole episode and "*all* [her] "platonic" affairs—always with Women . . . sickening," and probably they did not amount to much more than crushes.[33]

In 1870 and '71 Hattie had worked in her father's private office in the state house. Then in 1872 Robinson appointed his daughter his regular assistant, and she took her place beside him at the clerk's desk, the first female to hold an official position in an American legislative body.[34] The surprised gaze at first of more than two hundred representatives demanded a show of dignity on Hattie's part, but soon she felt at ease, writing for dear life and seldom looking up. Besides copying, she filed papers, indexed records, and noted the votes.

Hattie was compensated $750 for a four-month session, more than she could earn elsewhere. Her counterpart in the state senate, a young man who did no more work than she, was paid $900; he had been elected, whereas Hattie was only appointed.

During a special session occasioned by the Boston fire of 1872, the senate clerk earned an extra $100. The house clerk, too shy to ask for her money, got nothing.[35]

Hattie hoped to continue in this good situation for another year, but lost the job when her father was turned out. She then applied to the Robinsons' good friend Frank Sanborn, of the American Social Science Association, where she did office work for five years, meanwhile planning to go into journalism.[36] Hoping to be a correspondent and reporter like her father, Hattie began a long and unremunerative career as a newspaper writer.

She wrote children's stories, several of which were published, at the rate of $2 or $3 each. She got a short-lived job with the *New England Monthly*, writing editorials and making selections for $5 a month.[37] She wrote long reports of the proceedings at the Concord School of Philosophy for several summers in the 1880s. These highly praised accounts—which went on for column after column—were published in the Boston *Daily Transcript*, and Hattie was sent postage or very modest expense money for her trouble; she received 75¢ in 1882.[38] She wrote a regular uncompensated column for *The Transcript*, under the name of Simes. She conducted a column called "The Woman's Hour" in the Ewing (Nebraska) *Item* for three years, for which she was not paid. She contributed articles and letters to the Boston *News* and *The Woman's Journal*. Hattie worked every morning at her writing and amassed an impressive collection of articles, stories, poetry, letters to the editor. For these she received an occasional fee and some complimentary letters from editors (as well as rejection slips), noting that she had talent, that she could "poke fun artistically."[39] But she did not make a living at it.

Eventually Hattie published six books. The dramatization of *Our Mutual Friend* came out in 1870 and enjoyed modest sales for more than thirty years. *The Story of Dante's Divine Comedy*, a retelling for young people published in 1887, resulted from the articles she had written about the Concord School of Philosophy. *Little Folks East and West*, a collection of her children's stories, was published in 1892. Hattie wrote three books on parliamentary law, which sold thousands of copies and brought her considerable success and profits. Combining her experience in the state house, her knowledge as a club and suffrage worker, and her lucid writing style, these books helped educate a generation of emerging women for leadership roles. She wrote *The Woman's Manual of Parliamentary Law* in 1891, *Shattuck's Advanced Rules of Parliamentary Law* in 1898, and *Parliamentary Answers* in 1914.

One magic day in January of 1877 Hattie was left alone in the parlor with Sidney Doane Shattuck, and they "found each other." Shattuck, a slight, dapper young man, as articulate and bookish as Hattie and as good-natured and comfortable around the house as her father had been, became her husband. The relationship was a love match, as "fervant and staunch" as any in a book.[40]

The wedding took place on June 11, 1878, in Malden. Hattie had written her own service and, befitting an independent young woman with literary aspirations, the vows were graceful and egalitarian. Sid and Hattie promised to love, comfort, and honor each other, to choose each other alone from all the world as their best earthly friends, to cultivate for the other's sake all virtues, and to assist the other in life's work.[41] Hattie had lost fifteen pounds not long before and was a pretty bride in her wedding finery. After the church ceremony, a reception—where they feted their guests with twelve pounds of wedding cake—and a wedding trip to Manomet, the young Shattucks were back at home in Malden on Lincoln Street with Hattie's family.

Hattie quit her part-time job at the Social Science Association and stayed home. Sid was making only $800 a year and her $30 a month would have helped, but she later commented that her continuing her job would have caused a sensation and humiliated her husband. As she grew older and more conservative, Hattie wanted young women to follow her example. The "modern idea of a married woman going on with her work—if outside her home—is demoralizing all the girls,"[42] she said. Her writing at home qualified as appropriate for a housewife.

Two intelligent and handy women of the house, mother and daughter, whose major interests lay elsewhere could make light work of household routine. Harriet and Hattie began a pattern that was to last them for many years. They took turns catering and cooking for a week at a time, giving them each an "off week" in the culinary department.[43] They lived together in the Robinson house (along with Sid Shattuck) in apparent harmony until 1887, when growing prosperity allowed the Shattucks to buy a house within walking distance of Lincoln Street. This imposing frame structure, perched on a rocky crag, was elegant and fashionable. Harriet moved in with them.

చు.చు.చు

Family members were surprised that Hattie, the stout and independent one of the sisters, should marry first. All signs had pointed instead to Lizzie, so soft and demure, so tasteful, deft, and not without gumption.[44] Hattie described Lizzie as growing prettier and more loving daily, and she had numerous swains.[45] Unfortunately, however, she had bad luck with her boyfriends, engaging herself to one who was arrested for a crime and another who jilted her.

Lizzie had been attracted to kindergarten teaching by the work of Elizabeth Palmer Peabody, but William's death and the family's subsequent limited finances prevented her receiving special training. She taught a district school in Maine for a time, boarding around at the homes of her pupils, kept a small private school of her own, tried bookkeeping, and learned to set type. She even considered telegraphy.[46] She finally accepted a position as the kitchen maid in a charity kindergarten in Boston's North End, where the manager took an interest in her and allowed her to get some training. She graduated from Miss Lucy H. Symond's class in 1883 and taught locally, before moving to Waterbury, Connecticut, where she introduced the kindergarten program at the Hillside Avenue School.[47] She worked hard, feeling sorry for herself after her aborted romances. By this time Lizzie was thirty-one years old, well on her way to spinsterhood.

Romance nonetheless bloomed, with one George S. Abbott, a Waterbury bookkeeper and builder. The relationship deepened, and Lizzie was told by her mother to invite him to Malden for Christmas if he was "serious."[48] After the visit Harriet sent a guarded greeting his way: "Best wishes to Mr. Abbott. I am glad that we all like him, since he is to continue a friend of yours."[49] By mid-January an engagement had been accomplished.

Plans for the wedding and particularly the trousseau—to consist of a wedding dress, a walking dress, two white dresses, a

simple silk for all occasions, and two house dresses—were speed-
ily made.[50] Lizzie and George were married on May 14, 1885, in
Malden by the Rev. John Wesley Hanson, D.D., the bride's uncle,
who had come from Chicago to perform the ceremony. Lizzie
and George were "at home" at Lincoln Street before returning to
Waterbury, where they took up residence in a two-family house
in Valley View Park.[51] Lizzie was thirty-two and George thirty-
one. Both Hattie and Lizzie married late and were older than
their husbands.

When Harriet visited in Waterbury, she rejoiced to see her
daughter's prosperity.[52] Lizzie's nicely furnished flat was financed
by George's building enterprises. He was renting out a large brick
block of shop and office space he had built. He was also construct-
ing two dwellings and tearing down an old church. More than ten
men and boys were on his payroll.[53]

In 1888, when Lizzie had been married three years, she became
pregnant with her first child. "I never knew a woman so absorb-
ingly happy in the thought of becoming a mother. It is beautiful
to see," said the contented Harriet.[54] Lizzie was now thirty-six.

Lizzie labored long and painfully to bring forth her first child,
during which her brave comments gave way to despair. At first
she said, "How wonderful . . . is the production of a human being.
. . . I would not have missed this experience for the world." Later
she said, "O mother, now I know what you have suffered for me. I
never thought it, never knew how great it was." After more
painful hours, she said, "No more children. It is too much. I
would not suffer what I have today for a million dollars. . . . If the
baby does not live, it will be just as well."[55] Harriet sat at Lizzie's
bedside, sympathizing, encouraging, and recording Lizzie's remarks.

When, after ninety-six hours of hard labor, the baby did not
progress toward birth, the three doctors in attendance decided to
deliver him with instruments. Lizzie was chloroformed, and tiny
William Robinson Abbott was brought forth—dead. The child,
which was very large for the mother's pelvis, had turned to a
difficult presentation. The doctors repeatedly told the family that
the baby could not have been born alive and the mother saved;

they had apparently crushed the child's skull in order to deliver him. George and Harriet mourned together.

Lizzie's recovery concerned them next, for in this precarious period she was susceptible to infection and depression. Harriet remained in Waterbury to assist the full-time nurse. The doctor put Lizzie on quinine and the nurse administered vaginal douches and enemas. Lizzie was fed hourly—cold food, milk, champagne, eggnog, coffee or tea, light soup. Her menu expanded to include mutton chops and broiled chicken, with blancmange and whipped cream, custard, and ale. With these meals arriving hourly at her bedside, Lizzie began to put on flesh. She ate heartily and still her stomach cried for more. During that hot July the windows were kept open and she was bathed with alcohol and turpentine because of her heavy perspiration. Her douches of "very hot water" and carbolic acid may well have prevented puerperal fever.

After three weeks Lizzie was allowed to sit up for twenty minutes, which she "bore very well." Two months after the ordeal, she came to dine at the table.[56] Harriet thought Lizzie had never looked better. She was approaching her mother's size, about 160 pounds; as she was little over five feet tall, she must have been very round. Lizzie gained another six pounds during a month at the seaside, where she continued her recovery, and Harriet thought she was a "splendid looking matron."[57]

Despite Lizzie's bad experience, the Abbotts tried again, and this time produced a fine healthy son, Robinson Abbott, to be called Robin. He was born July 3, 1891, and about two years later, on May 28, 1893, a little sister, Martha Harriet, completed the family. Harriet prophesied of her first granddaughter, "If she lives she may be the greatest comfort of all, and the one to lean on,—as I was, to my mother." Martha was eventually the mainstay of her family.[58]

The Abbotts had fallen on hard times. The panic and depression of 1893 made it all but impossible for George to sell the houses he had built. He would have filed for bankruptcy if Lizzie had let him; she insisted that he pay his debts honestly, and he tried to do so. In his preoccupation with business, George disregarded his wife. Harriet extracted a promise from him to spend more time with his "three darlings"; if she felt obliged to interfere in family matters, the situation must have been serious.[59] By the end of 1894 Harriet could report that so far George had been saved from bankruptcy and that "Lizzie is brave and true and holds up both his hands."[60] George eventually bought a farm in Oakville, Connecticut, and his family joined him in hard labor. The Robinsons' opinion was that Lizzie had a great deal to put up with. As for George, his side of the story was never recorded.

෯෯෯

Young Warrie Robinson broke his mother's heart by dropping out of school at sixteen, during his father's illness. "I am not going to have my mother support me,"[61] said he. Harriet knew that curtailing his education was a mistake, but she hoped he would nonetheless be a good man, if not a learned one. "You are always my pride and joy my *only* son, and your progress in life is all in all to me."[62] Though sore tried by Warrie's diffidence, his mother never gave up on him.

Warrie went to work as a clerk in a bookseller-stationer's shop. His handwriting did not improve much, despite his mother's constant admonitions to practice. Given the precarious financial situation of the 1870s, the unskilled Warrie was frequently out of work. Harriet contented herself with a son who did well to keep a clerk's job.

When he was twenty-seven, still casting about for a place in the world, Warrie went off to Denver and got work in a stationer's store there. He engaged himself to Mary Elizabeth Robinson, a young Englishwoman, soon to be Mary Robinson Robinson. Harriet pronounced her "just the one" for Warrie.[63] Warrie was thirty-four at the time of his wedding. He had been married less than a month when his employer sold the business, and Warrie was again out of a job.[64] His mother sent him money, called on her friends, and wrote letters to influential acquaintances; it was six months before Harriet managed to get him a job. John Forbes's letters to the Denver and Rio Grande Railroad resulted in a position as a part-time express messenger. The next year Warrie and Mary moved to Pueblo, Colorado, where a permanent job awaited him. It was there that little Harriet Hanson Robinson II—"born to freedom" in a state with suffrage for women—came into the world. Such an advent was not to be missed, and Harriet, thanks to Sid's generosity, made a pilgrimage to Pueblo to see her namesake.

Harriet hoped to be godmother to her granddaughter, whom she wanted baptized into the Congregational Church. Considering Harriet's past and her skeptical attitude toward religion, this desire represented a watershed. Warrie and Mary never went to church, and the baptism was of little concern to anyone but Harriet. The stumbling block was that she was not a church member.

The Congregational minister brushed aside Harriet's doctrinal difficulties with immediate and fixed judgment, the Immaculate Conception, the virgin birth, and even the Trinity—but baptism was required; she must be baptized to stand as godmother to the child. Harriet, however, was unwilling to embrace the whole creed for the purpose of becoming little Harriet's godmother.

But several days later she woke with a start and the realization that she had been baptized back in that ill-fated Lowell revival. She dashed off a note to the minister describing the event and the unfortunate sequel—how she had been dismissed from the church for disbelief and nonattendance—which she supposed disqualified her. The minister thought otherwise. He was "much pleased" that she could serve as godmother to the child.[65]

How ironic that the ceremony that had meant little to Harriet as a girl, and which had brought her considerable pain and ostracism since, now gave her the means to serve as godmother. "Is there not an element of grim humor to the idea,—of that old sprinkling process of fifty-five years ago," she wrote her daughters, "which meant nothing to me then (and worse than nothing since because I did not understand its true meaning) being the weight (dead) in the balance as against all my other qualifications."[66] The early baptism incident had touched off Harriet's war with organized religion, a war that had lasted almost a lifetime. Yet in her maturity it was that incident which made it possible to participate in a church ordinance of great importance to her, when all her virtues and experiences counted as naught.

෴෴෴

In 1892 Harriet had been living on Murray Street, site of the Shattuck's elegant house, with Hattie and Sid for five years. She was determinedly happy about her pleasant large room and the setting close to the woodsy Felsway, where she often walked, gathered wildflowers, and called on friendly neighbors. With rental income from the Lincoln Street house, she was quite well off.

In 1892 Sid began to suffer business reverses.[67] His firm, Yates Brothers and Shattuck, engaged in a liquor trade with Africa, a practice that Hattie opposed and which Sid had promised to discontinue at his marriage. This volatile and perhaps illegal trade contributed to a business crisis that required Sid to relocate in Waterville, Maine, closer to his operations.

Harriet, who had in fact been pining for the old home, then concluded to move back there; she felt it calling to her like an old hen gathering her young under her wings.[68] Harriet took the lower floor for herself and rented the upper. The Murray Street house was broken up, and Sid sold it at a loss.[69]

Hattie got her husband settled in Maine and then moved back in with her mother. This break in propinquity apparently meant no break in cordial relations. Sid's was a temporary remove, which marked a retrenchment, rather than an expansion, and served to discourage a major relocation.

At this time Hattie suffered from a variety of nervous disorders, headaches, and backaches; her eyes hurt, her voice gave out, and she had bronchial problems. She was treated for several years by Dr. Richard Kennedy, finding herself almost wholly dependent on his daily care.[70] Kennedy, a former associate of the famed Lydia Pinkham, did nothing more than rub the top of her head, hard, for an hour or more, but he seemed to have some gift for healing; he could bring Hattie out of her nervous prostration, and Sid out of his rheumatism.[71] Because of her condition, Hattie could not leave her doctor when Sid went to Maine. Nor could she leave her work as a teacher of parliamentary law, nor her mother.

Back home in her own domain, where she was queen of the roost, Harriet contemplated a celebration. She would soon be seventy and decided to observe her anniversary—February 8, 1895—at home in a festive manner, much as she had celebrated the nuptials of her children. If no one had occasion to honor her at a party, she would do it herself.

The party seemed a fitting climax to this period of Harriet's life. Eight hundred cards reading "1825–1895, Mrs. Harriet H. Robinson, At Home on her Seventieth Anniversary" were mailed out. Harriet received guests from two in the afternoon until ten at night. She had made "the old ark look as well as possible," by putting in a front bell, bringing electricity into the house, mending the wallpaper, whitening the walls and ceilings, replacing the straw carpets and lampshades, and adding silk curtains. A caterer was on hand to simplify the food arrangements and clear up the remains.

A generous crowd—250—gathered, despite the furious storm outside. The house had been transformed into a temple to honor the chief priestess, "stately and handsome" in her gown of dove-gray silk and Brussels lace. Daughters and friends, all in costumes worthy of mention, received, ushered, or served, according to rank, as the guests moved to the dining room for confectionery, chocolates, sandwiches, and cake, served by black waiters; to the parlor, where frappé was available and the beautiful gifts were displayed; to the sitting room, where the queen held court.[72]

The newspaper listed some of the people who had sent regrets and letters of congratulation (these tended to be more distinguished than those present). The clubs Harriet belonged to were heavily represented at the fete: Members of Old and New, the Boston Political Class, and the Wintergreen Club attended, and the clubs sent gifts of silver and gold.[73]

Everyone was pleased with the event but Hattie, who resented Harriet's high-handed arrogation of her daughter's time, energies, and resources. Hattie was unwell and doubted she could get through the "wear and tear" of the party.[74] At the end of the year she commented, "Mother had her 70th anniversary party. I paid the bills."[75] This resentment of a strong mother who dominated

her life surfaced from time to time throughout Hattie's life—
"How tyrannical and selfish a good woman can be where her
children are concerned. The *mother* must be first!" said Hattie of
her own mother.[76] Hattie remembered the celebration as the time
"mother about killed me by her 70th anniversary."[77]

Friction but also mutual support characterized Harriet's family. Though William was gone, Mrs. Hanson was dead, and the
children were all settled with families of their own, the mother
and daughters and son retained the closeness of the earlier years.
But the physical distances separating them became a trial for
Harriet. "All is scattered, even my children. And I have to wander
in order to put my hand on them. All but Hattie. She is spared to
me yet,"[78] mourned Harriet. Harriet laid a heavy hand on them
all, even from afar.

Financial problems plagued all the Robinsons during the twenty years after William's death. But if they did not prosper, they
endured, building worthwhile if not notable lives from small
achievements. When Harriet visited her family's graves in Concord, she noted, "My youth was buried in Willie's grave." "My best
friend lies in my mother's grave." "But my life was buried in my
husband's grave."[79] These losses notwithstanding, Harriet was
still far from quitting.

X

Suffrage

🙟 *The Woman's hour is struck or is striking.*

—*"Warrington"*

🙟 *I feel at such meetings as if I too had a thing to say.*

—*HHR Diary, 1 February 1872*

The woman-suffrage movement, which in the United States began officially in 1848 with the Seneca Falls Convention, enlisted only a few far-sighted individuals, mostly drawn from the ranks of the abolitionists, until after the Civil War. The story has been told before of how in 1869 Elizabeth Cady Stanton and Susan B. Anthony, urging a woman-suffrage amendment to the Constitution, broke away from their dismayed colleagues of the American Equal Rights Association. Believing that their cause had been betrayed by its divorce from black suffrage, they moved swiftly, gathering their followers in the new National Woman Suffrage Association, for women only. This group, known as the Nationals, espoused wide-ranging plans for reform that went beyond suffrage.

More conservative in ambition was the rival American Woman Suffrage Association, or Americans, organized in Cleveland later that same year. This group, headed by the old abolitionists James Freeman Clarke, Thomas W. S. Higginson, Julia Ward Howe, and particularly Lucy Stone and her husband, Henry B. Blackwell, centered their efforts on state legislatures and admitted only delegates from "recognized" associations to their midst.

For twenty years—until 1890, when the two groups were united under the name National American Woman Suffrage Association—the leaders fought among themselves while battling the apathy of the populace and the growing militance of the antisuffrage groups. The split had an ideological basis, in the differing approaches to securing suffrage, but the real cause of friction was style: the Nationals offended the Americans' canons of respectability; they were too familiar with disreputable people.[1]

Against this background of reformer infighting, Harriet Hanson Robinson played out her public ambitions. She found the personal and institutional power she sought in the suffrage movement, and in strengthening it, she strengthened herself. Working in concert with her daughter Hattie—who actually superseded her in importance in the movement—Harriet found a platform where she was respected and listened to.

Harriet had been "converted" to the movement in 1869, when the organizations split. Her subsequent interaction with the two groups reveals inner workings of the movement that are generally missing from the official accounts.

෨෨෨

As a young wife, Harriet had been occupied with her babies and house while her husband fought center-stage for political reform. Such zeal as developed in Harriet was silently borne and unrecognized. Harriet recorded a telling incident from the Lowell days when some influential Republicans spoke in town and met afterward in the Robinson parlor-library-nursery: The reformers carried on a spirited dilation on the wrongs done to the slaves and the need for immediate action. "The young wife sat there, minding the baby in the cradle . . . listening, with her soul on fire," to the tales of the return of fugitive slaves to their "inhuman" masters. "At the close of this exciting conference, which she had heard silently (for women in *those days* were said not to be capable of politics), one of the gentlemen, speaking to her for the first time during the visit remarked—on the unpleasantness of the weather."[2]

Harriet made nothing of the incident at the time, but her official nonexistence must have rankled her, as it did in 1869 when as a matron of forty-four with two almost grown daughters she was introduced to Wendell Phillips as Warrington's wife. "Your wife!" sang out the incredulous Phillips. "I did not know you had a wife! I thought you were a crusty old bachelor!"[3] Such experiences as these might well cause a woman to wonder whether housekeeping was a dead end. Harriet was understandably susceptible to a cause that promised advancement to women individually and as a group.

The significant moment arrived in 1868. Young Hattie was at the state house, copying the house journal for her father. A hearing on the subject of woman suffrage was held before the Judiciary Committee, and Hattie went in to listen to speeches by Lucy Stone, Phoebe Hanaford, and Olympia Brown. At home she told her mother, who had been sewing all day on a carpet, how Lucy Stone had "put down every argument against the question," although the committee had not been convinced.[4] Harriet accompanied her daughter to Lucy Stone's next appearance, where she heard an "eloquent clear and exhausting speech . . . full of law logic and illustrations." The green room was crowded with gentlemen and "strong minded women."[5] "Mother liked it very much," said Hattie. "Of course I did."[6]

Lucy Stone could initiate Harriet into the new life because of her credentials as a legitimate domestic wife, who made bread and butter[7] and who had a little daughter she hated to leave. Lucy Stone was a housewife with a mission, a more attractive model to Harriet than an embittered spinster, a type she described as "Poor, forlorn soul, wearing out for the want of getting married and having babies."[8] Lucy Stone legitimized suffrage for Harriet, who dated her conversion from November of 1868 at the New England Convention of the American Equal Rights Association.

This *"rousing"* convention appealed to Harriet in another way, for it was headed by the famous old reformers William Lloyd Garrison, James Freeman Clarke, and John Greenleaf Whittier. When the New England Woman Suffrage Association was formed at this convention, Julia Ward Howe, so impressive as a social leader and literary figure, was elected president. Mrs.

Howe, gushed Harriet, "sacrificed the literary leisure so dear to her; and, in defiance of conventional traditions and usages, came to work upon an unpopular platform, for a weak and doubtful cause."[9] If Lucy Stone made membership in the association possible for Harriet, Julia Ward Howe made it desirable. Her presence dignified the movement when it was still weak enough that the members felt set apart as pioneers.[10]

The hall was crammed for most of the time by "thoughtful and intellectual looking men and women. Thoughtful and sincere and earnest looking as if they meant something."[11] This group compared favorably with the yawning, vapid groups Harriet had observed at church meetings. She transferred some religious imagery to the suffrage event, for here she experienced the conversion she had not yet found in the church: she was "reawakened into the spirit," as a "living witness."[12]

Harriet joined the New England Woman Suffrage Associations, and she was among the organizers of the Middlesex County and the Malden Woman Suffrage Associations, which were formed that year. She belonged to town, county, state, regional, and national groups, with their overlapping memberships and single purpose. All the associations did the same work of publicizing and proselytizing. Hearings, mass meetings, printed tracts, and lectures were the business of the day. Members raised money and organized new groups. This complex structure, without a recognized hierarchy, allowed everyone to be a boss, but it also made duplication and internal power struggles inevitable.

Harriet's principal suffrage duty in 1870 and '71 was working in the restaurant for the mammoth suffrage bazaars held by the New England group. Many states and towns were represented at tables where donated sewed or baked items were sold to raise money for the cause. The bazaars made it possible to begin publication in 1870 of *The Woman's Journal*, an American suffrage newspaper edited by Lucy Stone, Henry B. Blackwell, and Mary Livermore.

Harriet spent her free time in December "begging" for contributions of money or goods for the bazaar. As she went from door to door she met "many pleasant women" with a "look of yearning in their eyes . . . as if they longed for 'something better than they had known.' " She found women "greatly overworked and 'underdeveloped.' "[13] As manager of the restaurant in 1871, Harriet was a confident *chef de cuisine*, who provided an excellent bill of fare at modest prices and ordered her thirty-five assistants about efficiently. She sold ads to sympathetic businessmen for her menu card—interspersing the ads with choice women's right squibs and descriptions of the victuals—for which she collected $120.

Harriet's whole family participated in the bazaars, William editing a neat little giveaway newspaper, *The Bazaar Gazette*, and all the Robinsons saving their Christmas money to spend there.[14]

Calling on indifferent businessmen for contributions to the bazaar caused Harriet to define herself against the apathetic public. She resented both the businessmen and the women who were "well enough off"; poor women who ate the "bitter bread of servitude are nought to them."[15] She could not bear the "sickly sentimentality" women showed by subscribing to the "Dumb Animal" fair going on concurrently and not to suffrage. Women were supposed to have their turn after the Negro (black-male suffrage was achieved in 1870), but Harriet feared that after the Negro cause would come that of "all the cats, dogs, pigs and so on; then the fishes, then all the vermin, and the fowls of the air, then if nothing else comes up, *the women*."[16] She had joined the women's-rights movement to be *for* something, but she came instead to be against a great many others.

Harriet's café registered a profit of $856 the year she managed it. She discovered that hers was the only profitable department of the bazaar. The grateful committee presented her with a pair of handsome cranberry-colored vases from Paris (which had not sold).[17]

After her bazaar success, Harriet accepted the presidency of the Middlesex County Woman Suffrage Association, and in 1875 she held lively and well-attended conventions in Malden, Melrose, and Concord. In Malden Harriet invited Julia Ward Howe, Lucy Stone, suffrage agents Mary F. Eastman and Huldah B. Loud, and Henry B. Blackwell to speak, along with herself. The Melrose convention featured these famous speakers as well as Julia E. and Abby H. Smith, of Glastonbury, Connecticut, whose cows and land had been forcibly sold to pay taxes; taxed but unrepresented, the sisters doubted not that they would be better off with a king, for "King George himself never attached woman's property in so unfeeling and cowardly a manner as has been done to us."[18] The Concord convention again defended unrepresented taxpayers. Lucy Stone dramatically climaxed her speech with "If I were an inhabitant of Concord, I would let my house be sold over my head and my clothes off my back and be hung by the neck before I would pay a cent of it!"[19] The standard speakers were joined by Ralph Waldo Emerson and Bronson Alcott.

Harriet was proud of these successful meetings, which featured colorful speeches and converted new supporters to the cause. She had had the opportunity to show her skill as an enthusiastic leader who produced good results. Unfortunately, however, the three conventions triggered a major falling-out among reformers. Harriet had organized all three meetings, invited the speakers, and paid the bills. Lucy Stone, of whom she had always thought so highly, and her husband, Henry B. Blackwell, spoke at each convention. They charged Harriet $200 for their expenses between Malden and Boston. This extravagance could have been borne, but Stone committed a worse sin. In her account of the Concord convention in the *Woman's Journal*, she did not mention Harriet's name.

William Robinson was very angry about the slight, knowing that his wife had carried the show with no help. He stormed into *The Woman's Journal* office and pointed out the omission. Harriet, who was also present, described the scene: "Mr. B. expressed surprise that my name had been left out and said it was not intentional. Mr. R. told him that 'he lied and he knew that he lied. that the slight was intentional and of a piece with his usual treatment of people who could do better suffrage work than he and his wife could.' Mr. Blackwell flared up, and hot words passed between them. Mr. Robinson did not retract what he had said." Blackwell ordered him out of the office. Before the Robinsons left, Blackwell calmed down and tried to excuse himself. That same day he sent Harriet a note of apology for "losing control of his temper." Blackwell regretted Robinson's "direct & repeated contradiction of [his] positive statement," and noted that the intentional omission of Harriet's name would imply a "meanness" of which neither Blackwell nor Stone was capable. He pointed out that Harriet's name had been added to articles in the past when she had not requested their inclusion. Harriet granted that his tone was entirely conciliatory.[20]

Stone sent her apologies, too, saying that the extra work of speaking at the conventions as well as getting out the paper had caused her to neglect giving Harriet the "credit which you so much deserve." She was only too glad of the "rare good help" Harriet brought "not to wish to make the most of it before the enemy." Indeed, Stone and Blackwell had often discussed the "discretion and strength" Harriet brought to the common cause, and they hoped to do her justice.[21]

Had Lucy Stone compensated by publishing a correction to the article or by doing a feature piece on the capable president of the Middlesex County organization, the breach might well have been healed. But the personal apology did not compensate for the original slight, which denied Harriet respect and recognition. The conventions planned for Lowell and Somerville were canceled.[22] Henceforth, Stone and Blackwell were the enemy.

❧❧❧

This conflict resulted in a realignment between Harriet and the National Woman Suffrage Association. Despite Lucy Stone's entreaties that Harriet come down to the *Woman's Journal* office so they could "go to the [Boston] Common and have it out,"[23] leaving behind Blackwell and Stone and the American Woman Suffrage Association, Harriet joined forces with Elizabeth Cady Stanton and Susan B. Anthony and in 1878 was listed as a National officer.[24]

Anthony treated Harriet differently than Stone did and the contrasting styles of these two leaders go far toward explaining why Susan B. Anthony has become the personification of the suffrage movement. Anthony skillfully manipulated Harriet to give her utmost to the cause, rewarding her with praise and good speaking opportunities. And Harriet followed dutifully in Anthony's wake. Cool where Stone got hot, welcoming where Stone backed off in disdain, Anthony did not rise to Harriet's indignant letters. Harriet's demands were not granted when they did not fit into the leader's larger view; Anthony explained her disappointing decisions in ways that Harriet could not gainsay. Instead of fighting with her followers, Anthony focused them and encouraged their work.

The planning for the thirteenth annual meeting of the National Woman Suffrage Association, held in Boston in 1881, demonstrates Anthony's skill. Under her direction, Harriet made the local arrangements. Unable to reserve the Tremont Temple for both specified days, Harriet engaged a smaller, darker hall, called the Meionaon, for the first day. Anthony stewed about the implications of the meeting place for several letters. When her complaints were lost on Harriet, Anthony wrote directly to the Temple and engaged it for two other days. Harriet was told later.[25] Anthony soothed her ruffled lieutenant by promising "a *very strong force* of our *grandest women*" for the occasion, and insisting that she could not enter Boston "after this '*Stone*' banishment of a whole decade in any but *tip-top* style." The "Widow of 'Warrington' " was her only helper in that "big 'hub.' "[26] Harriet could only sputter and obey.

Nevertheless, the call to the convention went out with neither Harriet's nor Hattie's (another key worker) name on it, and the disregarded Harriet sent her usual scathing letter. Anthony was apologetic and confused as to how the oversight had occurred. The two Robinson women had certainly been included on the list *she* approved. She then skillfully turned this apology into a demand for further work, by throwing out a sop: she asked Harriet to set up some more New England conventions, and "perhaps, if we dont frighten you away from us at our Boston meeting—you will go to some of them with us."[27] She also asked Harriet to be a subscription agent for the massive suffrage history, the first volume of which had just been published. Anthony wanted a "brave agent" at Lucy Stone's next convention; did Harriet know a "good woman?" Would she ask Stone if she objected to such an agent? "Would *you* dare to do it?"[28] Harriet became the agent.

The contrast between Anthony and Stone was equally noticeable in connection with the compiling of the chapter on Massachusetts in the suffrage history, which Harriet was invited to write. The Nationals would have preferred Stone to write the chapter, but she refused to have anything to do with it. She deplored the Nationals' connection with such questionable people as the financier George Francis Train, the outspoken feminist Victoria Woodhull, and the polygamous Mormon women from Utah. She hoped to be left entirely out of any history "those ladies" might publish, and with "entire kindness" warned Harriet against them.[29] Elizabeth Cady Stanton commented that Lucy Stone considered it "desecration of her immaculate being, to be even mentioned by such profane lips as ours."[30] Stone excluded the unsuitable from her circle and ignored them.

The Nationals refused to take offense even when it was so deliberately given. After Harriet accepted the commission for the chapter, she discovered that she was to furnish facts to an editor, who would reword her piece and include it without her final approval and perhaps without her name.[31] The widow of Warrington—he who had based his career on saying whatever he pleased—drew herself up in full indignation. "Am I to understand . . . that the Mass. Chap. if written by me, will go into your History—as part and parcel of it, without any credit being given to me as its author? and that it is likely to be altered or changed in any way? If this is so (and I am sure I hope it is not) I am afraid I must decline to furnish you with such a chapter."[32] Harriet decided to write and publish her own book.

Susan B. Anthony kept at Harriet, discussing and negotiating, even though she would not cooperate. "Will you send us what you have written—and let us see it—and take such points, if any there be, as we have missed & add to ours—or perhaps yours may be so entirely unlike ours that we may put yours in as Mrs. H. H. Robinson's reminiscences."[33] And later, "—but if you do not feel willing to let us see & read yours—or would not—on reading ours—add yours to it—why, we shall have to go to press with what we have. . . . How much would you charge us for *every fact you have*—that we have not?"[34] But Harriet would not yield, and the Nationals did not see her manuscript until it was first published as a book.[35]

These negotiatons went on for some time. *Massachusetts in the Woman Suffrage Movement* was published in 1881. When volume three of the big suffrage history went to press, in 1886, the

Massachusetts chapter was Harriet's work. Both sides had compromised. Harriet consented to the cuts Anthony made in her
best rhetoric and paid for the handsome engraving of herself that
accompanied the article.[36] The Nationals displayed her name
prominently and allowed the chapter fifty-five pages, when they
had planned on only forty.[37] They virtually republished Harriet's
book with only a few deletions, a little expatiation, and a new
ending. So both parties won in this skirmish. Harriet and the
Nationals exploited each other as best they could, accomplished
useful work, and maintained mutual respect.

Massachusetts in the Woman Suffrage Movement reveals Harriet's
interest in the suffrage movement as being emotional and personal rather than intellectual. Arguments for or against women's
rights have no part in this book. She noted in the introduction
that the "doctrine of woman's rights" would not be treated, as it
would be "impossible to do justice" to such a subject.[38] In fact, the
arguments interested her less than the narrative of events and
lists of people involved. What concerned her was who would get
the credit for suffrage work. She was willing to forgo profits if the
book would claim her a place in history.[39]

The book—running less than 200 short pages, with another
100 or so pages of undigested appendices—is a highly personal
memoir, which documents the role of the Robinsons in the movement. Although the narrative begins with the nation's independence, the book picks up spirit in 1868, when Harriet began her
suffrage activity, and the story is often centered in Malden, where
the most dramatic episodes were experienced by the author herself. References to and quotations from the Robinson clan and
their friends are prevalent. Harriet herself appears six times in
the index, William (as Warrington) rates eleven entries, and
Hattie has four. Further Robinson references are not attributed,
so that the reader is unaware how very personal this book is.

Prejudiced as always, Harriet indicated that the Nationals were
doing the best suffrage work. Most of the book's bias against the
Americans is substantiated by a selective use of the facts; Harriet
verified her information, but she told only the story she knew,
rather than researching widely. Lois Merk, in her subsequent

history of Massachusetts suffrage, found the Americans active in the same areas as the Nationals and felt obliged to emphasize their contribution as a corrective to the "glaring omissions" in Harriet's book.[40]

Harriet's style was to intersperse dry accounts of conventions, lists of speakers, and names of correspondents with paragraphs of fiery rhetoric that revealed her feelings. The language of martyrdom lent itself well to her purposes:

What sacrifices, domestic and social, did not some of these devoted souls make, that they might show the faith that was in them! Many of them are forgotten, and their names have travelled "the way to dusty death," but the flame they helped to kindle, like a "Candlestick set in a low place, has given light as faithfully, where it was needed, as that upon the hill." It is well to keep the "memory green" of those who thus early took up the cross when it was a cross, in this weak, and as it was then often called, ridiculous movement.[41]

No newcomers could hope to measure up to the pioneers, whose contribution was more valuable because it was more difficult.

In a dramatic account of Malden women who dared to stand at the polls and give out handbills recommending pro-suffrage candidates, Harriet used some of her best religious language. The women, keenly aware that they were affronting society by going to the polls, naturally shrank from this "last test of faithfulness." But they had "fortified themselves with brave words, and some of them with prayers and tears, for they were in earnest, and 'having done all' were determined to 'stand.' " The picture she paints of the women "crowned with honor . . . pleading" with the few black men who came to the polls to vote for the women who had so "faithfully" worked for them in the past is memorable.

And so these women stood at the polls and saw the *freed slave* go by and vote, and the *newly naturalized fellow-citizen*, and the *blind man*, and the *paralytic*, and the *boy of twenty-one* with his newly-fledged vote (HE did not believe in Woman Suffrage), and the *drunken man* who did not know Hayes from Tilden, and the man who read his ballot upside down. All these voted for the men they wanted to represent them, but the women, being neither colored, nor foreign, nor blind, nor paralytic, nor newly-fledged, nor drunk, nor ignorant, but only *women*, could not vote for the men they wanted to represent them.[42] [Italics hers]

Although the "Woman Suffrage Ticket" was resoundingly defeated, garnering only 41 votes out of 1300 cast,[43] Harriet had
framed her categories so that the chosen few were victorious.

Harriet dramatically played on the betrayal of women by Irish
politicians in the 1880s (suffrage opponents no longer argued the
case, they just said "no!"): "It was enough to make the women who
sat in the gallery weep to hear the 'O's' and the 'Mc's' almost to a
man, belch forth the emphatic 'no.' " Men who a few years before
had had "hardly the right to live and breathe" voted away the
rights of the women of the country in which they found a "shelter
and a home."[44]

If the betrayal of the Irish was bad, how much worse the
faithlessness of the Yankees, Harriet's own people. It was enough
to "make angels weep" to hear them vote against their women.
"Far better that their revered names should never be heard of
again, than that they should be found with those who vote against
the rights of the people." When the "blue blood" joined the
immigrants against their women, treachery was indeed afoot.[45]

Having vented her spleen on all those who disagreed with her,
Harriet invited the endorsement of her book by the American
Woman Suffrage Association. She gave the Americans the difficult choice of subscribing to an interpretation of suffrage history they did not support or publicly admitting a division in the
ranks. Harriet sweetly invited Thomas Higginson to review the
book, assuring him that she would be "glad of any criticism you
may make."[46] Higginson, although recognizing that Harriet had
"done useful work with her little book," found that her association with the Nationals was nonetheless a "calamity to the movement." He mentioned her name no more.[47]

One critic noted that controversy had been the author's aim:
"People read [the book]; investigated disputed points, and this
sort of discussion led to the discussion of the principles in whose
interest the volume was published."[48] The response encouraged a
revised edition, published two years later, in which the challenged Harriet added new matter and verification of material in
question for "those who are as anxious as I am to have the history
of the movement correct, but who have not, like myself, gone to

the proper sources of information to substantiate them."[49] Her evidence was irrefutable. She angered and silenced her foes.

This suffragist infighting was not necessarily visible to others. The Boston *Evening Transcript* innocently noted that Harriet had told her story "fairly and impartially, and in so purely an historical spirit. . . . No person . . . has so thorough a knowledge of the . . . movement as she."[50] Though financially unremunerative, the suffrage book was eminently successful from Harriet's point of view. It shaped history, "kept the memory green," and brought her the pleasant notoriety of controversy.

Harriet again treated the women's-rights theme, this time in a delightful drama, entitled *Captain Mary Miller*. She tossed off the charming play during a visit to Lizzie in September of 1886, and it was published the next year by Walter H. Baker & Co. The work, filled with names and fragments of incidents from her past, had figured in Harriet's mind for some time before its composition. In the suffrage book she had declared that playwrights spoke too feebly in favor of women—"No modern successful dramatist has made this 'humour' of the times the subject of his play. . . . It is to be regretted that the stage still continues to ridicule the woman's rights movement and its leaders.[51] Harriet leapt into the breach when others remained silent.

In *Captain Mary Miller*—which is based upon an actual case, in which a Mrs. Mary Miller applied for a steamboat license—Harriet considers whether a woman can carry out a man's job in her own right. Mary takes over as captain of a Mississippi River boat when her husband, the captain, falls ill. She manages well, but the owner disapproves of a female captain and threatens to take the ship away unless she can get a license. After the standard difficulties, Mary is awarded the license, just as her recovered husband returns to the ship. Will Mary resume her secondary role? No! The theme that women will not only endure but prevail is struck by her proud husband. "She shall be captain still; and I'll be her mate. It won't be the first time a man has sailed through life under the orders of a brave and true-hearted women,—nor the last, I hope."[52]

Mary and her husband are stock characters and the story line is predictable, even to the ritual heroine-villain scenes with Mr. Romberg, the owner. But notably, Mary extricates herself from her difficulties without the standard hero to save her. *Captain Mary Miller* is really Harriet's story again, the tale of the wife left alone who proves she can carry on.

Mary apparently asks only to be able to support her family in peace until her husband is well. But her superior talents and leadership ability shine through. When the black cabin boy Josephus is asked whether Mary has *really* commanded the vessel, he sings out, "Yas, saar-e! ebryting! She bos' steamboat. She bos' Pats [the first mate]. She bos' Hank [the cook] and me. . . . W'y! mis' could bos' you, bos' de President 'nited States, be cap'n ob ebrybody."[53] Harriet, re-creating her world to make women equal, went on further and made them superior. Mary's performance earns the respect "ob ebrybody."

The play integrates many feminist pronouncements into the conversation. "If [H]e did creat' men an' wimmin ekal," Mary's mother Lorany notes, "an' call their name Adam, just as we call aourn Gandy, one of us has no right to sell the things that belong to both without askin' each other's leave."[54] As Mary signs the application for a license—signs it "Mary Miller"—she realizes "(sighing) that I must hereafter stand alone,—legally, at any rate, and take the responsibility of all my actions. No more hiding behind a husband's or a father's name."[55]

When Captain Gandy, Mary's father, appears in the fifth act— his ticket to New Orleans earned by his daughter's millinery business and his wife's boarders—he delivers a long speech showing the conversion of the sensible Everyman. "Sence a woman can't allus hev her husband or her father tew take care on her, she ort to have the right to take care o' herself, an' then she can use it or not, as she wants tew. An' so I begin to think that I don't care if we do let 'em vote."[56]

This short and entertaining play was first performed in the Union Hall in Boston on January 26, 1888. Hattie Shattuck was featured as Lorany Gandy, and tickets could be purchased for 50¢ and 35¢.[57] A reviewer for the Boston *Herald* noted that the play was "not a very pretentious one, but it is interesting and remarkably well told, the dialogue being bright or forcible as the situation demands."[58] Harriet herself thought the play was "a success though not a 'roaring one.' " A lady told her that the author "ought to be crowned with laurels."[59]

෨.෨.෨.

Having made a place for herself as a women's-rights spokeswoman and having been an officer of the National Woman Suffrage Association for four years, Harriet, together with Hattie, took the next dramatic step. On February 6, 1882, they organized the National Woman Suffrage Association of Massachusetts, in the very shadow of the headquarters of the American Woman Suffrage Association. The converts from the conventions that Harriet had organized became the core members.

The alarmed Lucy Stone urged them to reconsider and work in cooperation with her better way. "You say . . . that you are 'not trying to antagonize the work done by others.' But when you form another State Society, where one already exists, and which is open for work of every kind for the cause, you *do* antagonize."[60] When the miscreants failed to recant, Stone began a whispering campaign against them.[61] A friend reported that she thought Stone "a little jealous" of the Robinson women.[62]

Meanwhile, Susan B. Anthony decreed that Hattie should be president of the new group, a severe blow to Harriet's ego. Anthony reasoned that the state president should be a national vice-president, as Hattie was, and that vigorous young women were needed as leaders, around whom new members would gather. Although Hattie herself supported her mother's candidacy, Harriet did end up as recording secretary, sustaining her daughter in office and feeling somewhat cast off and worthless about it.[63]

The suffrage activities of the new organization paralleled those of the regional American group. Both Harriet and Hattie spoke at all the conventions. The two presented a dramatic appearance. Harriet, who was "very positive in her manner," played her pioneer role to the hilt, earning the title of the "venerable Mrs. Robinson of Malden." With her heavy black brows, dark eyes, and white hair and skin above a sturdy and fashionably clothed body, she was a commanding figure.[64]

Hattie was acclaimed for her beauty. The young woman

deemed too womanly in comparison with her girlish peers did very well when grouped with reformers a full generation older than she, as the steady stream of compliments on her appearance indicates. A journalist called her one of the "most winsome of the sisterhood."[65] Another referred to her "very pretty figure," and a third remarked that the "handsome face of Mrs. Shattuck, of Boston, and her tasty dress were also noticeable."[66] Yet another noted that Hattie's pretty brown eyes, which "sparkle with charming intelligence"—expressing her "gentle sarcasm, under which her masculine opponents must writhe in unutterable torture at times"—made her "altogether an ornament to the cause."[67] Even a hostile newspaper described Hattie as "tolerably good looking" and "about as creditable a delegate . . . as the convention afforded."[68] No wonder she tired of such references: "Mrs. Harriet Shattuck, of Boston, does not care to have her personal appearance described, which is certainly a remarkable circumstance, since she is a very pretty brunette, with a shapely head, indicative of good sense as well as feminine beauty, lovely dark eyes, and an expression so unusually sweet that she is well worth describing and looking at too."[69]

Harriet and Hattie contrasted in their public speaking as well as their appearance. Harriet had been warned by her husband before his death not to "make an ass" of herself about women's rights, and she considered herself a "Boston moderate," finding the reckless spirit of some of the more radical women's-rights speakers terrifying.[70] She was "positive, outspoken," and firm in her opinions, but she did not call for outrageous change. What she wanted was representation in the government, the simple vote.[71] Harriet spoke for herself in a contentious tone.

She was always at the center of her own speeches, as in her popular address "Who Represents Me?" She was a woman of "ripe culture and experience" who had no say in government. She was one of the 66,000 solitary women who headed households in Massachusetts and who had no one to speak for them in casting a vote. Although unrepresented in the government, she herself strengthened her position by speaking for other spinsters and widows.

Harriet argued more to put men in their place than to convince them. Woman had "finer instincts than man." She was "centuries ahead" of man in keeping "gratification of senses" under control. The human race was below its potential because the "mother element has been kept subordinate to the father element" for so many years. Speaking for herself, as always, Harriet said that "Past seclusion makes [a mother] when the necessity for [mothering] is over, all the more eager to take a wider interest in public matters, or to attempt to fulfill some cherished aspiration of her youth, a time long deferred, but patiently looked forward to." Harriet scolded for her rights, in the belief that she had been mistreated.[72]

Hattie's speaking sounded more objective, rational, measured, submissive. She appeared willing to accept that men were her masters and to beg prettily for her rights. She played on the "humiliation" women feel when disregarded. She asked men to put themselves in women's place in her speech "The Golden Rule": "We feel our degradation, gentlemen, and we ask you to lift the burden from us and to make us free. We have been and will still be patient. Do you then be just," implored Hattie. She spoke of "slights on [our] dignity," of the need for respect and the means of making oneself respected. Much of her public speaking was "lady talk," appealing to the condescension of all-powerful men; such arguments were designed to make men feel more powerful and masculine should they raise women up a little. Gentle and graceful in her manner, with her low, rich voice enhanced by elocution lessons, Hattie was a convincing orator. She insisted that "we must show men that women will not lower but elevate politics, and what is more important in their minds, that she herself will not be harmed by taking part in the government."[73] "Man has not been consciously unjust to woman in the past, nor is he now; but he believes she is in her true sphere, not realizing that he has fixed her sphere, and not God, as he imagines."[74]

Hattie seemed to be as conciliatory and eager to please as some of the more respectable American Woman Suffrage workers. But she also argued coolly from the Constitution, the Declaration of

Independence, and from moral right. Women should vote because in a republic every human being should have the right to
make the best use of his or her faculties. The government of the
United States was founded on the will of the people and theoreti-
cally on the equality of all, including women.[75] Hattie was smart,
well versed, and thoughtful, more conservative than radical. She
was eager to please and persuade rather than to demand and
offend. Suffrage was a vehicle for her rather than a religion.

Because of her ability, Hattie was recruited as a stump speaker
for the Nebraska suffrage campaign. From September to November in 1882 she took to the road throughout the northwest
corner of Nebraska, speaking four or five nights a week to ranch
men, cowboys, and their families. She threw away her prepared
talks and learned to think on her feet. Posters featuring her name
caused her to shrink with horror, but she carried on.[76] The
Nebraska campaign, along with referenda in fifteen other states
to win the ballot for women by the popular vote, was unsuccessful. Of the seventeen state referenda held between 1870 and
1910, only two were victorious.[77] The Omaha *Herald*, an antisuffrage paper, noted that the "suffering sisters are howling over
woman's rights on the stump." Somehow it is difficult to imagine
Hattie as one of a "shrieking sisterhood."[78] Though her views and
activities were more liberal than those of the majority of American women, she was a cautious and conservative suffragist.

During the eighties, Hattie presided over and spoke at many
state conventions and sessions of national conventions. She was
successful in having the "age of consent" for girls raised from ten
to eighteen in Massachusetts, making punishable acts of seduc-
tion and unlawful sexual intercourse with young women. Working in concert with the Women's Christian Temperance Union,
she popularized the age-of-consent issue, with circulars and
through the newspapers.[79] Hattie studied law for three hours a
day for a year before founding the Boston Political Class. She
spoke at the dedication of the Statue of Liberty from a special
suffrage boat in New York Harbor.[80] She was the first woman in
Massachusetts to apply for tax assessment, so she could pay her
poll tax and vote for the school-committee slate.[81] She directed

the canvassing of 814 Malden women on their feelings about suffrage, finding twice as many strongly in favor as opposed.[82]

Harriet was also busy, giving speeches wherever invited. On January 21, 1882, she was the first woman to speak before the special U.S. Senate Committee on Woman Suffrage in Washington, D.C.; the committee had been formed thanks to the persistence of her old friend Senator George Frisbie Hoar of Massachusetts. The faces of the committee, which at first registered "toleration, indifference and scorn," gradually changed to "interest mingled with surprise,"[83] another triumph for Harriet. She boldly petitioned Congress to "restore" her rights and make her a citizen, an act that brought her some attention from the press.[84]

All this individual and local activity was prelude to annual trips to Washington, where the Robinson women were notable members of a national sisterhood. In 1888 the International Council of Women met directly after the National convention and united participants in something thrilling and significant. A religious service conducted entirely by women attracted 3,500 women. At one session thousands of voices sang the suffrage song written by Harriet.

> Hark! the Sound of Myriad Voices
>
> (Tune—"Hold the Fort.")
>
> Hark! the sound of myriad voices
>   Rising in their might;
> 'Tis the daughters of Columbia
>   Pleading for the right.— *Chorus*
>
> Raise the flag and plant the standard,
>   Wave the signal still;
> Brothers, we must share your freedom,
>   Help us, and we will.
>
> Think it not an idle murmur,
>   You who hear a cry;
> 'Tis a plea for human freedom,
>   Hallowed liberty!— *Chorus*

O our country! glorious nation,
   Greatest of them all;
Give unto thy daughters justice
   Or thy pride will fall.— *Chorus*

Great Republic! to thy watchword
   Would'st thou faithful be,
All beneath thy starry banner
   Must alike be free.— *Chorus*[85]

The women stayed up late, talking into the night, after sessions of inspiring speakers. The suffrage pioneers were feted and interviewed. Harriet recorded the proceedings and telegraphed them to the Boston *Journal*. She thought the suffrage meetings and the International Council the "most wonderful gathering of women that the world has ever seen."[86] The unity and energy of those present impressed her more than what was being said.

By contrast, the annual meetings of the Massachusetts Woman Suffrage Association, Lucy Stone's American group, were rather lifeless. Harriet, who attended the meeting shortly before leaving for Washington, found good speakers, but a hall sparsely filled. A "dreadful dead calm" prevailed.[87] Negotiations were now under way for a union between the American Woman Suffrage Association and the National Woman Suffrage Association, initiated by Lucy Stone and smoothed by her daughter Alice Stone Blackwell and other second-generation workers too young to remember the feud.

Hattie was invited to be one of the "Sacred Seven Suffrage Saints" to consider Lucy Stone's union propositions, which included national headquarters in Boston, male and female membership, and merger or recognition of the original state group where two societies coexisted. The Robinson women opposed the union, which foretold the end of their N.W.S.A. of Massachusetts, and when Hattie made her opposition clear, she was replaced as a negotiator.[88] Harriet felt that the "unholy alliance" was being railroaded through by a small minority of suffrage workers, and that Lucy Stone should return to the fold as a penitent rather than be dictating conditions.[89] Susan B. Anthony was inclined to compromise for peace and unity. The Robinsons felt abandoned by their "lost leader," who had joined forces with the "enemy."[90]

At the N.W.S.A.'s first executive session of 1889, on January 21, the union proposition was brought forward. After some heated discussion, the vote showed thirty for and eleven against. The union was "consummated" on the National side, Harriet bitterly recorded, by the vote of thirty members.[91]

Harriet vowed never to work under Lucy Stone again in this or any other world. According to Harriet, Blackwell and Stone were

untrustworthy, unreliable and dishonest in all their methods of work. (I suppose one can speak the truth in ones diary?) and it would be the greatest misfortune that could happen, to have them at the head of the woman suffrage movement in America. Nothing but disaster could follow. And I shall oppose it to the "bitter end." How strange that I should be called upon to do what I have done to oppose these people! And yet. No one else would have done it at the time. And for this they hate me backbite me and try to undermine my work, and my influence. They even tried to run my woman suffrage play off the track, and substitute another in its place. . . . How poorly history must have been written, if leaders have always had the weak spots we find in the characters of those of our day.[92]

Harriet and Hattie continued their N.W.S.A. of Massachusetts, and despite the merger were able to maintain a membership almost as large as Stone's.

Harriet's violent outpouring reveals much about her attitude. It shows that she had been personally crusading against Stone, rather than working for suffrage, a subject only incidentally mentioned. She felt required to attack Stone and Blackwell, and then reacted bitterly to their lack of friendliness. The union represented real defeat to her. The situation was reminiscent of Warrington's battle with Butler. In both cases the Robinsons felt they were engaged in equal battle and had been brushed aside by more powerful opponents. Harriet could only invoke history to expose her enemies in the end.

The union in 1890 of the rival National Woman Suffrage and American Woman Suffrage Associations into the National American Woman Suffrage Association marked the beginning of the end of suffrage activity for the Robinson women. In 1891 Hattie wrote Susan B. Anthony, the chosen leader of the combined group, a sad little letter regretting the narrowing of national policies and wondering whether her organization in Massachusetts should send delegates to the convention in Washington. Anthony, looking as always at the whole picture, urged the two state groups to unite.[93] In 1892 Hattie resigned her presidency of the N.W.S.A. of Massachusetts, "being engaged in work more imperitive." Harriet also resigned.[94] Suffrage goals were, at the last, less important to them than personal relations.

Both Hattie's romance and her disillusion with the suffrage movement can be found on one page of her scrapbook. In 1881 she had written a letter to the newspapers that was very complimentary of Susan B. Anthony. Anthony sent her a nice letter in return. The clippings were pasted in and accompanied by these comments:

I received many compliments for [my letter] but wrote it because I so thoroughly admire Miss Anthony. She has been my inspiration and has helped me to focus my purpose—at last decided on—namely, to *work for Suffrage till it comes.* [1881]

Two comments were added later to the page. "I'm afraid I shan't" (1902). "For it won't come" (1907).[95]

XI

Club Work

[At the Boston Political Class] we never have outside talent but do our own speaking and singing and our own work generally, in the class. This can be said of perhaps no other women's club in Mass.

—*HHR Diary, 1 May 1902*

The complex network of women's organizations spun out in the United States after the Civil War resulted in part from the new halfway position many women occupied. Somewhat freed from their household labors by inexpensive household help and improved domestic contrivances, a significant group of relatively prosperous women aspired to higher education and admission to the man's world of public affairs. That such admission was denied or grudgingly accorded is evident from the discouraging efforts to secure suffrage. As many women had left the hearth forever and were never to reach a chair in the boardroom, a netherworld of women-only organizations arose. Women led women and listened to women in a world that excluded men except as occasional guests.

During the war women had been much involved in the Sanitary Commission, nursing the wounded and providing backup supplies and services. Peace left them casting about for some equally worthwhile activity. In 1868, not directly as a result of the Sanitary work, but as the spontaneous creation of many minds in

reaction to the times, the New England Women's Club was organized in Boston.[1] The stated purpose of the N.E.W.C. was to
provide a meeting place where like-minded women could discuss
subjects of general interest. The "cheap wit" and "scorn and
sneers" of the press that greeted the formation of the club served
only to unite the women further.[2]

Julia Ward Howe, who had become friendly with Harriet
Robinson through suffrage work, invited her to join the club
during its second year. Flattered beyond belief to be included,
Harriet made her first evening foray into Boston without her
husband and recorded the event for posterity. Ednah Dow
Cheney presided over the club tea, consisting of bread and butter, apples, dried fish, cake, and tea with cream, "all for $.25."
Then the fifty women present indulged in "conversation and
social intercourse." Miss Elizabeth Peabody provided the program by amusing them all with some anecdotes about the eccentric Mary M. Emerson of Concord.[3] For some time Harriet basked
in her acceptance by the rich, educated, and high-minded women
who made up the club's membership. Then she began to find
fault.

Harriet found the group to be snobbish, the atmosphere re-
pressive, the decisions made by secret committees. "There is
always an exasperating element there which I cannot describe."
Mrs. Cheney dominated the discussion time, making "feeble remarks" or some "gambols with her elephantine wit."[4] Abby May,
"whom no one particularly likes," was elected as president of the
club, "no one knows when or how."[5] Harriet's suggestion that
they get up a "Woman's Club Cook Book" to sell at the French
Fair met with an awkward silence—such a book, unbeknownst to
Harriet, had already been planned at a secret meeting. Harriet
was invited to send in her best recipes; "I did *not*."[6] This dissatisfaction was of a piece with other situations in which Harriet felt
herself disregarded.

Her disapproval of the proceedings was silent, however, as it
was not until a discussion concerning halftime schools for factory
children that Harriet spoke out at a club meeting.[7] From then on
she took part in discussions and tried to broaden the number of
those participating, as well as loosening the staid club procedures.

She felt she spoke for many of the ladies who did not like the way things had been managed and were glad the "opposition" had begun to express itself. Julia Ward Howe could not abide the open talk, telling Harriet that "certain women who spoke ought to be rid out of the club," and that such outspokenness was "naughty." "Oh, no Mrs. Howe," countered Harriet, "It is only a necessary thunder shower."[8] The group never could stay on a topic or reach a consensus, according to Harriet, but "the waters were stirred *some*."[9]

Harriet was also uneasy about distinctions in class that she felt were made by club leaders. Even Mrs. Howe, who was a suffrage officer, referred to servants as "those people" and to working women as "women of that sort." Women who had risen from those categories obviously could not feel real acceptance.[10]

Just as women who found no place in the man's world founded clubs, so women who were discontented with existing clubs founded their own. In 1878 the Robinson women established Old and New, a twelve-member Malden-based organization, with Hattie Shattuck as president and Harriet and Lizzie as officers. Hattie had just returned from the yearly meeting of the Association for the Advancement of Women and was filled with enthusiasm for a club. The family and friends she assembled to discuss it drafted a constitution and elected officers.

The primary object of the club was "to secure to all women better moral, mental, physical, and social conditions, with a more thorough understanding of the questions of the day and a confidence to utter their own thoughts." This lofty aim, which differed from other club manifestos in its emphasis on the building up of the members, was in fact realized. After a year of meetings the club officers claimed that most members had been enlightened in the areas of housework, dress, health, and marriage, and that women wrote and spoke who never thought they could before. By the time of the tenth-anniversary party when almost all the members had spoken very well, Harriet thought that the talent had developed wonderfully.[11]

The name Old and New characterized a club aiming at wide diversity. The symbol, suggested by Lizzie, of the superimposed old and new moons, recognized the combined idealistic and sentimental strivings of the women for self-improvement—certainly for Harriet the idea of rejuvenation through study and writing must have been there from the beginning. Old and young women considered a broad range of subjects, both ancient and modern, particularly the literature of Old and New England. Lectures were divided among ethics, social economy, art and literature, and science. Once monthly, on the evening of the full moon, regular female members gathered with male associate members for a lecture and a social evening.

The Robinson women were the best-known members of the club. No other early participants achieved the celebrity of Harriet and Hattie, except perhaps Hattie's friend Mary Perry, a teacher at the Malden high school and an unsuccessful candidate for the Malden school committee. The club consisted of friends and neighbors with modest and comfortable financial backgrounds who were generally unknown in Boston or in suffrage circles. Whereas Harriet had ranked among the lowly in the New England Women's Club, she was clearly ascendant amongst those in Old and New.

The club necessarily reflected the Robinsons' interests. A desire for democratic leadership, missing in the New England Women's Club, inspired the principle of rotation in office, a principle in women's clubs that Harriet was later to introduce on the national level. This concern for wide participation led to the early abolition of the private directors' meetings: from the early days of Old and New, all business was discussed in executive session by the whole club. Rotation in office gave everyone a chance to lead, but it also meant that the Robinson women could not always control their club. Of course they were frequently critical of the innovations of new leaders, and Harriet complained to her diary about the quality of the speakers. She was known to sulk, skip meetings in protest, or threaten to resign, but to her credit she did allow the club to be led by others.

Suffrage was not to be a major concern of either the N.E.W.C. or Old and New. Suffrage was still not generally respectable when the N.E.W.C. was established, and the controlling women were determined to keep the subject quiet.[12] As late as 1865 Harriet herself was not so sure she wanted to vote and doubted that most women wanted to; certainly, she noted, the subject was seldom discussed. She thought then that there was a "sort of opprobrium" attached to the women's-rights women and that men had "sneered [suffrage] into bad odor." The climate changed rapidly, and Harriet noted in 1872 that a majority of the women in the N.E.W.C. favored suffrage.[13] When Dr. Oliver Wendell Holmes, a very small man, lectured the club on the physical inferiority of women, Harriet was amused—he reminded her of an old hen who had hatched out of a brood of ducks and wanted to protect them from the water. "Don't, ladies, don't, go near the water," he seemed to say to this large group of great, stout women. Harriet commented that "Any of us could have 'licked' him."[14] Such discrepancies between theory and actuality finally persuaded many intelligent women that they were capable of public life.

Despite their original intentions to the contrary, both the N.E.W.C. and Old and New played important roles in the achievement of suffrage, albeit limited, in Massachusetts. The N.E.W.C. women supported a broad range of educational reforms, and in 1872 a movement to have women elected to local school committees gathered strength. The concern of the N.E.W.C.'s Education Committee (which included such luminaries as Abby May, Lucia Peabody, and Lucretia Crocker) was, however, children's rather than women's rights; many people who opposed general woman suffrage thought it quite proper for women to vote for and to serve on school committees, as an extension of woman's traditional motherly role. The Education Committee supported kindergartens and better schools for girls, and in 1873 four women, all members of the N.E.W.C., ran for the Boston school committee and were elected. Two years later there were six of them.[15]

In 1878, when Abby May was defeated as a member of the Boston school committee, an old movement to secure woman suffrage for the school committee took on new strength, and in 1879 a bill was passed giving Massachusetts women the right to vote for members of their town school committees.[16] It is ironic that this single suffrage achievement should have been brought about by people to whom woman suffrage was not a major issue. Many serious suffragists repudiated the measure, demanding full equality or nothing at all.

The leaders of Old and New, who were determined to keep the focus of their club broad rather than to concentrate on suffrage, temperance, or literature, did support the new school-committee measure. The combination of self-improvement and women's rights that it represented seemed to merit the attention of the club. To vote for the town school committees, women without property needed to pay a poll tax of $2, a rather high price to exercise a small privilege. Still, the club encouraged its members to register and vote, recognizing the "new position in this commonwealth which woman now holds," and fifteen of the fifty Malden women who voted in the next town election were from the club.[17] Hattie Shattuck was the first Massachusetts woman to register, and she published in the newspapers several accounts of how that alien activity could be accomplished. She assured women that neglect of their voting duty would "bring shame to [their] own consciences in the future,"[18] and urged them to stand for school committee "no matter how unpleasant it may be" to have their names emblazoned publicly.[19] Hattie was also the first local woman to vote.[20]

This suffrage activity brought some prominence to Old and New. Even without that, the club had gained a certain stature, for it legitimized many of the otherwise random activities of women and made their lives seem more significant; the club helped structure the week of the members, filling their spare time with useful, entertaining, and improving activities. Old and New functioned well as a vehicle for self-importance. Harriet, as a leader, had standing among a group of admiring women. She had access to the important guest speakers who came to lecture. The club enlarged her sphere of influence and gave her opportunities to perform, something she did very well.

One of her special interests was reflected in the organization of the writing group, an offshoot of the club that was limited to twelve members who met monthly to read and criticize one another's writing. The group provided an incentive for composing papers, critics to help get them in shape, and later an audience to deliver them to. This was no casual activity; much of the group's output was eventually published. Harriet dominated the writers, and because of her usual sharp comments, the members in turn judged *her* work with vigor, if not with skill. When she submitted a sonnet on Louisa May Alcott, she noted that they "all 'went for me' as they always do because I criticise so much."[21] Each of the women adopted a flower name. Harriet chose the columbine and significantly fastened on the motto "Resolved to win!" One of her flower friends penned a tribute recharacterizing the dainty flower as an ensign for the contentious Harriet:

> Hurrah, o, hurrah, bloodthirsty flower,
> With spurs like the birds of prey!
> With talons strong catch the crimes of man
> And bear them in wrath away![22]

Here is another suggestion that Harriet saw herself as Warrington's successor, writing and speaking out as he had done.

It was in fact her club life and her consciousness of following after William that inspired much of Harriet's literary work. William had always encouraged her writing;[23] he told her that she wrote well enough for the press and needed only a little practice.[24] In a pitiful letter written near the time of his death, he expressed his regret that she had not written more:

Do you know I have always felt a sort of self-reproach lest I have kept you from literary life & perhaps fame. It was selfish in me—but we have been *pretty* happy—have we not? I should like that we should have a few more years "thegither"—& to see the children happy also. Life is *so* good that it seems impossible that it should be wholly interrupted by death.[25]

Robinson's confidence in his wife's ability and his encouragement counted heavily with Harriet. And even more important were the opportunities for writing and performing that club life afforded her.

☙☙☙

Harriet's factory work, along with its attendant cultural advantages—a re-creation of an idealized female community of the past—was her best subject. She spoke on it often at club meetings: a woman's topic for women's groups.[26] She had treated the subject before, in a thirteen-page appendix to the suffrage history, and she was to use it again, in *Early Factory Labor in New England* and *Loom and Spindle.* The three books, published over an eighteen-year period, contain many identical paragraphs, moved into new relationships like building blocks. Harriet did not think through her books so much as she assembled them; it is indicative of her skill at transitions and rhetoric that the three accounts have different themes. The section on factory work in the suffrage book stresses feminism, *Early Factory Labor* aims at reform, and *Loom and Spindle,* which she had planned to call "A New England Arcadia," is a nostalgia piece.

The books were written as a result of Harriet's other activities. When Harriet's friend Lucy Larcom published her idealistic *Idyl of Work,* in 1875, Harriet wrote a review essay recalling some of her own experiences in a realistic vein. The piece was submitted to several newspapers before it was finally published by the New York *Independent.*[27] Lucy responded gracefully to the piece, praising Harriet's work and her historical insight. She encouraged Harriet to get the mill-girl epoch on paper and "fully before the public." "The style of your article is admirable," she wrote, saying that Harriet should keep up that sort of writing.[28]

The eventual outcome of this encouragement, *Early Factory Labor in New England* (Harriet's third book), had its genesis in an invitation to speak at the American Social Science Association in Saratoga, New York, in September of 1882. In a session with Carroll D. Wright, chief of the Bureau of Labor Statistics, and Lucy Larcom, Harriet delivered her mill-girl reminiscences now sharpened by presentation at several women's-club meetings. Her talk was praised in the press and in 1883 it was published as part of the *14th Annual Report of the Bureau of Statistics of Labor,* as well as on its own.[29]

Loom and Spindle developed from both suffrage and club work. Susan B. Anthony, fastening on the idea of having a history compiled of the Lowell *Offering,* as an example of early feminist activity, tried unsuccessfully to persuade Mrs. Abel Thomas, widow of the minister who had organized the Improvement Circle, to write it.[30] Lucy Larcom also declined to do it; she thought it was "getting a little tiresome, this *posing* as factory-girls of the olden time."[31] Harriet decided to do the job herself. She even published the book herself, after four publishers had turned it down, financing the project out of Henry L. Pierce's useful bequest (the $5,000 this old friend of William's had left her in 1897).

In all her accounts of factory life, Harriet aimed to show that female operatives were as good as everybody else—that they were equal to and indistinguishable from others. Further, she would show that the girls were actually better than everybody else. Harriet divided and defined the society so that she, as a former poor working girl, could be at the top.

In support of her contention that the workers were as good as—or better than—others, she cited their superior, though impoverished, social standing:

Some of these [operatives] were daughters of professional men or teachers, whose mothers, left widows, were struggling to maintain the younger children. A few were the daughters of persons in reduced circumstances, who had left home "on a visit" to send their wages surreptitiously in aid of the family purse. And some were the granddaughters of patriots who had fought at Bunker Hill, and had lost the family means in the war for independence [e.g., Harriet]. There were others who seemed to have mysterious antecedents, and to be hiding from something; and strange and distinguished looking men and women sometimes came to call upon them.[32]

Clearly, the looms of early Lowell were operated by princesses in disguise and others working beneath their station. Even the troops of farm girls often had "good New England blood, and blood tells even in factory people."[33]

Though Harriet could argue that there were no class barriers, her own evidence made clear that others were eager to have such demarcations maintained. The girls who were as good as anybody were "often accused of looking like ladies." Some complained that in church no one could tell the difference between the factory girls and the "daughters of some of the first families in the city."[34] The "most favored" girls were sometimes invited to dignitaries' homes, and "thus the line of social division was not rigidly maintained."[35] The girls "sometimes, perhaps, married into some of the best families,"[36] though Harriet had not a case to cite.

Having shakily established her thesis that the workers were equal to the higher classes, Harriet proceeded to show that their differences actually made them superior. Hidden nobility was to prevail, for this "class" would teach others that mill labor was not "degrading," that operatives were capable of "virtue" and of "self-cultivation."[37] The working girls showed up the "ladies" by being more simple and pure.

> They earned their own bread, and often that of others. They eked out their scant education by their own efforts, and read such books as were found in the circulating libraries of the day. They sought to help one another. They were wholly untroubled by conventionalities or thoughts of class distinctions, dressing simply, since they had no time to waste on the entanglements of dress.[38]

So Harriet pretended to dismiss the social distinctions that were in fact of great concern to her.

The hard-working girls transmitted money and culture to the backwoods, improving society. "Into the barren homes [which Harriet unwittingly admits were tawdry after all] many of them had left, [the money] went like a quiet stream, carrying with it beauty and refreshment."[39] The workers' little magazine, the Lowell *Offering*, was a beacon light. "It made its way into lonely villages and farm-houses and set the women to thinking."[40] Truly, Harriet saw this as a golden age.

When Harriet wrote *Loom and Spindle* (publishing it in 1898), she based it substantially on *Early Factory Labor in New England*, which became chapters four through eight. To these she added three new chapters that dealt with her education and early religious experiences. *Loom and Spindle* is a sprightly Harriet-centered memoir, which speaks in rich detail of the "good old days."

Her original plan for *Loom and Spindle* included selections from *The Offering* and photographs of several of the original writers, taken in the 1840s, as well as her narrative and sketches of the girls' later lives. Space and expense forced the elimination of the pictures and the *Offering* selections and a shortening and tightening of the remaining text, while Harriet retained her own reminiscences.

She did include a description of the early days of *The Offering*, having collected firsthand information from the aged ladies who had graced its pages in the 1840s. That Harriet thought *The*

Offering was a high literary achievement can be seen in her evaluation of the writers. "These authors represent what may be called the poetic element of factory-life. They were the ideal mill-girls, full of hopes, desires, aspirations; poets of the loom, spinners of verse, artists of factory-life."[41] She indicates that these ideal girls, who spent fourteen hours a day at their tasks, lived their real life in poetic fantasies. But few girls were actually involved in *The Offering*. Harriet identifies fifty-eight (she enumerates fifty-seven).[42] She wrote sketches of fourteen of them. Few of those involved continued to write; only four went on to produce books in their maturity. The gifed Harriot F. Curtis wore out her life caring for infirm relatives.[43] Lucy Larcom, the major literary figure to emerge from *Offering* days, succeeded perhaps by avoiding entangling personal relationships, and Harriet began her literary career only as a widow.

Harriet had an ax to grind in telling the story of *The Offering*. The credit for the newspaper had largely gone to or been assumed by Harriet Farley, at the expense of Harriot Curtis, Harriet Hanson (Robinson)'s special friend. Farley, according to Harriet, "is and always was false all through." She used some of the other girls' pen names so that she could monopolize the space of the paper, excluding other contributors—in one number she wrote all the articles, when there were plenty of other contributions. Moreover, she treated several of the girls "very shabbily." The vindictive Harriet Robinson "almost desire[d] to tell the whole truth about her."[44]

Harriet performed an essential service in collecting the *Offering* material in *Loom and Spindle*, her most important book, for much of this historic early club and literary movement might well have been lost to us without her labors. At the time she wrote it, in the 1890s, there was hardly a complete set of the papers in existence and *The Offering* was virtually forgotten.[45] Her perhaps self-aggrandizing overestimation of the significance of this little publication has served to make it remembered today. With her usual penchant for writing herself into the center of history, Harriet traced the New England Women's Club as the direct "descendant of a small woman's club of Lowell factory operatives," an improvement circle.[46] The book, largely made up out of her head and written some fifty years after the fact, is misleading if read as objective history. Nevertheless, the story is lively and convincing, and the book's sunny vision of an industrial arcadia still, after all this time, shapes our perceptions of early Lowell."

ᏁᏁᏁ

When Old and New's writing group was dissolved, Harriet moved into a remarkable study of the classics. The Bible, Greek drama and philosophy, and Shakespeare, along with history and commentaries, made up her subject matter. When she had been only fifty-nine, Harriet had determined that if she had the time she would take up some "good hard study" and "continue it to the end of my days—like Astronomy, Greek or anything."[47] By 1902 she noted that anyone who could see her desk would think she was either "quite learned or else determined to know something." Piled in front of her were Latin, French, and English dictionaries, Bunsen's *God in History*, Bulfinch's *The Age of Fable*, and Aeschylus.[48]

Her serious study was a final effort at significance, a desire to be associated with the best of all time. The classics soothed and uplifted her soul, opening to her the wisdom of the ages. She felt better and stronger, rising above the petty difficulties of her own life to commune with the great minds.

Harriet was fortunate in being able to study the classics in a social context. Old and New—which by the early 1900s had thirteen large committees, its usual programs, and many special-interest groups—was offering sections on Shakespeare and other selected poets. These sections met weekly to hear lessons prepared by rotating group leaders.[49] The classes enabled Harriet to attempt her long-unfulfilled ambition to write some memorable poetry. She offered *The New Pandora*, a feminist neoclassical blank-verse drama, as her claim to immortality.

It happened that Harriet was reading Plutarch (for her poets class) in the garden one day, musing on the arbitrary condemnation of women by the Greeks. She concluded that women never had been a curse to mankind, and wrote the play to prove it.[50] She used as her prologue a translation from Hesiod's *Works and Days* of the story of Pandora, the beautiful maiden created to bring sorrow to man by scattering evils throughout the world. Harriet's play then proceeded to tell how Pandora brought beauty, civilization, children, and hope to the world. Not content to revise history, Harriet had set out to revise myth, as well.

Pandora is a spiritual sister to Harriet's mill girl. No evil temptress, she is an ideal being who has been given a disagreeable chore. Though supposedly inferior to those around her, she is actually superior, and refuses to be tainted by the rude men she is sent to corrupt.

> I live and do as they? I, who have been
> The blest companion of the white-winged gods?[51]

By force of character, and some nagging, Pandora civilizes the savage masses, making them cook their food and eat at the table, as the gods do.[52] Her life is hard, but through sorrow and other suffering, she is refined and ennobled. Harriet is again writing her own story.

She thought that the play, written sometime prior to 1884, was good. She loved every line of it.[53] Thomas Niles, editor for Roberts Brothers, a Boston publisher, found the play admirable but was unable to swallow the "moral education." Harriet reluctantly modified that part and limited the "strong doses of Womans Rights." She wanted the book to be popular. "The world ought to hear all there is in it, but whether it wants to is another thing."[54]

She continually reworked the play, culling some things "which on severe and cool examination seem to me to mar the beauty of the whole,"[55] and submitting it to various publishers for four years before she consigned it to the bottom of the trunk. "But I know it is good and I am glad I wrote it. It is as much a part of me as one of my children. Bone of my bone, flesh of my flesh, spirit of my spirit."[56] Finally, she published *The New Pandora: A Drama* at her own expense, in 1889.

The book is a notable achievement, an imaginative reinterpretation of old materials. The characters are well drawn. The diction is apt and unpretentious; the lines scan. The familiar ideas are rather elegantly couched in poetry of high accomplishment.

> For in my heart
> Doth something truly say, that far away
> In some unclouded land we cannot see,
> The feet we miss, now bound and still, unchained
> Will be, and free. And when our earthworn steps
> Have reached their journey's end, they'll follow where
> To higher paths the little child doth lead.[57]

Unfortunately, however, the drama reads like a classical work in eighteenth-century translation, which was, after all, Harriet's model. The poetry sounds particularly archaic considering that it was published in 1889, years after some of America's most vigorous literature had been written.

The familiar feminist sentiments sound stilted in this affected language:

> Who loves, forgets himself, oppresseth not
> The one he loves; doth more than clothe and feed,
> And find a home for his own mate. He doth
> Consult her wishes, honor her, respect
> Her feelings, as they were his own. True love
> Sustains the mind and makes the spirit thrive;
> Uplifts the earthy toward the spiritual part.
> It makes the dullest clod a thing of life;[58]

But Harriet was in deadly earnest. The humor in transposing the nineteenth-century womens'-rights debates onto the prehistoric forest glade was lost on her. Harriet did not intend the play to be parody, but the result was very close.

The play has some very nice moments: Pandora is dramatically created from a "dainty clod" of clay.[59] Later, when she is settled in her unhappy marriage, her little firstborn child drinks bitterness from the mother's breast and dies.[60] At the end of the play, as Pandora wanders up a pathway to rejoin the immortals, Aetes, the rude mate now thoroughly devoted to her, springs after her and falls; Pandora turns, raises him, and they continue together. She has truly been his salvation.[61]

The play echoes much of Harriet's personal life—the lost child, the younger son who could not buckle down to work, the husband elevated by the wife's efforts. Pandora also voices her creator's tortured need for accomplishment and for remembrance:

> But this I ask, that I may be allowed by thee
> To do one single thing to make my kind more good,
> More happy for that I have lived.[62]

Pandora is Harriet's imagined classical reincarnation.

Review copies of *Pandora* were dispatched far and wide, and the book received many compliments. *The Woman's Journal* noted that "In working out Pandora's mission to civilizing man, there are touches of real poetic genius and occasional felicities of expression that will give this work a permanent place in literature. [Some] lines and passages are almost Shakespearian in their rhythmic beauty." Another reviewer found the work "highly imaginative," with "entertaining originality."[63]

Other critics were more guarded in their praise, the felicitous beauties of the book falling on rather deaf ears. The California *Argonaut*'s reviewer regretted that "This is not the age of long poems . . . and few will dive down into its five acts to find the gems it bears."[64] *The Englishwoman's Review* faintly praised the "pretty descriptions of nature," but confessed that "we have not grasped the idea which [the book] is intended to convey."[65]

Several reviewers were both critical and amused. *The Congregationalist* found that

As poetry it is of good quality, without rising to any dizzy heights of excellence, and as a plain yet kindly delineation of the natural, although not hopeless, baseness of man, and of the moral, and intellectual superiority of woman, it will thrill with admiration the heart of every woman suffragist in Boston.[66]

The Literary World called the play both womanish and womanly and regretted that "so much reason for amusement" was found in a poem so "well intended, and so painstakingly executed." The reviewer continued to regret that a "quicker sense of appropriateness and of the humorous in the author had not prevented the unconscious comedy of setting forth Pandora as a propagandist of woman's rights."[67]

Harriet was doomed to undercut her best literary gifts, aspiring to an erudition she could not sustain. Her writing is primitive.

Her power came from instinct and emotion rather than training and intellect. She had little schooling, and though she was widely read, she had no serious critical help. If William had lived to criticize her work, it would have been better, as she needed an objective editor, who had some distance from the subjects. But William was gone and his literary friends took little interest in her. No editors or publishers snapped up her productions; they hedged and allowed her to publish them at her own risk. For a sounding board she had only women's groups, in which the members were either uncritically supportive or afraid of her, intimidated by her superior manner. When read carefully, Harriet's work is badly organized, superficial, and lacking objectivity. What generally saves it is passion and a taste for specific detail; indeed, the general effect is often dazzling. But she was not at her best in *The New Pandora*, a purely imaginative work. Once more fame and money eluded her pen.

Club work enabled Harriet to avoid the lonely miseries of old age. Reading, study, writing, and handwork filled the time that otherwise would have hung heavy. She had little gift for friendship and compassion. Harriet pleased a friend once by telling her that she loved her; Hattie wryly noted that Harriet's spontaneous affection was a thing to be pleased at—"She loved so few."[68] Occasionally Harriet would be moved enough to have "tears in her voice," but, again, Hattie noted that tears were "seldom in her eyes."[69] She shunned sentimentality and reserved affection for her family. Without clubs to structure her life and institutionalize her friendships, Harriet's life would have been lonely indeed.

Club work gave a shape to the months from October to May. Organizations met regularly during that period. Each day had its meeting, with preparations and performances extending the hours devoted to the club. This heavy activity contrasted with the long summer months from May to October, when writing her books, visiting the family, gardening, and vacationing took up long uninterrupted periods of Harriet's time. Order and society gave way to freedom and creativity at a stated time each year. This contrived schedule seemed as immutable as the seasons and set up parameters for women who had passed beyond the natural rhythms of women's traditional work.

Harriet belonged to several groups besides the New England Women's Club and Old and New. She joined the Wintergreens, a club made up of elderly former club leaders. The venerable veterans did little active work in this club, spending their time, instead, visiting. Among these better-known women—including Julia Ward Howe, Mary A. Livermore, May Sewall, and Julia K. Dyer—Harriet cut a much narrower swath than in her own groups.[70]

Hattie's Boston Political Class, which had been organized in 1884 when some of the women of the National Woman Suffrage Association decided to study politics together, also figured in Harriet's schedule. When in 1892 Hattie resigned from suffrage work, the class, which studied parliamentary law and current events, became an independent club. Like Old and New in its early days, the group took responsibility for studying topics and leading discussions; Harriet knew of no other club that did all its own work.[71] Hattie continued to teach parliamentary law as the club was reorganized several times. In addition, from 1902 to 1912 she and a friend, May Sheldon, ran the Shattuck and Sheldon Club, a group of such closeness that the members continued to meet annually as late as 1927, even after Hattie had moved away and the club had disbanded.[72]

Harriet and Hattie also belonged to a small strictly social group, dubbed by Hattie's husband, Sid, the Paragons. The eight women, all members of other clubs, took turns inviting one another for luncheon and to spend the day with "speeches, discussions, and stories," along with the reading of original poems. These well-aged maidens—Harriet was in her seventies and Hattie over fifty—enjoyed "great larks" together, going on picnics and outings to Castle Island and Revere Beach.

Besides these official and social gatherings, the Robinson women had church and suffrage activities, and weekly whist games with an invalid friend. Harriet and Hattie averaged one scheduled activity a day, often supplemented with a cultural event in the evening.

This intense local activity qualified Harriet for office in nation-

al organizations. Having been organized in 1878 and incorporated in 1889, Old and New participated in the formation in 1890
of the General Federation of Women's Clubs, for which Harriet
traveled to New York City as her club's representative. She
accepted an appointment on the committee for bylaws of the new
Federation, and she suggested her pet idea of rotation in office, as
well as some of the language used in the constitution. She went on
to hold several offices in the G.F.W.C., serving on the first advi-
sory board and on the board of directors, but declining nomination to the latter in favor of Julia Ward Howe (whose New England Women's Club voted to join the Federation soon after it was
established). Harriet was then elected auditor, a position she held
until 1894, when at the age of sixty-nine she ended her connection with the G.F.W.C.[73]

This national exposure through suffrage and club work made
Harriet more valued at home. She had the sweet satisfaction of
Ednah Dow Cheney's recognition after a speech in Washington.
This snobbish leader of the New England Women's Club, who
was "more than affable," called on her to speak in a "very flatter-
ing manner," saying that her speech had made the "hit of the
day."[74] Having failed to impress the leaders of the N.E.W.C. on
their own turf, Harriet brought back her achievements in other
places for the same effect.

෨෨෨

The female network that had its bones in club work and study
groups was all in all to these often solitary women, bypassed as
they were by the political and financial dealings of the "real
world." They honored one another in their limited sphere, giving
celebrations that sometimes made the social pages but would go
no further. On the twentieth anniversary of the founding of Old
and New, in 1898, the six original members who remained (three
of them Robinsons) were feted by a banquet, speeches, and
gifts—rituals that paralleled those of the legislative bodies Harriet had observed. Lizzie, Hattie, and Harriet, who were "all
women together—more than Mother and Daughters,"[75] gathered
for this occasion, and Hattie indicated how such fellowship would
strengthen them against their real difficulties: "We will all have a

good time together and forget, if we can, our trials and troubles or talk them over and help each other to bear them."[76]

Ritualistically dressed in black figured satin with real Brussels lace and fresh red roses, and wearing an onyx-and-pearl pin that had been a gift from William (serving as a talisman to unite her with an important past), Harriet ventured forth to these annual celebrations—exercises in self-importance—and "tried to 'grace the occasion.'"[77] If she had failed to earn a place in the outside world, she had created another world where she reigned as a queen.

The Last Years
and Those
Who Came After

❧ *I shall never be half as good and useful as [Grandma] is at her age. I am too uneasy and aspiring.*

—HHR to William Robinson, 11 August 1875

❧ *I am in my sixtieth year and "come to nothing yet." Yet I have done a little.*

—HHR to Lizzie, 3 April 1884

❧ *O there is so much that I wanted to do, so much that I might have done and the day is so far spent. If I had stuck to one thing as [Lucy Larcom] did I might have done better work in one line at least. But I am content. All is well.*

—HHR, end of year 1898

❧ *I wonder if I shall have to make as many alterations in my outfit this year as I did last? First I had to discard all my shoes & boots "of commerce" and have a new lot made to order, at large expense. Then my teeth false began to fall out, & new ones were put in, upper, while as to under ones I was obliged to have a new set made,*

and "lastly" so far three grades of spectacles were needed to help me
see my advancing years. I wonder what will be the next "sufficient
warning."

—*HHR Diary, 3–5 January 1904*

Harriet confronted the problems of old age with equanimity. She
had put away the contentiousness of her middle years. Death held
no terrors for her, and she moved gracefully toward that final
climax. Her belief in immortality had led Harriet to make peace
with organized religion. For several years she had regularly
attended the Episcopal chapel, and yielding more to her own
sense of fitness than to a conversion experience or to the
preaching of Mr. Edwards (an English-born minister, whom she
did admire), she decided in 1898 formally to ally herself with that
church.

I have been thinking for some time that I would better join the Church,
and so show my colors . . . as I call myself a Christian, I should be enrolled
among them. I have a great deal of faith but not so much belief as I
supposed was required by the Episcopal Church. But Mr. E[dwards] has
shown me that, to join the church is not the end but the beginning of a
Christian life, and so I enter it. . . . I feel that I need to work with
Christians rather than with unbelievers.[1]

Harriet was prepared to submit herself to church discipline for
social and spiritual support and identity. After her long battle
with organized religion, her peacemaking had a finality to it.

Her daughter Hattie, who came to the church at the same time,
had an intellectual conversion. The study of philosophy had led
her to Christ. Dr. William Torrey Harris's presentations at the
Concord School of Philosophy convinced her of the truth of the
Trinity, and later Dr. Elisha Mulford's *Republic of God*, which she
read in 1885, convinced her of the truth of the Incarnation.[2]
Hattie believed. What remained was for her to acknowledge her
dependence. A friend told her she ought to "let [her]self down"
and join the church.[3] Hattie herself thought she should "give in"
to her need for spiritual help,[4] as she had admitted her physical

reliance on Dr. Kennedy. On Easter of 1897, April 17th, Hattie was baptized.

Harriet and Hattie were confirmed members of the Episcopal Church on January 23, 1898. Lizzie had been confirmed some months before. Harriet described her first communion two weeks later—a "solemn occasion, very pleasant"[5]—in comfortable rather than ecstatic language. This experience marked the peak of her commitment to organized religion.

For even after confirmation, Harriet's accustomed stance as a "creedless Christian" superseded her new Episcopal identity, and she continued to judge those she was supposed only to sustain. Mr. Edwards, her religious leader—who preached "elegant" sermons[6] and astonished a temperance meeting with his "brew of human rights and true temperance," persuading Harriet that "a brave and true man is our rector"[7]—had had much to do with her confirmation. But before long that crusader began to disappoint her. His sermon was "rather sensational." "The virtue had gone out of him." His "feet of clay" were visible. He gave a "begging" sermon. Mr. Edwards, it seems, cared more for the temporal than the spiritual needs of his people. "He is a great disappointment to me."[8]

Harriet's difficulties with the church flared whenever she sensed ambition or hypocrisy in its leaders. She had gone as far as to join the church, but soon thereafter returned to her critical attitude, choosing to think for herself rather than to accept the sermons she heard.

While I find some religious help I do not find that ethical & moral standard set up there as I might have expected. But I can get along & go my own way as always in these matters.[9]

A year later she was staying home from church, "distressed by some of its [social] problems" and finding the Trinity seldom "upheld."[10] Complete loyalty to the church required a submission she could not quite muster.

※※※

Money shaped the possibilities of Harriet's life. Her literary efforts did not earn her an income. Aside from an occasional fee as a guest lecturer or payment for a newspaper or magazine item, she earned nothing. She had the house and rent from the tenants; Hattie, who was living with her, made some money from her parliamentary-law classes; Sidney sent what he could spare from Maine. The household was maintained on minimal funds. In 1897 a wonderful windfall came Harriet's way. When Henry L. Pierce, one of her husband's old friends died, he bequeathed her $5,000. Pierce was an old Free-Soiler, a politician who had served as Boston's mayor and as a member of Congress. He was also a keen businessman, who died without heirs. Half of his large estate was apportioned to charitable, educational, and religious institutions, and the other half went to about twenty unrelated people, along with Harriet, who received small legacies. For this gift, Harriet blessed Mr. Pierce regularly. Carefully nurtured and doled out, the money made a cushion for her old age. Indeed, the family could scarcely have managed without it.

Up in Maine, the faithful Sid's business was rapidly deteriorating. True to pattern in the Robinson family, the breadwinner was defaulting. In August of 1900 he left Yates Brothers and Shattuck, which had "ill treated him." Apparently he was squeezed out. Sid returned to Malden, cheerful, self-effacing, but sadly defeated.

For two years he hunted for work and could find nothing. Finally he got a summer job at Revere Beach keeping account of the tickets sold to the bathers. He now carried a lunch bucket, a new thing for him. In the fall he began work for a book publisher, selling the latest publications door to door.[11] When he gave up on selling books, Sid accepted the offer of Mr. Edwards, the rector of the Episcopal chapel, to replace Ben, the church's black sexton and janitor. The job, which paid $7 a week, carried a distinct loss of status, and Harriet and Hattie suffered keenly. Sid showed a "very brave spirit."[12] "S[id] swept the church yesterday & found it hard. I should think so. 'o my goodness o my gracious,'" confided Harriet to her diary. Sid began to notice that male members of the congregation treated him differently. The women required him to "dance attendance."[13]

Harriet described Sid as the lame or vanquished "animal" whose companions gored him to death.[14] On the other hand, he was the "angel" entertained by the thoughtless unaware.[15] He was a treasured family member, but crippled and wounded: an embarrassment.

When his prosperous New York relatives heard of Sid's plight, they brought him down to see about a position in the telephone business in Brooklyn. The job, under one of his family members, promised no great pay but was considered a bonanza by the long-suffering Harriet and Hattie. Sid set off for a new start; he was almost fifty. He never came back to Malden to live. Within six months he was again out of a job. This time he retreated to the home of relatives in Maine, and it was several months before he secured a job, with the American Express Company. This job he owed to the good offices of yet another relative, Cousin Mary, of Salem, Massachusetts.

Throughout these trials Sid's relations with his wife remained good. Hattie preserved no word of discouragement about Sid's distance or unemployment, even though he was absent for long periods (when he managed a visit in 1908, he had been gone for more than a year). On the contrary, her infrequent comments about him were warm and loving—"Sidney came for two weeks and we had a *lovely* time." There is a "perpetual sense of comradeship between us."[16] His mother-in-law reported that he had "taken his medicine like a man. May I do as well!"[17]

In this unconventional family, members did not fill their expected roles. Sid provided neither a living nor a home. Hattie had no children and cleaved to her mother rather than her husband. Yet the family functioned well as a unit. All three pooled their resources and did not blame the others for their lacks. Family connections found Sid jobs when his own efforts failed. If he could not fulfill the traditional family responsibilities, he had certainly paid his dues. Harriet forgave him by saying, "I remember well his generosity to me and all, when he had the means to give."[18]

Sid's reverses demanded careful management of the family's other resources. When tenants moved away money flowed out fast until the rooms were filled again. At one difficult period of unoccupancy, Harriet was required to sell off seventy-two of her more valuable books to keep the "spectre of an aged persons home forever from my door."[19] The women compacted their quarters and rented out more rooms. They kept for themselves most of the first floor, two rooms on the second, and the two attics. With thrift, Harriet and Hattie could live without further spending their principal, which Harriet described as "in *reductio*, but not yet *absurdam*."[20]

Having to admit tenants into her domain offended Harriet, but she did it, accommodating as always to necessity and remaining a householder with some dignity. Once when prospective tenants came to look the place over, Harriet mourned, "O dear! I wish I did not have to rent rooms. No! I am thankful I have them to rent."[21] If she had refused to rent, she would have had to sell the house and join the ranks of homeless widows living in furnished rooms, a fate she refused to consider. The Pierce legacy enabled her to pay taxes, repairs, and heating costs, so that the house could provide the income.

Hattie preserved an account book for 1907. The figures are incomplete and do not balance, but they indicate just how close to the bone Harriet and Hattie were living. That year Hattie earned $208.69, Sid sent $121.00, and Harriet supplied $315.65, for a total of $645.34. House expenses without taxes and repairs came to $433.24. The women paid $200.88 for food, $52.91 for Hattie's clothes, $31.93 to the church, $78 for coal, $9.45 for ice, $56.90 for washing, and $70.50 for help. Amusement rated a paltry 50¢.[22] On this shabby genteel budget, the women counted the pennies, keeping personal expenses to a minimum. They were not, however, reduced to doing all their own housework, and in fact spent considerable sums on domestic help and laundry. The church was generously remembered. This careful accounting illustrates the determined respectability of women with standards in reduced circumstances.

The Robinsons carried on a structured, rather monotonous life with serious reading and not too much exertion. In 1907 Hattie, as a woman of fifty-seven, recorded her daily routine.

Rise 6:30 to 7
Carry drink of water up to mother & bring down slops. Get dressed in time to "receive" Mrs. Gateley [the help] at 7:20 or so. Go see to furnace, coal ashes & wood.
Get breakfast—very simple.

Breakfast at 8. See to fires, lamps etc. Get dinner & cook what is necessary—usually in the kitchen till 10:30 often all the forenoon Try to read something solid in the forenoon [such as] Thomas á Kempis.

Get dinner (at 11:30) dishes, etc.

Nap from 12:30 to 2:30 or less, except on Tues. & Fri. when start for Boston at 12:15. Back at 5 or before. Errands, marketing, sewing 'till dark. Whist to about 4:30.

Get supper (5.30)

Read News, N. Y. Times, or perhaps a story. Light up. Read & Sew or make calls on neighbors or write letters. Get *ready* for bed (begin to) at 9:30 (if I have a nap) 8:30 if I don't. (Psalter before bed) Get to bed 10 or 10:30. *Rarely* at 9:30 when *very* tired. Sometimes give out & lie down in evening or get off to bed at 8. leaving Mother to close up, which I don't like to do. She always has a long nap & likes to set up late.

Fires on my mind all day. Also cooking & planning ahead. Make doughnuts or cookies or cake once a week.[23]

Hattie had taken upon herself the burdens of running the household. She was her mother's mainstay, her comfort, her companion. She willingly, if not enthusiastically, accepted the responsibility.

Harriet's successful financial management in the face of bad times and failure testified to her ability to subordinate her wishes to unpleasant necessity. She was a survivor, the family banker, the rock that all relied on. She rather proudly related the story of her dependability, including the fact that she had sacrificed for others:

Let me record my thankfulness, that I have been permitted to do more for others than I have done for myself, even "from the beginning," and no doubt unto the end thereof.

First for my mother to help her fill our four hungry mouths, then for my brothers one of whom, my earnings in the factory helped to become a Universalist minister. Then my second brother, what help I gave him was never of any good to him. Then came my married life, a very happy one but one in the early part, full of cares & trials, and privations. Then the desire of my youth to write something of value (poetry) was laid aside and I became the help meet for a poor man & a reformer! And to prove that I was a true help meet, I will write his verdict. "I never could have done (or been) what I am but for your help." And so the time went on until he left me & Since then my children *all* can tell what I have been to them.

I may add that in the time of our greatest, early pecuniary stress, we had the care & the maintenance of both our mothers and though there were other men children in both families we never had any pecuniary help from them, and both mothers lived to a good age, died with us and were buried and just as they desired to be—And thankfully and willingly we did this duty, and now in my age, I remember this with gratitude and thankfulness. They were both good mothers, but my *own*. I cannot express here all her self-forgetfulness, all her help & all her goodness to me and mine.[24]

Harriet had cause for pride in her dependability and generosity. She was prouder of maintaining her family than of the six books she had written, and she put it on record for future information.

❧❧❧

Lizzie and her family, on the farm in Oakville, Connecticut, were enjoying comparative prosperity. They had weathered their threatened bankruptcy and paid their debts. The children, Martha and Robin, were growing up. Aunt Hattie found Martha "a perfect jewel of a girl," gentle but firm, "with a sweet low voice an ear for music & a love for being petted & cuddled."[25] The aunt and niece began a close relationship, which was to last for many years.

As the children grew older Harriet noted that they were "bright and natural."[26] Robin was very truthful; Martha, more imaginative, saw things in "an enlarged manner."[27] The children grew up on a farm without the civilizing influences of city, school, and church, and their exuberant manners sometimes offended their older, more reserved relatives. "They have plenty of good qualities but they need to go among other children who are well trained to add the necessary regard for externals, though they are not very bad."[28]

Lizzie herself, a "brave and capable"[29] woman, managed a busy life that included a fair amount of drudgery. She ran the milk business on the farm and also a school in her house. She did manage to do a fair amount of literary work in her clubs,[30] and was the prime mover in instituting a rural mail service in her area. Although Harriet felt that Lizzie was equal to the demands made on her, that her "back [was] tilted for the burden,"[31] Lizzie herself wrote that she longed for rest.[32]

Harriet began again to mention Lizzie's husband, George, in fond terms. He kindly invited his mother-in-law to his fiftieth-birthday party, and she noted that George was faithful and true and always good to her.[33]

Sometime later, however, there was another family crisis. No one elaborated on these "last few years of [Lizzie's] severe trials," but there was apparently a major conflict involving finances and the future of the children. Almost certainly Lizzie suffered some sort of nervous breakdown. But she pulled herself together and reopened the school, which was successful enough to pay Robin's tuition in the home-study program of a private school.

Harriet read trial and fulfillment into this sequence of events. She noted that Lizzie's "revolt ha[d] not only lifted her out of—where she was, but that George ha[d] been helped too and [was] really trying to help her." The reverses had reinitiated Lizzie into the family group of those who were tried and had prevailed. Harriet noted that Lizzie was more like herself than she had been for some time.[34]

❧❧❧

The Western branch of the Robinson clan had been settled in the mining town of Telluride, Colorado, since 1895. Warrie had found a steady job as deputy clerk of San Miguel County, an area in the southwest, of which Telluride was the county seat and most important community. Warrie was thriving with his nice office and improved salary, his "very attentive and hospitable" wife, Mary, and their bright and good-natured baby, Harriet.[35]

Warrie had now lived in Denver, Pueblo, and finally Telluride, working as a stationer, a railroad clerk, and a government official. He had little connection with Telluride's major industry, mining, which involved many of the evils of the textile factories in which his mother had grown up. Capitalization was largely furnished by absentee owners, whose primary interest, of course, was profit. Warrie was not one of the struggling workers, as his mother had been, playing instead a small part in the establishment.

Several months after Lucy Winyard Robinson was born to Mary and Warrie, in 1900, Mary took her new baby and her five-year-old Harriet on a train trip to Malden to show them off to their relatives. Their grandmother was charmed. Young Harriet was her namesake and very "quick and taking," but Lucy, "thick skinned," with hazel eyes and curly light hair, was "resolute and strong" with great determination. Lucy quite wound herself around her grandmother's heart. Harriet detected some of her own qualities—indeed, peculiarities—in the child.[36]

Lucy was "sweet as a rose," "more like our people"—"*my* people"—than her older sister, Harriet. "She will create." Looking at Lucy, Harriet saw the generations stretching back and before her. All of this was wishful thinking, for Lucy was well under a year at the time; the comments speak of Harriet's need to perpetuate herself. She seized on the newest grandchild after the others had seemed to her to be unlikely candidates. Certainly she did not see perfection, noting that both children, like their cousins, would need a great deal of training, as do all children of "pronounced personalities."[37]

When Mary reached home after the visit she sent back the happy news that Warrie had been appointed justice of the peace for the county and was to be called "Judge." He filled the unexpired term of a departed elected official. Warrie took his job seriously and began to read the law, settling small cases as they came up. The Telluride paper reported that "Justice Robinson seems to have the correct idea about bailing out accused criminals." His mother was proud.[38]

Telluride was a prosperous mining town settled in the narrow low lands between the jagged Uncompahgre and San Juan mountains. Several churches and large school buildings as well as a brick county courthouse had been built there in the 1880s. In 1890 the Sheridan Hotel, a three-story brick structure of generous proportions and luxurious appointments, was erected. In addition, gambling halls and lace-curtained brothels supplied all comers. The steady refrain during working hours was the tinkle of the bells of the burros as long strings of them negotiated the tortuous trails that clung to the cliffs; all day the burro trains ran, taking coal up the mountains and ore down again. The Smuggler-Union Mine dominated the business of the town.

In 1901 an angry strike occurred in Telluride. The strikers' union, the Western Federation of Miners, demanded recognition and an end to the "fathom" system, which meant that individual miners had access to the coal in the veins they were working, and so some miners had to work harder than others for their wages.

When scab miners were then hired, the strikers beat them up and sent them on their way. The owners gave up and the strike ended as a clear victory for the union men, who had won recognition, an eight-hour day at prevailing wages, and a three-year contract.

Warrie was not involved in this strike, but continued troubles in the mines eventually resulted in the imposition of martial law. Again the union had attempted to establish its dominance and to abolish nonunion labor. Local officials rounded up the strikers, and they were tried in the magistrate's court, on the bench of which sat Judge Warrington Robinson. The strikers were arrested for "vagrancy," and Warrie gave them the choice of paying fines and going back to work, or else leaving town within two days. The judge dispensed swift justice, settling thirty-eight cases in one day, twelve of them in just two hours. Most strikers complied and relative peace was restored. "Police Magistrate Robinson has the courage to do his duty," puffed the Telluride papers.

Harriet was elated about Warrie, "on the topmost wave just now." She believed that he had been "led" to the West to perform this particular duty. "Blood will tell," she declared, thinking of her crusading husband. Warrie, too, was pretty proud of himself, having proved to one and all "that when I [am] tried, I am not found wanting."[39]

Harriet—she who prided herself on having led a strike in her youth—had little sympathy with these strikers of her adulthood. Her desire to read triumph into her life—which encompassed the lives of her children—caused her to change sides in this case involving Warrie. She compared Warrie to her husband. But the elder Robinson would most likely have been on the other side. Robinson had always championed the worker and had campaigned hard for a reduction in the fourteen-hour day. He would have sympathized with the miners, who worked under dangerous conditions for bosses who considered human beings cheaper than safety precautions. The father had been fearless in espousing unpopular causes; his son, whose identity and livelihood were with the leaders of the town, was more cautious.

The strike heated up yet again and was not to be settled for many months. Warrie Robinson, however, would not be around to deport any more strikers: just after the beginning of 1904 he died of pneumonia. After more than forty years of fighting with asthma for his breath, he now breathed his last. His wife was devastated, and with good cause. A poor widow with two small children, she was miles away from family and without many friends.

Mary transferred her dependence from her husband to her mother-in-law. In response to Mary's steady stream of grieving letters with pleas for help, Harriet sent money and advice; but she did not feel the same responsibility for Mary that she had felt in helping her often unemployed son. Indeed, when Mary's own mother suggested that Mary be invited to Malden for a long rest, Harriet was a little put out. It "broke their hearts," Harriet responded, but she and Hattie decided it best that Mary not come.[40]

Hidden in this little incident were many deeper feelings. Family responsibility ran in blood lines. Harriet felt that Mary's family should be taking her back and smoothing her way. Moreover, to Harriet Warrie was always her little boy, not Mary's husband. Mary's abandoned grief offended Harriet, who had known Warrie much longer and believed she was grieving more deeply.

Harriet wanted to be free of reminders of Warrie's widow in order to build a monument to her eternal child. She mourned the comforting baby she had carried when her little Willie had died. She grieved for the boy whose painful breathing had kept him from sleep, for the many quiet times of closeness when all the rest were sleeping. Once he had said he would rather *die* than live with his illness. Later she noted the prophecy in his words.[41]

Harriet rationalized Warrie's life. Poverty and the other hardships of life were as nothing, she wrote, if "one's dear children live to do her honor."[42] Harriet's wishful thinking is probably responsible for contemporary family belief that Warrie was a Harvard man rather than a high-school dropout, and that he died by the gun of an angry miner in the courtroom rather than of pneumonia.[43]

Harriet wrote her last diary in 1908, three years before her death, at eighty-six. The diary provides the last pictures of this tart and stouthearted woman. She was sure that the country was

on its way to anarchy and the disruption of the republic. She saw
Theodore Roosevelt as a despotic ruler determined either to
"rule or ruin" the nation.[44] But, distant from the world of political
events, she did no more than complain to her diary. She was
frailer and increasingly lame, always tinkering with her unsatisfactory boots—"o feet! it's you that are to blame. Wanted: a new
pair of feet!"[45]

Nevertheless, "My home is very pleasant and I can do just as I
like in all things," wrote Harriet.[46] All rooms were rented out
except those she meant to "keep and die in."[47] The house was
repaired and kept in order, the frequent sound of the hammer
reminding her of her handsome father when he had walked on
the Boston Common with her eighty years before.[48]

She was busy with the usual routine. Writing, reading, sewing,
and twilight solitaire filled the day. She was still thinking that she
might try to write a great poem, the only unfulfilled ambition left
from her youth.[49] But her major literary effort at this time, apart
from her diary, was an amiable poem on the worth of age, "At
Eighty-three."

At Eighty-Three

Once, in the arrogance of youth,
　When all things good seemed made for me,
I thought one old enough to die,
　Who reached the age of eighty-three.
　　"　　　"　　　"　"　"　"　　"

But when I older, wiser grew,
　Enjoyed my blessings full and free,
I said, "I can't live half a life,
　Unless I come to eighty-three.
　　"　"　"　"　"　"

So I went on the "foot-path way"
　Till slow the pace has come to be,—
For Faith and Hope convoyed me on!
　They brought me safe to eighty-three.
　　"　　　"　　　"　"　"　"　　"

And when I pass the dividing line,
My immortal self I sure shall see,
To guide my way to things beyond;
No longer bound by eighty-three!
    "   "   "   "   "   " 50

On December 22, 1911, Harriet Robinson died. The Malden
Evening News reported the death—"after protracted illness of old
age and general breaking up"—on the first page. She would have
been pleased with the obituary, which praised her contributions
as a pioneer in several women's movements. Paragraphs were
devoted to her literary achievements and her club work, her
ancestry and her survivors. It was the kind of obituary Harriet
would have written herself. She practically did write it herself.
The paper drew heavily from information published at the times
of Harriet's birthday parties; these accounts had been written by
Harriet or by Hattie. The obituary presented Harriet as she
wished to be remembered: a person of solid, admirable achievements, well connected to an established family.[51]

Harriet's reputation, unfortunately, fell short of her desired
goal. A contemporary essay on important women of Malden
listed the recently deceased Mrs. Robinson as "the friend of Lucy
Larcom, and the inspirer of the gifted 'Warrington' in his work as
a publicist," descriptions that gave Harriet only a second-hand
claim to remembrance and made no acknowledgment of her own
accomplishments. The essay, read before Old and New, was
presented as praise of Harriet.[52]

This discrepancy between descriptions of Harriet by others
and by herself illustrates the gap between the way Harriet was
known and the way she wished to be known. She was grimly
ambitious, eager to leave her mark on the world. That some of
those most disposed to be kindly to her could not recognize her
achievements would have brought her some bitter hours of
reflection. Harriet failed to perpetuate her self-view among her
contemporaries. None of them kept her memory green. For
years she was forgotten.

If she was unsuccessful at securing herself an important place in history, she did succeed at sustaining her influence over the family. The house was maintained through four generations of the family, who lived and died there. Harriet left it jointly to her two daughters and to her daughter-in-law, Mary, as well. Lizzie and George wanted to live in it, so they paid $1,500 to Mary for her share and owed Hattie—who went off to Poughkeepsie, New York, to live with her husband—her share. With their children, Martha and Robin, the Abbotts left the Waterbury, Connecticut, area where they had been living for thirty years, to live in the family home.

The Abbotts' arrival on Lincoln Street can be seen as a retreat rather than as a tribute. George had taken on the job of building the Waterbury reservoir and, because of construction difficulties, had again lost money. Nevertheless, it is remarkable that the family should feel drawn back to the old home. They had not the resources to keep it up, and during their occupancy Hattie thought the place looked "forsaken and poverty stricken."[53]

The Abbotts did, however, succeed in preparing their children for the world in a way that the Robinsons had been unable to do. Robin and Martha both graduated from college, the first of the family to do so. Granted that the importance of higher education was increasing and that the young people both worked hard to get through, their family actively encouraged them in their schooling.

Robin, the elder child, majored in practical civil engineering at Tufts, where he was a twenty-three-year-old freshman. He made the transition from farm boy to college student successfully, joining the football team and the chess club as well as pursuing his studies in a serious way. He worked his way out of subsistence living into the professional class. He stayed on at Tufts as a professor of civil engineering and married Elsie Dustin, an aristocratic young blond woman his relatives considered "almost too faultless."[54] After a number of childless years Elsie and Robin adopted a "dear little blond boy" named David.[55] They made their home in Medford and later Winchester, more fashionable suburbs than nearby Malden, and their lives moved some distance from the Lincoln Street house, both physically and stylistically.

Martha Abbott later said she had spent all her life in schoolrooms, having helped with her mother's classes and then taught school when she herself was in high school, commuting to class on horseback from the Connecticut farm. She made enough money to put herself through college, and graduated from Smith in 1916. Her ambitions more closely reflected family interests than did Robin's. Martha wanted to write and produce plays, to act, and to teach. These interests, as well as the circumstances of the family, kept Martha close to the older relatives, whereas Robin spun off in new directions. Indeed, Martha was to become the central strength of the family, just as her grandmother Harriet had predicted upon her birth.

Martha was the true heir of the lively women in her family. Hattie found her "very satisfactory & remarkably efficient in many directions." Martha was a "writer, athlete, teacher, practical cook (in small way) dressmaker & milliner (natural gifts) & above all, an almost perfect daughter." Hattie found a visit to Malden a great success, "thanks to that little girlie, Martha."[56]

The theme of sacrifice of personal interests for family duty—the traditional theme of the Robinson women—was repeatedly sounded in Martha's life. Lizzie's poor health, possibly due to arthritis of the spine, confined her to a wheelchair for her last eleven years. She suffered from both pain and depression. Martha frequently dropped her professional activities, as the manager of a troupe of collegiate actors and as a teacher in Gambier, Ohio, and then Glens Falls, New York, to come home and care for her sick mother. She finally moved back and taught at Malden High School—eventually giving up the job altogether—in order to nurse Lizzie.

When Lizzie died, on September 27, 1926, at seventy-four, her front-page obituary in the Malden paper stressed her club work, identifying her as a founder of Old and New and of the women's club in Waterbury, Connecticut, where she was "prominent in society." She was also identified as the daughter of "Warrington," the "well known Boston journalist," whose accomplishments were described at length. Her mother, Harriet, was mentioned only by name.[57] After Lizzie's death, George and Martha continued to live in the old house.

❧ ❧ ❧

Hattie had reached the age of sixty-one when her mother died, and although she had been married for thirty-three years, she had never lived away from Harriet. She had been her mother's child, her mother's colleague, and finally her nurse. The mother-daughter relationship had taken precedence over her marital relationship; Sid was the "wandering star" in this group.

Hattie said in her diary that Martha's care of *her* mother, Lizzie, was no more than her "obvious duty,"[58] but Hattie's ambivalence about duty to aged parents came through. After her own mother's death, she missed Harriet's "espionage."[59] She regretted the "carefulness and unselfishness" of her own—Hattie's—life.[60] Martha was right to care for Lizzie, "But she will find that it will always be mother first (as it was with me) I fear," wrote Hattie.[61]

Whatever Hattie's bitterness at her sacrifice to her mother, she remained true to her duty as she saw it. Her marital union had been sundered by responsibility to family (along with Sid's difficulties in making a living), but the emotional bonds between mother and daughter remained strong. Harriet's death severed the cord of filial obligation and Hattie was now free to rejoin her husband.

After a series of short-lived jobs, Sid had developed a satisfactory career as a bookkeeper for P. A. & Son, a plumbing concern in Poughkeepsie, New York. Here he was a respected figure if not a powerful one. All day he stood at a high desk, working over his figures. He was absolutely honest, a man who had mastered the small things in his life when the large ones were out of his control. The company failed, however, in 1917, so that he was once again out of a job, this time for many months. Finally, through the kind offices of a friend, he procured a position with the Poughkeepsie Savings Bank.

Hattie moved into her husband's furnished flat. The apartment had a kitchen, and now a woman to run it, but the Shattucks preferred to take their evening meals at Mrs. Simpson's boarding house, with the good company that had made Sid's hitherto lonely exile pleasant. Indeed, even after Hattie rejoined him after so many years of separation, Sid's life continued much the way it had before.

Hattie had difficulty adjusting. Her health precluded many activities, forcing her to give up anything that required exertion. She voluntarily withdrew from life and then became bitter as she watched it pass her by. Whereas her mother had hung on to life, Hattie relinquished it. Hers was the grim story of the deterioration of social structures. In an effort to avoid responsibility and strain, she frequently told herself to "Exclude everything redundant—nothing essential."[62]

She listed the activities she allowed herself. She maintained the flat, got breakfast and Sunday suppers, ironed, mended, and kept the household in cookies. Her remaining social activities included calling on friends and neighbors and visiting the Old Ladies' Home. She corresponded with forty old friends and attempted to keep cheerful and merry at the table. For intellectual stimulation she went to the library weekly, whence she took out one solid and one light book; she read the religious lessons and the Psalter daily; and she kept up an old interest in astronomy.

Hattie also listed the things she did not do. She did no serious cooking, reading of religious literature, or writing of anything of "value or permanency." She took care of no one but herself and Sidney. She had no regular occupation. She did not "sew or knit or crochet or tat or embroider or paint or botanize."[63] She lived to stay alive, and her life was resolutely barren as a result.

The absence of serious responsibilities and activities led Hattie to be somewhat disconnected and morbid. She brooded a lot and came up with some strong and unexpected opinions. Notably she reversed her position on woman suffrage: "If suffrage is a right, women ought to have it. If suffrage is a privilege, women must earn it.—and want it.—Which is it.?"[64] This basic question troubled her. If every citizen had the right to vote, then it was of little use in improving society, for the Western states, where women could vote, had no better laws than Eastern states, and "some are worse." If the vote was a privilege, the small sample of Western women who had won the vote had used their privilege ill. In neither case did the voting of women improve the country. Votes for women would neither benefit the society nor the women themselves. Hattie was also convinced that women did not want to vote.[65]

She had come to believe in the superiority of man; equality was false in theory and reality. "I have achieved a great admiration for men. They are so strong & so protecting & so loyal & so loving."[66] She scorned the "wobbly" tendency of women and "their narrow vision." She believed that women could do their best work when supervised by men. " 'Harriette Shattuck! What Heresy!' " she heard her old friends exclaim.[67] She felt that women were unpleasant and unfeminine when they clamored for rights.[68] She opposed working wives. "You *cannot* serve God & Mammon, i.e. you cannot be a man & a woman too," by which she meant a wage earner and a housekeeper and mother.[69] She had become a defender of the old ways. Perhaps this antifeminism resulted primarily from years of service to a domineering mother.

She also took a strong stand against birth control. Her educated friends favored informing the "poorer classes" of the methods then known only to the initiated. For Hattie, birth control was a "euphonius name for *murder*."[70] These statements reflect on the intimate life of the Shattucks, who apparently did not practice birth control, not knowing how it was done. "I guess I shall have to find out and so be posted—though I hate the subject," mused Hattie. She still thought that people should have babies if they could, though she never wrote of yearning for children or seemed to feel unfulfilled because she was childless.[71]

Hattie adopted an abrasive attitude in her personal relations. She made a virtue of her outspokenness, saying her mission in life was to do and say disagreeable things, even though she was disliked as a result. This prickly nature antagonized the very friends she craved, but gave her an excuse when people were not attracted to her.[72]

Hattie's complaints about icy walks deviled Mrs. Simpson into forbidding her to come to her meals during winter unless the streets were dry; on bad days she thus dined at home alone, while

Sid went to the boarding house.[73] A friend to whom she had been reading daily, as a matter of duty, let it be known that she did not care for the service anymore; Hattie's grudging offering had been rejected.[74]

Some of this abrasiveness reflected Hattie's discomfort at being a woman of intellectual pretensions without a college degree in the territory of Vassar. She did not find the graduates particularly impressive, yet they possessed the badge of education that made them impossible to ignore. Once she said, "Sometimes I wish the Vassar contingent would all go away—& stay. They act as a conglomerate wet-blanket on the rest of us—poor ignorant non-collegians."[75]

Hattie did exercise the impressive credentials she had. Her successful books on parliamentary law were recommended as the authority for the National American Woman Suffrage Association, and for a while they had the endorsement of the General Federation of Women's Clubs. In 1916 the Shattuck Rules were turned aside in favor of the Robert Rules, which were in fact similar to Hattie's and had even adopted some of her rulings. The local Tuesday Club decided to adopt Robert as authority and Shattuck, which they found easier to understand, as acting authority.

Despite her withdrawal from activity, the success of Hattie's books and her expertise in the field led her to attempt once more the teaching of parliamentary law. She signed up twenty women and began a course of ten lessons for $4. But the effort brought back her old nervousness, and after only five lessons she canceled the class. She never taught again.[76]

How to keep human relations alive when institutionalized activity had stopped was a major problem for Hattie. She did maintain a large correspondence, and her extant letters are charming and entertaining; her best relations were with distant friends. The friends gradually fell away, however, with death or serious illness. And Hattie herself went out calling less and less often. The Shattucks moved twice in Poughkeepsie, upsetting amicable neighborhood relationships; an old lady who walked painfully with a cane could not comfortably visit old friends in distant parts of town. Hattie steadily moved toward isolation. Many days she opened or closed her diary entry with the notation "No callers today."

Hattie's loneliness caused her to rely heavily on her good-natured husband. "I can't imagine my life without him. We are one, if ever husband and wife were one. My life, before I knew him, seems like that of another person. . . . We were made for each other for time and for eternity."[77] As he started off for work each day, she prayed, *"Oh God, save him for me; save me for him; if it by Thy will and as it be Thy will."*[78]

Sid worked at the savings bank until 1930, when he requested a rest or his retirement. The bank granted a leave of absence to the tired man and Sid came home to rest, but he weakened rapidly. When Hattie felt unable to cope with his condition, she had him moved to the hospital. As the ambulance men took him away on a stretcher, Hattie saw her husband for the last time. She was informed of his death by friends from the bank, who made all the arrangements for his funeral and interment. Hattie's niece and nephew, Martha and Robin, came down to lend support.

Hattie admitted that "The whole world has stopped." The decisions that she had determinedly avoided were now thrust upon her. "What must I do? Where must I stay? God help me."[79] She decided to do nothing. Her poem "Sufficient unto the Day" underscored her determination not to borrow trouble from the future.

Sufficient Unto the Day

I lock the door on tomorrow
    I firmly withdraw the key
So, be it joy, or sorrow,
    I cannot, I will not, see.

I look not through that key-hole,
    I turn my eyes from that door,
I see just this day only,
    And not one moment more.

Then—all night long I slumber
    While the watchful stars hold sway;

And when I awake—it is morning!
Tomorrow? Oh no! Today![80]

༄ఌఌఌ

The bereaved widow, a deaf and halt old woman of eighty, in
fact became more self-sufficient. She cooked her own meals and
saw to the coal and the furnace. She took short walks, though
careful not to do much exercise. "My motto is *take care* of your
health *so as not to be a burden to your relatives.*"[81] In case of trouble
she had two family avenues of aid: go live with Martha in Malden
or write to Mary, Warrie's widow, in Colorado, to come and live
with her.

Since Warrie's death Mary had been eking out a living for
herself and two daughters by taking in boarders and doing nursing. They moved around for the nursing cases, always on the
edge of poverty, frequently writing the Robinsons for money,
which was sent less and less often. Once Mary mistook a burglar
for the demented old man she was nursing and was shot and
almost killed.

Mary was good-natured, hard-working, and resourceful. She
managed to bring up Harriet and Lucy and marry them off
respectably. In January 1925 Harriet Hanson Robinson II,
named for her grandmother, great-grandmother, and aunt, produced the first blood descendant of the next generation and
named her—Betty! It was a sure sign that the family traditions
were dying out.

Mary came East for a visit, and Hattie, impressed by her affection and helpfulness, renewed their friendship. Mary offered to
care for Hattie—eighteen years her senior—when she needed it,
proposing to come live with her at once; she could use Hattie's flat
as a base to go off on nursing jobs. Hattie thought she seemed like
a real sister, though she was only a sister-in-law, and was well
pleased while Mary worked around the flat, cleaning, cooking,
and sewing. But she began to murmur when Mary ran errands
and then got a nursing job away from Poughkeepsie. The two
subsequently fell out, Mary departing for Detroit to her daughter
Lucy's. "So I am alone again. But I'm used to it,"[82] wrote Hattie.
She had become as cantankerous an old lady as her mother could

sometimes be—demanding attention and paying for it with harsh words.

At the time of Sid's death, in 1930, Martha was a spinster schoolteacher. She was thirty-seven and taught English at Malden High. She also took care of her failing father, George Abbott. Martha's devotion to her aged parents is impressive. Long after her mother's death she would wake in the night thinking she heard Lizzie's voice.[83] Hattie gave her high marks for doing her duty: "She has grown older & not so pretty. Oh dear! She has the hardest row to hoe of anyone in our whole family, past & present. And such courage and so faithful to her task!"[84] George died in 1931, at seventy-eight years of age.

George, who figures as a rather shadowy, insensitive, almost villainous character in this narrative, was respectfully remembered in the Malden *Evening News*.[85] He was identified primarily as the father of the high-school teacher Martha and of Professor Robinson Abbott of Tufts. He was also listed as a member of the Centre Methodist Church (while all the women in his family had gone the Episcopal route, he had kept his old allegiance).

During his active life, George had been a contractor and builder. He had gotten the bid from the town of Malden to tear down a large house, and with the materials he had built the ugly house next to the Lincoln Street property. He had been obliged to mortgage the family house, which he left jointly to Martha and Robin.

With George gone, the way was opened for Hattie to move to Malden. Martha, the most solicitous of the nieces, convinced her aunt Hattie that she would come for her any time she was needed, though she did not object to Hattie's staying in Poughkeepsie as long as she was able. "She seems almost like a daughter even if only a sister's daughter," wrote Hattie, again distinguishing between degrees of loyalty due to blood kin.[86]

Martha's warm nature promised a close and rewarding relationship. When Hattie wrote that she had gotten a new wrapper, the supportive Martha replied that she hoped it had some red in it, "real dark, rich, wine-color threads to give you that *dark, brown-eyed beauty* which certain clothes which you wear always give you. Black makes you 'sparkley,' like a jewel."[87]

After her father's death, Martha perked up, had her black hair cut short and curly, and took off on a long trip to the West. Hattie stayed in Poughkeepsie for another two years, until Martha, concerned about her aunt's dwindling finances and health, suggested that she come back to the old house. Modest living in Poughkeepsie cost Hattie $100 a month.

Before she left Poughkeepsie Hattie was grandly written up in the Poughkeepsie *Star*.[88] The author described a vigorous pioneer in women's rights, the first woman clerk in the Massachusetts House, the author of six books, and a contributor to several newspapers. The reporter found her at eighty-two an "omnivorous reader" of classics, with a "ring of assurance in her voice." The accompanying photograph portrayed Hattie as a triumphant ruin: a grim, far-seeing old battle horse. "Horrid! Looks 90!" she protested.[89] Nowhere was there a sign of the petulant, introspective, morbid woman she revealed in her diaries. In fact, when a neighbor read the article and came over, identifying himself as an old schoolmate, she coyly noted, "Imagine it. Fortunately he's married!"[90]

For her last scene Hattie moved back to the family's Malden house, where she found her life less satisfactory than she had expected. Martha had been wonderful company while visiting in Poughkeepsie, but here her work kept her busy. The upstairs was rented out. Martha's boyfriend Zivan Simonian, a young man she had taught at the high school and who had chauffeured her on the Western journey, was in constant attendance. The household did not revolve around Hattie; she found herself frequently *de trop*.

Financially she was much better off, as she now paid $20 a month board and nothing for her room. Her meals from Mrs. Simpson in Poughkeepsie had been 35¢ each. Unfortunately, two problems led to conflict: Hattie expected to be catered to, and she spoke her mind. When she confronted Martha about her long absences or bossed Zivan—whom she called "a perfect gentleman" and a "dear boy"—she was answered back. Hattie tried to play the household tyrant and increasingly drew Martha's wrath down upon her head.

Hattie recorded her frustrations and helplessness in her journal. "Why can't I hold my tongue?" she agonized.[91] She genuinely appreciated Martha and knew she needed her—"Martha feeling better. Bossing. Glad of it. I need it!"[92] But "Sometimes it seems as if nobody cared to be *with me*—if they could be with somebody else. (This ought not to be written down) I must *write* to *somebody*!!"[93]

Martha and Zivan were wed in June of 1935, a move that cost Martha her job because of the rules against married teachers and the depression shortage of work. Hattie canceled the old $1,500 debt of the Abbotts on the house as a wedding present. The marriage brought very little change. Zivan moved in with Martha, but both were off at work or on unexplained visits most of the time.

Despite longer separations, the relations between the two generations continued to deteriorate. In despair Hattie set up her rules: "*Ask no questions. Keep quiet, stay in own room, don't open door to kitchen* (unless it is ajar.)" "Will not *do anything* or *touch anything* again unless I'm told I may!"[94] She fixed her own meals and ate them in solitude. "I desire to be *dead*! But I must 'carry on.' "[95]

Hattie would seem to have been the worst treated of the Robinson relicts. She recorded the most personal abuse and was ignored more than she felt was her due. She longed for the old days in Poughkeepsie, where she remembered having been happy, though she certainly did not think she was while she lived there. She remembered that in the past she had been "somebody." "And now? Just existing & trying not to think of the future."[96]

Her lot was probably not worse than her predecessors', however. While Hattie saw herself as pitiful and mistreated, Martha and Zivan probably saw a sharp-tongued, deaf, snoopy old lady. Whereas Hattie's grandmother Mrs. Hanson had worked hard for her keep in her old age, Hattie made no pretense of doing that. Hattie's mother, Harriet, had in her old age been the householder and dispenser of funds, and Hattie's sister, Lizzie, had been the lady of the house and direct blood kin to her daughter, Martha; that Hattie had been invited to Malden at all, rather than relegated to the Old Ladies' Home, testified to Martha's continuing the family tradition of responsibility for aged relatives. It was this tradition, as well as the goodness of Martha's heart, that provided a home for Hattie when she was old.

Hattie survived into 1937, trying to reconcile herself to her inglorious end. Her last diary entries recalled her relationship with Susan B. Anthony and her suffrage work.[97] By then her suffrage activities again counted as a source of pride rather than as a lost cause. Martha closed her aunt's last diary with Hattie's funeral notice, and the comment "*Auntie* buried today at Concord, Mass. Sunny day—just the sort she would have liked. Funeral expenses $254."[98]

Martha, the protector of the aged, lived only four more years. She died in 1941, at the age of forty-eight.

So closes the saga of the family of Harriet Hanson Robinson. Knowledge of this family's experience, its complexity, is a corrective to the generalities offered today about family life in the nineteenth century. When faced with the account of the devolution of one real family, historical categorization becomes difficult.

Much of this picture has been seen through the eyes of Harriet Robinson, whose whole life was a search for significance. Born into a family at the nadir of its development, a family that disintegrated when she was six, Harriet attempted to give herself a fixed place in society by reconstructing her past. She researched her genealogy, and using words, the only tool at her disposal, she built her history from collected bits, as well as her imagination. She wrote herself into historic movements in which she had marginal importance. She recorded her days and preserved the documentation. Most of her life can be read as a yearning for respectability, respect, and remembrance.

For some time it seemed as if Robinson's efforts were in vain. Though she lived for more than fifty years in Malden, Massachusetts, the family was virtually forgotten there. A recent town history does not mention Harriet, the author of six books, nor her crusading journalist husband, William. Even their daughter Hattie Shattuck, who founded the still-flourishing Old and New and was an author of national impact, has not been remembered there. A Malden authors' conference passed over them entirely.

But the situation is changing. Harriet Robinson may soon

achieve the respect and immortality that has eluded her dogged efforts. Her *Loom and Spindle*, a personal account of life in the early New England mills, was republished in 1976, almost eighty years after its original publication, in 1898. For some time the book has been developing a reputation as an early voice for women's rights, as well as a description of women's nineteenth-century working experience. Full of specific information and written in a forthright manner, the book has become a favorite for history and women's-studies reading lists. In her home town, where Harriet Robinson was once forgotten, the Malden Bicentennial Committee put a marker on her house—not as her husband's house, but as hers. Her now tattered and extensive papers, which were procured beginning in 1959, from Goodspeed's Book Shop because of their peripheral value for the history of the suffrage movement, have been microfilmed under a grant to Radcliffe's Schlesinger Library, for relative immortality.

Harriet Hanson Robinson, unable to find a firm niche for herself during her life, has now found a permanent position as a representative and commentator of her time.

APPENDIX
Geneaology

The Family of Harriet Hanson Robinson and William Stevens Robinson

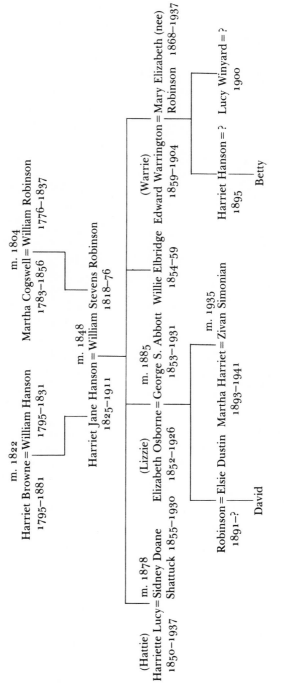

COGSWELL

Robert = Alicia
?–1581   ?–1603

|

Edward = Alice
?–1616

m. 1615
John = Elizabeth Thompson
1592–1669   ?–1676

m. 1650
William = 1. Susannah Hawkes
1619–1700

John   Edward   Mary = Godfrey Armitage   Hannah = Cornelius Waldo
1622–53   1629–?   ?–1649   1624–1704

Abigail = Thomas Clark   Sarah = Simon Tuttle   (daughter, stayed   Elizabeth = Nathaniel Mapleton
                            ?–1663   in England)   ?–1657

m. 1670
Elizabeth = Thomas Wade   Hester = 1. Thomas Bishop   Susannah = Benjamin White
1650–1726   2. Thomas Burnham   m. 1681

2. (another)

Sarah = William Noyes   William = Martha Emerson
                           1659–1708   m. 1685

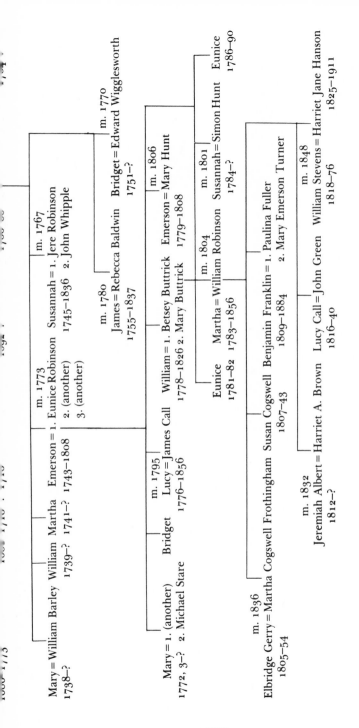

ROBINSON

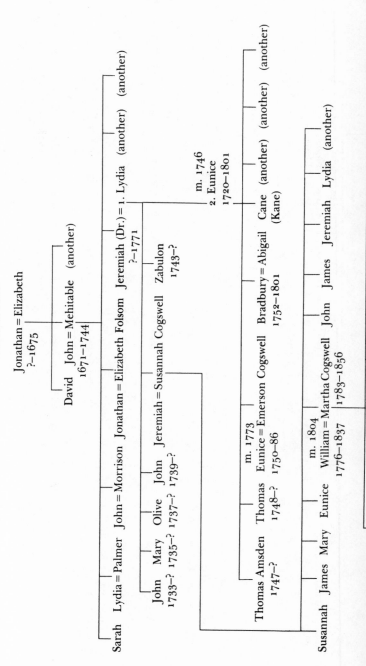

1812

1816–40

1825–1911

1818–76

BROWNE

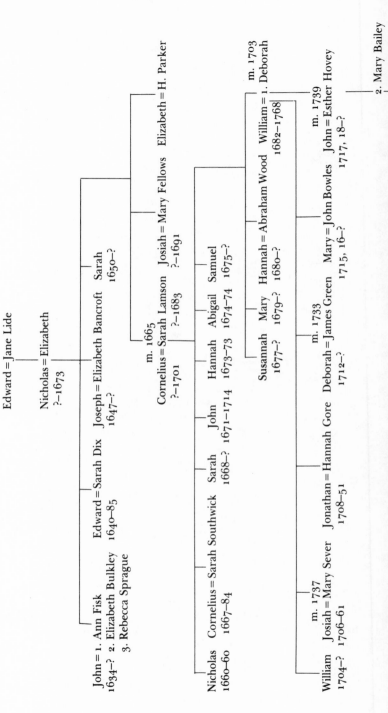

?–1809

2. Sarah Godding
1763–1802

Lucy Sally = 1. Varney Abijah Cynthia = Eben O. Hawes Benjamin Piper = 1. Taylor Charles Harriet = William Hanson
1789–1836 2. Crisp 1791–1872 1793–1843 1794–? 1795–1881 1795–1831
2. Martin m. 1822
3. Ladd

Isaac Cooper = 1. Palmer Angeline Cooper = 1. Cudworth William = Eliza Kingsbury Jane = Lowell Adams
1797–184? 2. Cook 1798–1882 2. Clarke 1800–31 1802–70
3. Call

229

HANSON

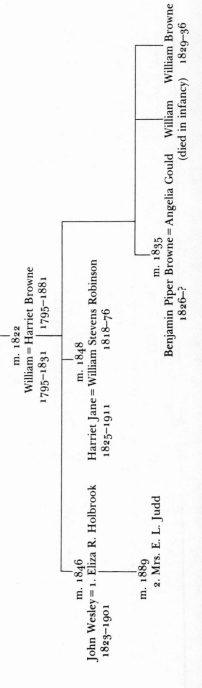

Thomas = ?

Thomas = ?

John = ?

John = ?

John = Sally Getchel

m. 1822
William = Harriet Browne
1795–1831 | 1795–1881

m. 1848
Harriet Jane = William Stevens Robinson
1825–1911 | 1818–76

John Wesley = 1. Eliza R. Holbrook
1823–1901
m. 1846

m. 1889
2. Mrs. E. L. Judd

m. 1835
Benjamin Piper Browne = Angelia Gould   William   William Browne
1826–?   (died in infancy)   1829–36

NOTES

Chapter I

1. Harriet H. Robinson, *Loom and Spindle, Or Life Among the Early Mill Girls, with a Sketch of "The Lowell Offering" and Some of its Contributors* (Boston: Thomas Y. Crowell & Co., 1898; reprint ed., Kailua, Hawaii: Press Pacifica, 1976), p. 25, hereinafter cited as *Loom.* Page references are to the original edition.

2. Genealogy Book, Box 2, Folder 24, in "HARRIET JANE HANSON ROBINSON, 1825–1911; HARRIETTE LUCY ROBINSON SHATTUCK, 1850–1937; Papers, 1833–1937," Collection A-80 in the Arthur and Elizabeth Schlesinger Library on the History of Women in America, Radcliffe College, Cambridge, Mass. All diaries, scrapbooks, and letters pertaining to the family, except those specifically noted, can be found in this collection. Harriet Hanson Robinson will hereinafter be cited as HHR and Harriette Robinson Shattuck as HRS.

3. HHR Genealogy Book; Harriet H. Robinson, "Nicholas Browne of Reading and Some of His Descendants," *New England Historical Genealogical Register* 44 (July 1890):281–2.

4. Ibid.

5. Ibid., p. 284.

6. HHR Genealogy Book.

7. HHR Genealogy Book.

8. HHR D.A.R. application in Genealogy Book.

9. HHR Genealogy Book.

10. Ibid.

11. Ibid.

12. HHR Diary, 24–25 October 1870, Robinson-Shattuck Papers.

13. HHR Genealogy Book.

14. *Loom,* p. 158.

15. HHR Genealogy Book.

16. *Loom,* pp. 25–26.

17. HHR Genealogy Book.

18. HHR Diary, 8–9 February 1904.

19. *Loom,* p. 26.

20. David H. Fischer's massive study of social change in America indicates that families became stronger and more responsible, presumably owing to longer life, in the period from 1790 to 1820. He presented this and other findings in a talk at Boston University, July 1977.

21. *Loom,* p. 26.

22. Ibid., p. 28.

23. Lucy Larcom, "Among Lowell Mill-Girls: A Reminiscence," *The Atlantic Monthly* 48 (November 1881):598. Also found in HHR Scrapbook, vol. 29, Robinson-Shattuck Papers.

24. HRS Diary, 11 June 1915.

Chapter II

1. *Loom,* p. 30.

2. Ibid., p. 31.

3. Hannah Josephson, *The Golden Thread: New England's Mill Girls and Magnates* (New York: Duell, Sloan and Pearce, 1949), p. 51.

4. *Loom*, p. 7.

5. Larcom, "Among Lowell Mill-Girls," p. 600.

6. This subject is discussed in Robert F. Dalzell, Jr., "The Rise of the Waltham-Lowell System and Some Thoughts on the Political Economy of Modernization in Ante-Bellum Massachusetts," *Perspectives in American History* 9 (1975):235, 242–44, notes 25–35.

7. Thomas Dublin, "Women, Work, and the Family: Female Operatives in the Lowell Mills, 1830–1860," *Feminist Studies* 3 (fall 1975):32.

8. *Loom*, p. 15.

9. Ibid., p. 76.

10. Lucy Larcom, *An Idyl of Work* (Boston: J. R. Osgood and Co., 1875), p. 34.

11. Lucy Larcom, "American Factory Life—Past, Present and Future," a talk delivered before the American Social Science Association, in HHR Scrapbook, vol. 36, p. 144.

12. F. G. A., A Lowell Operative, "Susan Miller," *Mind Amongst the Spindles: a Miscellany, Wholly Composed by the Factory Girls, Selected from "The Lowell Offering"; with an Introduction by the English editor and a Letter from Harriet Martineau* (Boston: Jordan, Swift & Wiley, 1845), pp. 81–92.

13. Larcom, "Among Lowell Mill-Girls," p. 610.

14. *Loom*, pp. 25–26.

15. Asa Briggs, "The Language of 'Class' in Early Nineteenth Century England," *Essays in Labour History*, Asa Briggs and John Saville, eds. (London: Macmillan & Co., 1960), pp. 43, 47

16. *Loom*, p. 14.

17. *Early Factory Labor in New England* (Boston: Wright & Potter Printing Co., 1883) (hereinafter cited as *Early Factory Labor*), p. 18; *Loom*, p. 72.

18. See, for instance, Josephson, and Norman Ware, *The Industrial Worker, 1840–1860* (Boston: Houghton Mifflin Co., 1924; reprint ed., Chicago: Quadrangle Books, 1964), particularly "The Degradation of the Operative," pp. 106–25.

19. Josephson, p. 207.

20. Robert George Layer, *Earnings of Cotton Mill Operatives, 1825–1914* (Cambridge, Mass.: Committee on Research in Economic History, 1955).

21. *Loom*, p. 71.

22. Thomas Dublin, *Women at Work: The Transformation of Work and Community in Lowell, Massachusetts, 1826–1860* (New York: Columbia University Press, 1979), discusses the two Lowell strikes in detail and offers many insights into the mill-girl experience.

23. John Clark, for Merrimack Co., and others, circular in Lawrence Corporation Papers, Baker Library, Harvard University.

24. William Austin to Henry H. Hall, 23 January 1834, Lawrence Papers. All following letters are in the Lawrence Papers unless otherwise noted.

25. Abbott Lawrence to "My Dear Sir," 11 February 1834.

26. Austin to Hall, 12 February 1834.

27. Austin to Hall, 14 February 1834.
28. Hall to Austin, 15 February 1834.
29. Ibid.
30. Austin to Hall, 15 February 1834.
31. Thomas Dublin, "Women, Work, and Protest in the Early Lowell Mills: 'The Oppressing Hand of Avarice Would Enslave Us,' " *Labor History* 16 (winter 1975):108–9.
32. "Reminiscences of Strike of '34," Boston *Globe*, 1883, in HHR Scrapbook 29:52.
33. Ibid.
34. Ibid.
35. Hall to John Aiken, 22 February 1834, Letterbook of the Tremont and Suffolk Mills Corporation, Tremont Mill Papers, Baker Library, Harvard University.
36. Austin to Hall, 1 March 1834.
37. Austin to Hall, 9 March 1834.
38. Aiken to Hall, 20 February 1834, Tremont-Suffolk Letterbook.
39. "Reminiscences of Strike of '34."
40. Between 1828 and 1836 the average wage of female operatives rose from $2.61 to $4.33 a week. By 1840 the wage had declined to $2.75. (Ware, *The Industrial Worker*, p. 112.) The old overseer said that his "smart, spry" weavers could make from $3 to $5 a week over their board, double the proposed amounts ("Reminiscences of Strike of '34"). The proposed equalized wage after the strike allowed speeders $1.90 a week above board cost; drawing girls, $1.55; lap winders, $1.67; spinners, $1.85; doffers, $1.85; warpers, $2.25; dressers, $2.25; drawers-in, $1.67; and weavers, $1.67 (Austin to Hall, 15 February 1834).
41. Lucy Larcom, *A New England Girlhood: Outlined from Memory* (Boston: Houghton Mifflin Co., 1889), pp. 152–53.
42. Hall to Robert Means, 24 September 1836, Tremont-Suffolk Letterbook.
43. *Loom*, p. 84.
44. Aiken to Hall, 4 October 1836, Tremont-Suffolk Letterbook.
45. Josephson, p. 238; Boston *Daily Advocate*, 5 October 1836; Boston *Transcript*, 4 October 1836, copied from the Lowell *Advertiser*.
46. Ibid.
47. Boston *Evening Transcript*, 6 October 1836.
48. Aiken to Hall, 14 October 1836, Tremont-Suffolk Letterbook.
49. *Loom*, pp. 83–86.
50. Ibid., p. 85.
51. "Proceedings in the City of Lowell at the Semi-Centennial Celebration of the Incorporation of the Town of Lowell, March 1st, 1876," (Lowell, Mass., 1876) in HHR Scrapbook 31:74.
52. HHR Scrapbook, vol. 39, p. 123.
53. *Loom*, p. 85.
54. Aiken to Hall, 7 October 1836, Tremont-Suffolk Letterbook.
55. *Loom*, pp. 67–68.
56. Ibid., p. 45.

57. Helena Wright, "Sarah G. Bagley: A Biographical Note," *Labor History* 20 (summer 1979):398–413; Ware, *The Industrial Worker*, pp. 90, 125.

58. *Loom*, p. 39.

59. Larcom, *A New England Girlhood*, p. 229.

60. *Loom*, p. 96.

Chapter III

1. HHR Diary, end of year 1867.

2. *Loom*, p. 39.

3. Ibid., p. 44.

4. Ibid., p. 8; HHR Scrapbook, vol. 31; Theodore Edson, *An Address Delivered at the Opening of the Colburn Grammar School in Lowell, December 13, 1848* (Lowell, Mass.: James Atkinson, City Printer, 1849), p. 23.

5. Frederick W. Coburn, *History of Lowell and Its People*, 3 vols. (New York: Lewis Historical Publishing Co., 1920), 1:19.

6. Edson, pp. 26, 29.

7. John Phillips Coolidge, *Mill and Mansion: A Study of Architecture and Society in Lowell, Massachusetts, 1820–1865* (New York: Russell & Russell, 1942), p. 200.

8. Edson, p. 34.

9. Samuel Adams Drake, *History of Middlesex County*, 2 vols., (Boston: Estes and Lauriat, 1880), p. 105.

10. Edson, p. 53.

11. Larcom, *Girlhood*, pp. 150–52.

12. *Loom*, p. 20.

13. Ibid., p. 19.

14. Ibid., pp. 19–20.

15. Ibid., p. 21.

16. Larcom, *Girlhood*, p. 155.

17. Ibid., p. 156.

18. Lowell, Massachusetts, Trades and Labor Council, *Lowell: A City of Spindles* (Lowell: Lawler & Co., 1900), pp. 29, 33–34.

19. Emit D. Grizzell, *Origin and Development of the High School in New England Before 1865* (New York: Macmillan Co., 1923), p. 77.

20. HHR Diary, 18 February 1864.

21. Grizzell, p. 78.

22. Ibid., pp. 79–80.

23. *Loom*, p. 42.

24. All of these compositions are found in HHR Papers, Box 2, Folder 18.

25. HHR Diary, 1–2 May 1908; *Loom*, p. 42.

26. Larcom, *Girlhood*, pp. 175–76.

27. Ibid., p. 181.

28. *Loom*, p. 43.

29. Fred Lewis Pattee, *The Feminine Fifties* (New York: D. Appleton-Century Co., 1940), p. 53.

30. *Loom*, p. 45.

31. Ibid., pp. 45–46.

32. Ibid., p. 41.

33. Larcom, "Among Lowell Mill-Girls," pp. 593–612.

34. "Petition for a Ten-Hour Workday," *Documents Printed by Order of the House of Representatives of the Commonwealth of Massachusetts During the Session of the General Court A.D. 1845*, Number 50 (Boston: Dutton and Wentworth, State Printers, 1845).

35. Duane Hamilton Hurd, ed., *History of Middlesex County, Massachusetts, with Biographical Sketches of Many of Its Pioneers and Prominent Men*, 3 vols., (Philadelphia: J. W. Lewis & Co., 1890), 2:233–37; *Catalogue of the Middlesex Mechanics' Association* (Lowell, 1860); Harriette Knight Smith, *The History of the Lowell Institute* (Boston: Lamson, Wolff & Co., 1898).

36. *Loom*, pp. 74–75. Donald M. Scott, "The Popular Lecture and the Creation of a Public in Mid-Nineteenth Century America," (*The Journal of American History* 66 [March 1980]:791–809). Scott suggests that the lecture-attending public was a self-elected American mainstream that consolidated the "collective cultural consciousness" (p. 809).

37. Henry A. Miles, *Lowell: As It Was and As It Is* (Lowell, Mass.: Nathaniel L. Dayton, 1847), p. 205.

38. Herbert G. Gutman, *Work, Culture, and Society in Industrializing America* (New York: Alfred A. Knopf, 1976). In chapter one Gutman discusses many of these tensions.

39. Miles, p. 42.   41. *Loom*, p. 103.
40. Larcom, *Girlhood*, pp. 170–75.   42. Ibid., p. 122.

43. William Robinson, whom she later married, encouraged the paper while he was an editor of the Lowell *Journal*. "In his zeal for the writers," he "went so far as to take one of the least known among them as his companion for life" (*Early Factory Labor*, note on p. 21).

44. *Loom*, pp. 101–2.

45. This poem and following ones by HHR can be found in HHR Scrapbook, vol. 30.

46. Larcom, *Girlhood*, pp. 213–15.

47. Gordon S. Haight, *Mrs. Sigourney, the Sweet Singer of Hartford* (New Haven: Yale University Press, 1930), p. 12. In Ann Douglas Wood's "Mrs. Sigourney and the Sensibility of the Inner Space," the author suggests seeking after death in poetry was a way of "anaesthetizing herself," of "sublimating her desires," of perfecting "the suffering and receptive sensibility" (*New England Quarterly* 45 [June 1972]:178).

48. *Early Factory Labor*, note on p. 21; Harriet Hanson Robinson, ed., *"Warrington" Pen-Portraits* (Boston: Mrs. W. S. Robinson, 1877), p. 41.

49. HHR to William Stevens Robinson—hereinafter cited as WSR— 23 September 1875.

50. Haight, p. 35.
51. Ibid., p. 36.
52. Ibid., p. 45.
53. Ibid., p. 99. Wood in her article "Mrs. Sigourney and the Sensibility of the Inner Space" reads Sigourney's career as a metaphor for "militant sublimation" rather than as a metaphor for power (p. 181), which is what Harriet thought it to be.

54. John Wesley Hanson to Harriet Jane Hanson, n.d., from Wentworth, N.H., Robinson-Shattuck Papers.

Chapter IV

1. Ibid., p. 49.
2. Ibid.

3. *Trumpet and Universalist Magazine* (1828–64).

4. Richard Eddy, *Universalism in America*, 2 vols. (Boston: Universalist Publishing House, 1886), 2:82.

5. *Loom*, p. 21; Coolidge, *Mill and Mansion*, p. 42.

6. HHR Diary, 29 January 1865.

7. Coolidge, pp. 56, 197; *Loom*, pp. 15–16.

8. *Loom*, pp. 21–22; Coolidge, pp. 201–2.

9. Coolidge, p. 49.

10. H. T., "Our Household," Lowell *Offering*, quoted in *Loom*, p. 92.

11. Larcom, *Girlhood*, pp. 8–9.

12. *Loom*, p. 49.   17. Ibid., p. 54.

13. Ibid., pp. 49–50.   18. Ibid.

14. Ibid., p. 50.   19. Ibid., pp. 54–55.

15. Ibid., p. 51.   20. Ibid., p. 55.

16. Ibid., pp. 52–53.   21. Ibid., pp. 55–56.

22. Ibid., pp. 55–58; Harriet preserved a certificate of honorable discharge in HHR Scrapbook 36:35.

23. *Universalist Leader*, 4 January 1902.

24. John Wesley Hanson to Harriet Jane Hanson, 3 May 1845, Robinson-Shattuck Papers, hereinafter cited as JWH and HJH.

25. JWH to HJH, 11 May 1845, from Wentworth, N.H.

26. JWH to HJH, 12 April 1845, from Fairlee, Vt.

27. JWH to HJH, n.d., from Wentworth, N.H.

28. JWH to HJH, 11 May 1845, from Wentworth, N.H.

29. JWH to HJH, 12 October 1845, from Wentworth, N.H.

30. JWH to HJH, n.d.; 27 November, 1845.

31. JWH to HJH, 12 March 1846.

32. JWH to HJH, 12 October 1845.

33. JWH to HJH, 14 June 1846, New Mills, N.H.

34. JWH to HJH, 13 November 1846, New Mills, N.H.

35. HHR Diary, 16 July 1908.

36. Ibid., 19 February 1867.

37. WSR, Valentines, Box 2, Folder 33, Robinson-Shattuck Papers.

38. *"Warrington" Pen-Portraits*, p. 35.

39. JWH to HJH, 12 September 1848.

40. John Wesley Hanson published more than thirty discourses, sermons, histories, and miscellanies for women between 1849 and 1900, as well as his journalistic work. His books include *Bible Proofs of Universal Salvation* (1877); *The Greek Word "Aion Aionios" Translated Everlasting, Eternal in the Holy Bible* (1875); *Historical Sketch of the Old Sixth Regiment of Massachusetts Volunteers* (1866), for which he served as chaplain during the Civil War; *Christian Chorals: A Hymn and Tune Book for the Congregation and the Home* (1879); and *A Cloud of Witnesses: Poetry and Literature for Universal Salvation* (1880). One of the Universalist colleges awarded him the D.D. degree, and in 1877 he was appointed president of the Universalist college Smithson. He died in 1901 while traveling west on a train. A picture of Hanson and a eulogy can be found in The *Universalist Leader* 5 (4 January 1902):12.

41. *Loom*, pp. 58–59.

Chapter V

1. *"Warrington" Pen-Portraits*, p. 7.
2. HHR Genealogy Book; Harriet H. Robinson, "William S. Robinson ('Warrington')," *The Historical and Genealogical Register* 39 (October 1885):313–24.
3. *"Warrington" Pen-Portraits*, p. 2.
4. Ibid., pp. 2–3.
5. At his death he left an estate valued at £2,973, including a "dwelling house, barns, buildings, and land," appraised at £1,500. He owned silver plate; clothing—including a £20 silk-lined green cloth suit, 13 pair of stockings, a silk sash valued at £12, 12 caps, 12 shirts, and a green velvet cap—28 pair of sheets; and four slaves, worth an estimated £310. (Will and inventory of Captain James Pecker, quoted in *"Warrington" Pen-Portraits*, pp. 565–74.)
6. William S. Robinson, "Sketch of Emerson Cogswell," delivered before the Social Circle, 1871, quoted in *"Warrington" Pen-Portraits*, p. 3.
7. Robert A. Gross, *The Minutemen and Their World* (New York: Hill and Wang, 1976), p. 174, discusses the importance of the Social Circle in stratifying an originally fairly homogeneous society.
8. *"Warrington" Pen-Portraits*, pp. 3–7.   10. Ibid., p. 8.
9. Ibid.   11. Ibid., p. 11.
12. Ruth R. Wheeler, *Concord: Climate for Freedom* (Concord, Mass.: Concord Antiquarian Society, 1967), p. 147.
13. *"Warrington" Pen-Portraits*, p. 8.
14. Records of the Grammar School, Concord, Mass., District 1, 1834–41, Concord Public Library, Concord Safe, Shelf 8, Item 20.
15. *"Warrington" Pen-Portraits*, p. 10.
16. Ibid.
17. WSR to William Robinson, 30 August 1835, Robinson-Shattuck Papers.
18. *"Warrington" Pen-Portraits*, p. 16.
19. Ibid.   21. Ibid., p. 18.
20. Ibid., p. 17.   22. Ibid., p. 17.
23. WSR to his mother, Martha Cogswell Robinson, 7 July 1838; "Articles by Warrington," Scrapbook, Boston Public Library, Department of Rare Books and Mss., Boston.
24. WSR to brother Jeremiah Albert Robinson, 23 June 1838, Robinson-Shattuck Papers.
25. Ibid.
26. WSR to Martha Cogswell Robinson, 16 November 1838.
27. WSR to sister Lucy Call Robinson Green, 25 February 1838, Robinson-Shattuck Papers.
28. *"Warrington" Pen-Portraits*, p. 18.
29. Ibid., p. 20.
30. Concord *Republican*, quoted in Ibid., pp. 18–19.
31. WSR to sister Lucy Green, 4 October 1839.
32. WSR to Martha Cogswell Robinson, 28 April 1839.
33. *"Warrington" Pen-Portraits*, p. 22.
34. Ibid., pp. 22–23.

35. WSR to Martha Cogswell Robinson, 17 January 1842; Lowell *Journal and Courier*, 18 January 1842.

36. Lowell *Journal and Courier*, 18 January 1842.

37. Boston *Daily Republican*, October 1848; *"Warrington" Pen-Portraits*, p. 186.

38. WSR to Henry H. Fuller, 27 January 1842, Robinson-Shattuck Papers.

39. *"Warrington" Pen-Portraits*, p. 28.

40. WSR to brother Benjamin Franklin Robinson, 27 March 1844, Robinson-Shattuck Papers.

41. *"Warrington" Pen-Portraits*, p. 29.

42. Lowell *Journal and Courier*, 25 September 1846.

43. WSR to Martha Cogswell Robinson, 4 September 1844.

44. WSR to brother Elbridge Gerry Robinson, n.d. (probably 1844), Robinson-Shattuck Papers.

45. WSR to Family, 16 March 1846.

46. WSR to Martha Cogswell Robinson, 11 February 1845.

47. *"Warrington" Pen-Portraits*, p. 31.

48. Ibid., pp. 32–33.

49. WSR to Benjamin Franklin Robinson, 27 March 1844.

50. *"Warrington" Pen-Portraits*, p. 36.

51. WSR to Martha Cogswell Robinson, n.d. (probably 1848).

52. WSR to Martha Cogswell Robinson, 4 November 1848.

53. HHR Diary, 30 November 1888.

54. WSR to Martha Cogswell Robinson, 2 December 1848.

55. HHR to Martha Cogswell Robinson, 30 December 1848.

Chapter VI

1. An analysis of a marriage with an even more improvident bread-winner can be found in Kirk Jeffrey, "Marriage, Career, and Feminine Ideology in Nineteenth-Century America: Reconstructing the Marital Experience of Lydia Maria Child, 1828–1874," *Feminist Studies* 2 (spring–summer, 1975):113–30; HHR Diary, 18 July 1865.

2. Henry Wilson to WSR, February 1849, quoted in *"Warrington" Pen-Portraits*, p. 41.

3. JWH to HHR, 28 March 1849.

4. "Opinions of the Press," Scrapbook, Boston Public Library, Department of Rare Books and Mss., Boston.

5. *"Warrington" Pen-Portraits*, p. 48.

6. Ibid., p. 50.

7. HHR to Harriet Browne Hanson, 29 June 1851, Robinson-Shattuck Papers.

8. *"Warrington" Pen-Portraits*, p. 49.

9. HHR Diary, 9 January 1865.

10. Ibid., 6 December 1902.

11. WSR to Martha Cogswell Robinson, 4 December 1850, HRS Scrapbook, vol. 100.

12. WSR to Martha Cogswell Robinson, 6 December 1850, HRS Scrapbook, vol. 100.

13. HHR to Harriet Browne Hanson, 29 June 1851.
14. HHR Diary, 6 January 1852.
15. Ibid., 20 January 1852.
16. HHR to Harriet Browne Hanson, 13 July 1851.
17. HHR Diary, 6, 13, 20 January 1852.
18. Ibid., 11 September 1904.
19. HHR to Harriet Browne Hanson, 29 June 1851.
20. HHR Diary, 7 January 1852.
21. *Loom,* p. 47.
22. HHR Diary, 14 December 1868.
23. Ibid., 21 April 1863.
24. Ibid., 12 February 1866.
25. Ibid., 15–17 February 1863.
26. WSR to Martha Cogswell Robinson, 8 November 1849.
27. WSR Diary, 4 January 1852.
28. HHR Diary, 6 January 1852.
29. Ibid., 5 May 1855, 12 February 1852, 7 April 1855, 4 May 1863; WSR Diary, 11 January 1852.
30. WSR Diary, 25 January 1852.
31. Lowell *American,* 4 August 1851.
32. HHR Diary, 18 March 1855.
33. *"Warrington" Pen-Portraits,* p. 65.
34. HHR Diary, 11 December 1854.
35. *"Warrington" Pen-Portraits,* pp. 67–69.
36. HHR Diary, 31 May 1864.
37. Ibid., 31 May 1855.
38. Ibid., 9 June 1856.
39. Harriet H. Robinson, *The North American Review* 140 (May 1885):479–80.
40. Dr. Bartlett said of William that he was a man of "the most perfect integrity and goodness," a man of the "most sterling character" (HHR Diary, 25 May 1855).
41. HHR Diary, 18 March 1855.
42. Ibid., 6 October 1854.
43. Ibid., n.d., February 1858.
44. Egbert Guernsey, *Homeopathic Domestic Practice* (New York: Boericke & Tafel, 1856), pp. 564–65.
45. HHR Diary, 25 April, 25 May 1855.
46. Ibid., 3 June 1855.
47. Ibid., n.d., February 1858.
48. Guernsey, p. 28.
49. HHR Diary, n.d., February 1858.
50. HRS Diary, 6 January 1929.
51. HHR Diary, 13 June 1896.
52. HHR to Elizabeth Osborne Robinson Abbott (hereinafter cited as Lizzie), 28 October 1884; Robinson-Shattuck Papers; HHR Diary, 28 August 1888.
53. HHR to children, 7 February 1884.
54. HHR to Harriet Browne Hanson, 19 May 1855.

55. HHR Diary, 16 November 1856.
56. Ibid., 24 April 1855.   58. Ibid., 8 April 1855.
57. Ibid., 7 May 1855.   59. Ibid., 23 June 1858.
60. *"Warrington" Pen-Portraits*, pp. 76–77.
61. HHR Diary, 23 June 1858.
62. Samuel Adams Drake, *History of Middlesex County*, 2 vols. (Boston: Estes and Lauriat, 1880), p. 134; The *Bi-Centennial Book of Malden* (Boston: Town of Malden, Mass., 1850), pp. 224–25. Three thousand five hundred twenty people lived there in 1850. When the town of Melrose was created out of part of Malden, in 1860, Malden still numbered 5,865 people. Even after Everett was also cut off in 1870, Malden's population had grown to 7,370. (Drake, pp. 134–35.)
63. *"Warrington" Pen-Portraits*, pp. 82–84.
64. Ibid., p. 85.   67. HHR Diary, 12 December 1868.
65. Ibid., p. 99.   68. Ibid., 23 June 1858.
66. Ibid., p. 85.   69. Ibid., 12–13 December 1868.
70. Compare this loyalty with that of Lydia Maria Child, who abandoned her husband to his impractical fancies for ten years. (Jeffrey, "Lydia Maria Child.")
71. HHR Diary, 23 June 1858.
72. *"Warrington" Pen-Portraits*, p. 89.
73. HHR Diary, 4 May 1859.
74. The Robinsons soon thereafter moved to the Lincoln Street house that they later bought. The family that then moved into the Ferry Street house lost two children and the father to disease by 1863. "They *must* believe now that the location is unhealthy," wrote Harriet (Diary, 19 September 1863).
75. *"Warrington" Pen-Portraits*, p. 87.
76. HHR Diary, n.d., February 1858, comment written in 1889.
77. Ibid., 30–31 December 1859.
78. *"Warrington" Pen-Portraits*, p. 88.
79. HHR Diary, 31 December 1865, 12 October 1864.
80. Lucy Larcom to HHR, 5 January 1860, Robinson-Shattuck Papers.
81. HHR Diary, 24–26 January 1864.
82. Ibid., 22 April 1855.   88. Ibid., 15 September 1872.
83. Ibid., 7 June 1871.   89. Ibid., 2 June 1872.
84. Ibid., 22 January 1865.   90. Ibid., 31 December 1865.
85. Ibid., 1 September 1866.   91. Ibid., 1 May 1871.
86. Ibid., 4 July 1869.   92. Ibid., 4 February 1872.
87. Ibid., 17 September 1871.   93. Ibid., 14 March 1869.
94. HRS Diary, 13 December 1868.
95. HHR Diary, 16–17 April 1871.
96. Ibid., 23 April 1871.   98. Ibid., 29 April 1888.
97. Ibid., 31 December 1865.   99. Ibid., 6 January 1857.
100. *"Warrington" Pen-Portraits*, p. 104.
101. HHR Diary, 9 January 1864.
102. Ibid., 12 December 1863.   104. Ibid., 24 April 1867.
103. Ibid., 9 January 1864.   105. Ibid., 6 May 1867.

106. Ibid., 7 May 1867.
107. HRS Diary, 3 August 1916.
108. HHR Diary, 8 February 1865.
109. Ibid., 20 July 1865, comment written in 1876.
110. Ibid., 17 June 1864, 4 December 1865.
111. Ibid., 24 November 1866, 11 April 1867.
112. Ibid., 22 July 1868.
113. Ibid., 26 January 1868.
114. Handy School Brochure, 1869–1870, HHR Scrapbook, vol. 35.
115. HRS Diary, 26 May 1917; HHR Diary, 28 Septemer 1868.
116. HRS Diary, 9, 17, 24 November 1868.
117. HHR Diary, 5 January 1871.
118. HRS Diary, 25 September 1871, 14 January 1872.
119. Report card of Edward Warrington Robinson (hereinafter Warrie), HHR Scrapbook, vol. 35.
120. HHR Diary, 31 December and end of year 1869.
121. Ibid., 29 September 1863.

Chapter VII

1. Ibid., n.d., 1852.
2. Ibid., 14 July 1868, 23 August 1875.
3. Harriet H. Robinson, "My Choice," Robinson-Shattuck Papers, vol. 30.
4. HHR Diary, 1–2 September 1863.
5. Ibid., 10 October 1864.
6. WSR to Martha Cogswell Robinson, 4 November 1848.
7. HHR Scrapbook, vol. 38.
8. WSR to Martha Cogswell Robinson, 29 November 1849.
9. WSR Diary, 4 January 1852.
10. HHR to Martha Cogswell Robinson, 29 November 1849.
11. HHR to Martha Cogswell Robinson, 12 July 1850.
12. HHR Diary, 31 March, 2 April 1855.
13. *"Warrington" Pen-Portraits*, p. 66.
14. HHR Diary, 25 January 1857.
15. In May 1855 Harriet recorded that they had paid off the last important *American* debt, $150; on June 9, 1856, she wrote, "Paid all old debts, bought $100 worth of furniture, saved $300." On January 27, 1857 they had $600 in the bank. (HHR Diary.)
16. Ibid., 18 June 1865.
17. Ibid., 16 April, 10 May 1855; 9 June 1856.
18. Ibid., n.d., May 1858.
19. Ibid., 13 May 1855.
20. Ibid., 3, 8, 30 December 1863; 4, 9 January 1864.
21. Ibid., 18 January 1864.
22. Ibid., 16, 24 February 1864.
23. Ibid., 16, 20 February 1864.
24. Ibid., 14, 27, 29–30 March 1864.
25. Ibid., 2–3 April 1864.

26. Harriet Beecher Stowe, "The Lady Who Does Her Own Work," *The Atlantic Monthly* 13 (June 1864):754, 758.
27. HHR Diary, 3 April, 21 November 1864.
28. Ibid., 20, 27 April 1864.
29. Ibid., 7 April 1868.   31. Ibid., 12 September 1859.
30. Ibid., 11 May 1866.   32. Ibid., 5 May 1871.
33. Ibid., 16 February 1866; 18 January 1864; 16 December 1865; 24 October 1866.
34. Ibid., 25–26 June 1869.
35. Ibid., 15 August 1865.
36. Ibid., 30 August, 2 September 1865.
37. Ibid., 4 March, 4 April, 18, 29 June 1866.
38. Ibid., 31 December 1867, 1 August 1868. Pierce had been a good friend for a long time, offering Robinson a desk in his office when Robinson was out of work from 1857 to 1859. Pierce said that he was more than repaid for any favor he bestowed on Robinson "by the juice he expressed" out of him. (*"Warrington" Pen-Portraits*, pp. 85–86.)
39. *"Warrington" Pen-Portraits*, p. 103; HHR Diary, 11 September, 27–28 December 1871.
40. HRS Scrapbook 104:1.
41. HHR Diary, 4, 12 September 1865; 26, 28 March 1867; 2 May 1868; 16 April 1866; 24 May, 15 November 1869.
42. Ibid., 23 October 1870; 4, 5, 10–11 November 1870.
43. Ibid., 23 (on page for 30) May 1867.
44. Ibid., 9 October 1873; 5 November 1868.
45. Ibid., 13 September 1865; 26 April 1866; 7–8 July 1869; 13 June 1868.
46. Ibid., 13 February 1865; 23 April 1866.
47. Ibid., 12, 21 May 1866.
48. Ibid., 18–19 January 1864; 14–15 February 1866.
49. Ibid., 7 September, 28 November, 8, 9 December 1866; 22 September 1868; 10 September 1869.
50. Ibid., 4 March 1864.   52. Ibid., 18 February 1869.
51. Ibid., 24 May 1864.   53. Ibid., 15–17 February 1863.
54. Ibid., 6 December 1867; 31 March 1869; 22 March 1871. When Lizzie held a luncheon for nine guests, she sent out to Parker's for a small boiled tongue, a pound of boiled ham, three pints of chicken salad, a dozen bread sticks, a quart of charlotte russe, a quart of wine jelly, three pints of frozen pudding, and a dozen rolls. This generous repast was supplemented with some items from home: potato croquettes, bouillon, "macaroon letters," currant and grape jelly, pickles, and "molasses chips." They had enough of everything but the charlotte russe. (HHR Diary, 12 January 1888.)
55. Ibid., 9 March 1864, end of 1864.
56. Ibid., 10 October 1864.
57. Ibid., 21 February 1868; HHR to Harriet Browne Hanson, 22 June n.y. (1858?).
58. HHR Diary, 2 February 1871.
59. Ibid., 8 July 1869.
60. Ibid., 29 December 1900.

Chapter VIII

1. George Frisbie Hoar, *Autobiography of Seventy Years*, 2 vols. (New York: Charles Scribner's Sons, 1903), 1:80.

2. Springfield *Republican*, 24 January 1856.

3. Richard Hooker, *The Story of an Independent Newspaper* (New York: Macmillan Co., 1924), p. 81.

4. Springfield *Republican*, 5 January 1860.

5. HHR Diary, 8 September 1865.

6. *"Warrington" Pen-Portraits*, p. 108.

7. Springfield *Republican*, 25 April 1861.

8. *"Warrington" Pen-Portraits*, p. 102.

9. Ibid., pp. 103–4.

10. Ibid., pp. 155–57.

11. HHR Diary, item pasted in front of page 1865.

12. *"Warrington" Pen-Portraits*, p. 80.

13. Ibid., pp. 79–80.

14. HHR Diary, 29 November 1900.

15. *"Warrington" Pen-Portraits*, p. 81.

16. Ibid., p. 99.

17. HHR Diary, 9 May 1864.

18. Dumas Malone, ed., *The Dictionary of American Biography*, 15 vols. (New York: Charles Scribner's Sons, 1963), 8:1:443–44.

19. Ibid., 8:2:326–27.

20. *Francis William Bird: A Biographical Sketch by His Children* (Boston: privately printed, 1897) (hereinafter *F. W. Bird Sketch*), p. 2.

21. HHR Diary, 23 August 1864.

22. *F. W. Bird Sketch*, p. 35.

23. Ibid., p. 49; *"Warrington" Pen-Portraits*, p. 93.

24. *"Warrington" Pen-Portraits*, p. 423.

25. Ibid., p. 439.

26. Ibid., p. 387.

27. Ibid., p. 118.

28. *F. W. Bird Sketch*, pp. 76–79.

29. Paul Goodman, "The Eclipse of a Whig Elite: Politics and Social Change in Massachusetts, 1830–1877" in Richard L. Bushman et al., eds., *Uprooted Americans: Essays to Honor Oscar Handlin* (Boston: Little, Brown, 1979), gives an excellent background for this section.

30. Robert S. Holzman, *Stormy Ben Butler* (New York: Macmillan Co., 1954), p. 206.

31. Robert Werlich, *"Beast" Butler: The Incredible Career of Major General Benjamin Franklin Butler* (Washington, D.C.: Quaker Press, 1962), frontispiece.

32. *"Warrington" Pen-Portraits*, p. 133.

33. Ibid., p. 441.

34. William S. Robinson, "General Butler's Campaign," *The Atlantic Monthly* 28 (December 1871):745.

35. Ibid., pp. 748, 750; *"Warrington" Pen-Portraits*, p. 134.

36. Lowell *American*, 25 June 1852.

37. *"Warrington" Pen-Portraits*, p. 137.

38. HHR Diary, 13 December 1872.

39. *"Warrington" Pen-Portraits*, p. 138.

40. Ibid., pp. 132–33.

41. *F. W. Bird Sketch*, p. 81.

42. HHR Diary, 22 September 1869.

43. Ibid., 26 January 1873; *"Warrington" Pen-Portraits*, pp. 139–40.

44. William S. Robinson, *The Salary Grab: A History of the Passage of the Act Increasing the Salaries of Members of Congress; with Full Lists of the Yeas and Nays in Both Branches: with a Sketch of the Debates and a Review of the Apologies for the Bill; with Special Reference to the Responsibility of Gen. B. F. Butler . . .* (Boston: Lee & Shepard, 1873).

45. Howard P. Nash, Jr., *Stormy Petrel: The Life and Times of General Benjamin F. Butler 1818–1893* (Rutherford, N.J.: Fairleigh Dickinson University Press, 1969); Robinson, *The Salary Grab*, p. 75.

46. *"Warrington" Pen-Portraits*, p. 143.

47. Hoar, pp. 349–50, 352.

48. Benjamin Butler, *Autobiography and Personal Reminiscences of Major General Benjamin Franklin Butler: Butler's Book* (Boston: A. M. Thayer & Co., 1892), p. 78.

49. HHR Diary, 31 December 1872.

50. Ibid., 3 October 1869.

51. *"Warrington" Pen-Portraits*, p. 145.

52. HHR Diary, 31 December 1873.

53. HHR Travel Journal, vol. 13, Robinson-Shattuck Papers.

54. HHR Diary, 3 November 1874.

55. *"Warrington" Pen-Portraits*, p. 142; Robinson, *The Salary Grab*, p. 5.

56. HRS Scrapbook, vol. 104; *The Woman's Journal*, 7 October 1882.

57. *"Warrington" Pen-Portraits*, p. 153.

58. Ibid., pp. 153–55, published 23 January 1875, Boston.

59. WSR to HHR, 16 October 1875.

60. WSR to Frank Bird, quoted in *"Warrington" Pen-Portraits*, p. 159.

61. *"Warrington" Pen-Portraits*, p. 158.

62. Ibid., pp. 163–65.

63. HRS Diary, 11 March 1917.

Chapter IX

1. HHR to WSR, n.d. (probably 1875).

2. HHR to WSR, 8 August 1875 and n.d.

3. HRS Scrapbook, vol. 108.

4. HHR to Mr. Knapp, 16 June 1877, Robinson-Shattuck Papers.

5. HHR to children, 17 June 1877.

6. HHR to children, 28 June 1877.

7. HHR to children, 14 July 1877.

8. HHR to children, 24 July 1877; HHR to "Diddie" (Lizzie), 23 June, 1 July 1877.

9. HHR to children, 15 July 1877.

10. *"Warrington" Pen-Portraits*, pp. 32–33.

11. Ibid., p. 85.   14. Ibid., p. 104.

12. Ibid., p. 108.   15. Ibid., p. 9.

13. Ibid., p. 131.   16. Ibid., note on p. 9.

17. Ibid., p. 25.
18. Ibid., p. 37.
19. Ibid., p. 125.
20. "Book of notices of *"Warrington" Pen-Portraits*," Scrapbook, Boston Public Library, Department of Rare Books and Mss., Boston. Includes orders for the book and an autograph letter of W. S. Robinson.
21. HHR to Lizzie, 15 April 1884.
22. HHR to WSR, 17 September 1875.
23. HHR to WSR, 11 August 1875.
24. HRS Scrapbook, vol. 102.
25. Harriet Browne Hanson to WSR (dictated to Warrie), 21 July 1875.
26. HRS Scrapbook 105:51.
27. HRS Diary, 10 November 1916.
28. HHR Diary, 8 September 1865.
29. Ibid., 7 September 1865.
30. HRS Diary, 26 August 1928.
31. Ibid., summary of year 1871.
32. Ibid.
33. Ibid., 26 May 1916; 7 May 1916. Hattie indicated that Emma was "sexless or rather double sexed. (She has no nipples.)" and blamed her for any irregularity in the relationship.
34. *"Warrington" Pen-Portraits*, p. 133.
35. Speech at Rochester meeting of the National Woman Suffrage Association, July 1878, in HRS Scrapbook, vol. 101.
36. HHR to WSR, 9 September 1875.
37. HRS Scrapbook, vol. 100.
38. Ibid., vol. 104.
39. Ellen Harman to HRS, n.d., HRS Scrapbook, vol. 100.
40. HRS Diary, 9 February 1918.
41. Wedding service of HRS and Sidney Doane Shattuck, written by Hattie Robinson, in HRS Scrapbook, vol. 100.
42. HRS Diary, 22 August 1916.
43. HHR Diary, 22 January 1888.
44. Ibid., 29 April 1872.
45. HRS Diary, summary of year 1871.
46. HHR to Lizzie, 28 August 1879.
47. Frances E. Willard and Mary A. Livermore, eds., *A Woman of the Century* (Buffalo: Charles Wells Moulton, 1893), p. 2.
48. HRS to Lizzie, 10 December 1884.
49. HHR to Lizzie, n.d. (probably early 1885).
50. HHR to Lizzie, 18 March 1885.
51. Boston *Evening Transcript*, 15 May 1885.
52. HHR to HRS, 25 August 1885.
53. HHR to HRS, 9 August 1885.
54. HHR Diary, 21 March 1888.
55. Ibid., 24–25 June 1888.
56. HHR to children, 5 August 1888.
57. HHR Diary, 7 September 1888.

58. HHR to HRS, 30 May 1893.
59. HHR to HRS, 7 June 1893.
60. HHR Diary, summary of year 1894.
61. Malden *Mirror*, 16 January 1904.
62. HHR to Warrie, 9 September 1875, Robinson-Shattuck Papers.
63. HHR Diary, 25 September 1893.
64. Ibid., 4 December 1893.
65. HHR to HRS and Lizzie, 38 September 1895.
66. Ibid.
67. HHR to HRS, 14 May 1893.
68. HHR Diary, 13 July 1893.
69. Ibid., 11 July 1893.
70. HRS Diary, 24 January 1895.
71. Ibid., 13 January, 19 March 1930.
72. HHR Diary, 31 December 1894; 1 February 1895.
73. Ibid., 4, 7, 8, 11, 21 February 1895; Malden *Mail*, 9 February 1895.
74. HRS Diary, 13 January 1895.
75. Ibid., summary of year 1895.
76. Ibid., 9 February 1918.
77. Ibid., 6 April 1916.
78. HHR Diary, 10 February 1888.
79. Ibid., 20 September 1899.

Chapter X

1. Eleanor Flexner, *Century of Struggle: The Woman's Rights Movement in the United States* (Cambridge: Harvard University Press, 1959), which spans the whole period, is still the best study. Aileen S. Kraditor, *The Ideas of the Woman Suffrage Movement, 1890–1920* (New York: Columbia University Press, 1965), deals briefly with the period, concentrating on the ideology of the time after the two parties united. Lois B. Merk, "Massachusetts and the Woman-Suffrage Movement" (Ph.D. dissertation, Radcliffe College, 1958), deals primarily with the American wing of the suffrage movement and is an effort to correct Harriet H. Robinson, *Massachusetts in the Woman Suffrage Movement* (Boston: Roberts Brothers, 1881), in which Merk found the American wing slighted. Merk's original intention had been to take up the story where Robinson had left off, in 1881, but finding Robinson's history incomplete and slanted, Merk went back to 1868 to set the record straight (Merk, p. 6). Robinson's book is hereinafter cited as *Woman Suffrage*.
2. *"Warrington" Pen-Portraits*, p. 56.
3. HHR Speech, *The Woman's Journal*, 1878, HHR Scrapbook 50:81.
4. HRS Diary, 7 April 1868.
5. HHR Diary, 15 April 1868.
6. HRS Diary, 15 April 1868.   8. Ibid., 15 May 1863.
7. HHR Diary, 9 October 1871.   9. *Woman Suffrage*, p. 50.
10. Mrs. Howe found sisterhood and power in the suffrage movement, as did Harriet. Julia Ward Howe, *Reminiscenses* (Boston: Houghton Mifflin Co., 1899), p. 372. Harriet was not mentioned in Mrs. Howe's memoirs.

11. HHR Diary, 19 November 1868.
12. *Woman Suffrage*, p. 48.
13. HHR Diary, 7–8 December 1870.
14. Ibid., 1 January 1871; HHR Scrapbook, vol. 35.
15. HHR Diary, 4–5 December 1871.
16. Ibid., 12 December 1871.
17. Ibid., 2 January 1872. The first bazaar had netted more than $7,000. The second was not a pecuniary success. (HHR Diary, 20 December 1871; *Woman Suffrage*, pp. 255–56.)
18. *Woman Suffrage*, p. 223.
19. Ibid., pp. 225–26.
20. HHR note describing Blackwell incident and Henry B. Blackwell to HHR, 21 May 1875, both in Box 3, Folder 58, Robinson-Shattuck Papers.
21. Lucy Stone to HHR, 23 May 1875.
22. HHR to WSR, 6 October 1875.
23. Lucy Stone to HHR, 6 July 1878.
24. HHR Scrapbook 50:41.
25. Susan B. Anthony to HHR, 20 December 1880, 14 October 1880, others, Robinson-Shattuck Papers. Hereinafter Anthony is cited as SBA.
26. SBA to HHR, 20 December 1880.
27. SBA to HHR, 7 April 1881.
28. SBA to HHR, 16 May 1881.
29. Lucy Stone to HHR, 4 March 1879.
30. Elizabeth Cady Stanton to HHR, 1 November n.y.
31. SBA to HHR, 11 August 1879.
32. HHR to Matilda Joslyn Gage, 18 May 1879.
33. SBA to HHR, 14 October 1880.
34. SBA to HHR, 19 November 1880.
35. At the 1884 National Woman Suffrage Association Convention, the plan of work includes a list of books that every society should own "to provide ammunition for arguments and debates": Theodore Stanton, *Woman Question in Europe*; Elizabeth Cady Stanton, Susan B. Anthony, and Matilda Joslyn Gage, *History of Woman Suffrage*; Harriet H. Robinson, *Massachusetts in the Woman Suffrage Movement*; T. W. Higginson, *Common Sense for Women*; John Stuart Mill, *On Liberty. The Subjection of Women*; and Frances Power Cobbe, *Duties of Women* (Stanton et al., *History of Woman Suffrage*, 4 vols. [Rochester: Susan B. Anthony, 1886], 4:26).
36. SBA to HHR, n.d.
37. SBA to HHR, n.d.
38. *Woman Suffrage*, p. x.
39. Profits were to go to suffrage work. The publisher doubted the book would make any money. (Thomas Niles of Roberts Brothers to Louisa May Alcott, 14 February 1881, Alcott Papers, Houghton Library, Harvard University, Cambridge, Mass.)
40. Merk, p. 6.
41. *Woman Suffrage*, p. 23.
42. Ibid., pp. 84–86.
43. Ibid., p. 84.
44. Ibid., p. 123.
45. Ibid., pp. 122–24.
46. HHR to T. W. Higginson, 14 November 1881, Boston Public Library, Department of Rare Books and Mss., Boston.

47. T. W. Higginson to Mrs. M. R. Brown, 14 April 1882, Boston Public Library, Department of Rare Books and Mss., Boston.

48. Indianapolis *Times*, 8 April 1883, HHR Scrapbook 34:4.

49. HHR Scrapbook 34:1; Boston *Evening Transcript*, 27 March 1883; *Woman Suffrage*, p. xi.

50. Boston *Evening Transcript*, 27 March 1883.

51. *Woman Suffrage*, pp. 170–71.

52. Harriet H. Robinson, *Captain Mary Miller* (Boston: Walter H. Baker & Co., 1887), p. 47.

53. Ibid., p. 35.   55. Ibid., p. 31.

54. Ibid., p. 12.   56. Ibid., p. 41.

57. HHR Scrapbook 39:107.

58. Boston *Herald*, 27 January 1888; HHR Scrapbook 34:16.

59. HHR Diary, 27 January 1888.

60. Lucy Stone to HHR, 3 May 1882.

61. Lucy Stone to Mrs. M. R. Brown, 2 March 1882; G. W. Bashford to Mrs. M. R. Brown, 2 April 1882; Robinson-Shattuck Papers.

62. Frances Tudor to HRS, n.d.

63. SBA to HHR, 20 January 1882.

64. HHR to children, 10 February 1884; Lowell *Daily Citizen*, 31 January 1879.

65. HHR Diary, 9 March 1884.

66. HHR to Lizzie, 1 February 1885; HRS Scrapbook, vols. 38, 68.

67. HRS Scrapbook, vol. 70.

68. Ibid., vol. 104.

69. HHR Scrapbook 70:13.

70. HHR to Lizzie, 22 May 1892.

71. Lowell *Daily Citizen*, 31 January 1879; HHR Scrapbook 28:56; HRS Scrapbook, vol. 72, loose clipping at p. 36; HHR Scrapbook, vol. 50.

72. "Who Represents Me?," Lowell *Daily Citizen*, 31 January 1879; HHR Scrapbook 28:56.

73. "The Golden Rule," HRS Scrapbook, vol. 109.

74. HRS Scrapbooks, vols. 78, 113.

75. HRS Scrapbook, vol. 105.

76. HRS Scrapbooks, vols. 104, 105, 106.

77. Flexner, p. 175.   79. Ibid., vol. 111.

78. HRS Scrapbook, vol. 105.   80. Ibid., vol. 113.

81. HRS to assessor, 5 May 1879, HRS Scrapbook, vol. 101.

82. "We canvassed four localities in the city of Boston, two in smaller cities, two in country districts and made one record also of school teachers in nine schools of one town. The teachers were unanimously in favor of woman suffrage, and in the nine localities we found that the proportion of women in favor was very much larger than of those opposed. The total of women canvassed was 814. Those in favor were 405, those opposed, 44; indifferent, 166; refused to sign, 160; not seen, 39." (Stanton et al., 4:36.) Lucy Stone praised the canvass as a "remarkable series" and a "mathematical test of strength" (Woman's Journal, 9 February 1884). Harriet, who worked on the canvass, demonstrated a little noblesse oblige by canvassing the opinions of "help," saying that Bridget's vote was as good as anyone's (ibid.).

83. HRS Scrapbook, vol. 104.

84. HHR Diary, 19, 30 December 1888; Boston *Daily Globe*, 21 December 1888.

85. HHR Scrapbook, vol. 30.

86. HHR Diary, 26 March 1888.

87. Ibid., 1 February 1888.

88. Merk, p. 36.

89. HHR Diary, 9, 21 January 1888.

90. Notebook concerning the union of the National and the American Woman Suffrage Associations, 1889, Box 3, Folder 61, Robinson-Shattuck Papers.

91. Ibid., pp. 30, 33.

92. HHR Diary, 14–15 December 1888.

93. SBA to Clara Bewick Colby, 22 September 1891, Robinson-Shattuck Papers.

94. Stanton et al., 4:752.

95. HRS Scrapbook, vol. 103.

Chapter XI

1. Ednah Dow Cheney, *Reminiscences of Ednah Dow Cheney* (Boston: Lee & Shepard, 1908), p. 155. New York's Sorosis Club was organized at just the same time, another true child of the times.

2. Ibid. Ednah Dow Cheney, *Memorial Meeting of the N.E.W.C.*, Boston, 20 February 1905 (Boston, 1905), pp. 12–13.

3. HHR Diary, 8–9 March 1869.

4. Ibid., 8 November 1870; 17 January, 13 February 1871.

5. Ibid., 17–18 January 1871.

6. Ibid., 14 February 1871.

7. Ibid., 10 April 1871.

8. Ibid., 22–24 May 1871.

9. Ibid., 9–10 May 1871.

10. Ibid., 9 May, 9 December 1872.

11. Ibid., 17 April 1888; HHR Scrapbook, vol 38; Jennie June Croly, *The History of the Woman's Club Movement in America* (New York: Henry G. Allen & Co., 1898), pp. 652–55.

12. HHR Diary, 22 May 1871.

13. Ibid., 5–7 March 1865; 8 April 1872.

14. Ibid., 1 July 1873.

15. Polly Kaufman, "Boston Women and City School Politics, 1872–1905: Nurturers and Protectors in Public Education." Boston University (unpublished Ph.D. dissertation, 1978), pp. 31, 42.

16. *Woman Suffrage*, p. 104.

17. Croly, p. 654; HHR Scrapbook, vol. 38.

18. HRS Scrapbook, vol. 101.

19. Ibid., vol. 103.

20. HHR Scrapbook, vol. 38.

21. HHR Diary, 8 November 1888.

22. "WRB," poem in HHR Scrapbook, vol. 38.

23. HHR Diary, 2 December 1888.

24. WSR to HHR, 3 August 1875.

25. WSR to HHR, 6 August 1875.

26. She listed the subjects on which she would lecture in 1899: "*Loom & Spindle*, Woman Movement in the US from 1840 to the Present, Wordsworth, Browning, and readings from *The New Pandora*." (HHR Diary, 11 August 1899.)

27. HHR Scrapbook 28:2–3.

28. Lucy Larcom to HHR, n.d. (1875?), in HHR Scrapbook 28:4.

29. Ibid. 39:3, 52.

30. SBA to HHR, 10 February 1881.

31. *Loom*, p. 177.

32. *Early Factory Labor*, pp. 6–7; cf. *Loom*, pp. 63–64, 66–67.

33. *Early Factory Labor*, p. 7.

34. Ibid., p. 16; *Loom*, pp. 89–90.

35. *Early Factory Labor*, p. 9; *Loom*, p. 71.

36. *Early Factory Labor*, p. 8; *Loom*, p. 62.

37. *Early Factory Labor*, p. 6; *Loom*, p. 61.

38. *Early Factory Labor*, p. 18; cf. *Loom*, pp. 88, 89–90.

39. *Early Factory Labor*, p. 12; *Loom*, p. 76.

40. *Early Factory Labor*, p. 21; *Loom*, p. 117.

41. *Loom*, p. 117.

42. Ibid., p. 118.

43. "Harriot Curtis was out and spent a night with me. She was in the slough of despond, and looks broken enough. I had a hard time to talk with her and 'pour oil into her wounds' but I succeeded after a measure and sent her home comforted. She had really got a fancy that she had left her home not to go back. What trials sensitive women have and how this monotonous dogtrot life wears upon the spirits and nerves and all for lack of a little change and amusement at the right time. I pity her. She has buried her talent in a napkin." (HHR Diary, 13 April 1871.)

44. Harriet Hanson Robinson, compiler and corrector, "Names and Noms de Plume of the Writers in the Lowell Offering," Malden, Mass., 1902, in the library of the University of California, Berkeley; HHR Diary, 2–3 September 1897; 18–21 August 1902.

45. *Loom*, p. 120.

46. *Woman Suffrage*, pp. 168–69.

47. HHR to Lizzie, 9 March 1884.

48. HHR Diary, 31 January 1902.

49. Old and New Club Calendars, Rare Book Room, Boston Public Library, Boston; Edwin P. Conklin, *Middlesex and Its People: A History* (New York: Lewis Historical Publishing Co., 1927), p. 344.

50. "Women Who Make Books," *The Business Woman's Journal*, quoted in the Boston *Traveler*, n.d. (probably 1889), in HHR Scrapbook 36:73.

51. Harriet Hanson Robinson, *The New Pandora: A Drama* (New York: G. P. Putnam's Sons, 1889) (hereinafter cited as *Pandora*), p. 20.

52. Ibid., p. 26.

53. HHR to Lizzie, 2 March 1884.

54. HHR to Lizzie, 23 March 1884.

55. HHR Diary, 6 November 1888.

56. Ibid., 7 February 1888.

57. *Pandora*, p. 62.

58. Ibid., p. 60.

59. Ibid., p. 11.

60. Ibid., p. 38.

61. Ibid., p. 149.

62. Ibid., p. 139.
63. "Templeton," Hartford *Courant*. These references are from a Putnam leaflet advertising *The New Pandora*, HHR Scrapbook 39:153; 34:22.
64. HHR Scrapbook 34:50.   66. Ibid., p. 26.
65. Ibid., p. 51.   67. Ibid., p. 29.
68. HRS Diary, 6 October 1915.
69. Ibid., 11 July 1916.
70. HHR Diary, 20 February 1908.
71. Ibid., 25–26 February 1902.
72. HRS Diary, 21 September 1917; 7 September 1918; 26 October 1927.
73. HHR Diary, 30 June–2 July 1908.
74. Ibid., 1 May 1888.   76. HRS to Lizzie, n.d. 1898?.
75. Ibid., 5 January 1888.   77. HHR Diary, 30 March 1908.

Chapter XII

1. HHR Diary, 12–14 January 1898.
2. HRS Scrapbook 108:1.
3. HRS Diary, 20 July 1895.
4. Ibid., 9 July 1895.
5. HHR Diary, 23 January, 6 February 1898.
6. Ibid., 17 April 1897.
7. Ibid., 22 November 1897.
8. Ibid., 27 May, 30 October, 20 November, 4 December 1898.
9. Ibid., 1902 end of year.
10. Ibid., 8–9 March 1903.
11. Ibid., 1 September 1902, 1 October 1902.
12. Ibid., 10–11 November 1902.
13. Ibid., 13, 16, 26–27 November, 21 December 1902.
14. Ibid., 27–28 November 1902.
15. Ibid., 2-3 February 1903.
16. HRS Diary, December 1907.
17. HHR Diary, 27 January 1904.
18. Ibid., 8 February; 12, 16 October 1908.
19. Ibid., 28 August 1903.   27. Ibid., 17–18 July 1902.
20. Ibid., 11–12 June 1904.   28. Ibid., 21–22 July 1902.
21. Ibid., 1 September 1903.   29. Ibid., 10 September 1903.
22. HRS Account Book, 1907.   30. Ibid., end of 1903.
23. Ibid.   31. Ibid., 12 November 1899.
24. HHR Diary, end of 1903.   32. Ibid., 9 June 1900.
25. HRS Diary, 2 July 1895.   33. Ibid., end of 1904.
26. HHR Diary, 10 July 1902.   34. Ibid., 7 January 1908.
35. HHR to Lizzie, 13 July 1898.
36. HHR Diary, 7, 10, 20–21 May 1900.
37. Ibid., 28–30 June 1900.
38. Ibid., 21–22 July; 3, 14 August; end of year 1900.
39. Ibid., 23 September, 11–12 December 1903.
40. Ibid., 8–10 March 1904.

41. Ibid., 18–20, 31 January; 18 April 1904.
42. Ibid., 31 July 1904.
43. Private communication with Zivan Simonian, November 1977.
44. HHR Diary, 1 January 1908.
45. Ibid., 22 March 1908.
46. Ibid., 7 November 1904.
47. Ibid., 24 May 1904.
48. Ibid., 24 July 1908.
49. Ibid., 3 January 1908.
50. Written 8 February 1908; in HHR Diary, 11 February 1908; published in Springfield *Republican*, 19 February 1908; HHR Scrapbook, vol. 30.
51. Malden *Evening News*, 22 December 1911.
52. Mary Lawrence Mann, "Some Notable Women in the Annals of Malden," read before Old and New, in the *Malden Historical Society Registers, 1911–1912* (Lynn, Mass., 1912).
53. HRS Diary, 10 June 1916.   55. Ibid., 1 October 1926.
54. Ibid., 7 October 1918.   56. Ibid., 9 October 1916.
57. Malden *Evening News*, 28 September 1926.
58. HRS Diary, 1 September 1916.
59. Ibid., 28 October 1915.   62. Ibid., front of 1926.
60. Ibid., 9 August 1916.   63. Ibid., 6 October 1915.
61. Ibid., 1 September 1916.   64. HRS Scrapbook 115:48.
65. HRS Diary, 13, 28 October 1915.
66. Ibid., 5 January 1916.   73. Ibid., 6 December 1926.
67. Ibid., 24 October 1915.   74. Ibid., 21 April 1928.
68. Ibid., 28 October 1915.   75. Ibid., 7 July 1916.
69. Ibid., 3 June 1916.   76. Ibid., 29 March 1916.
70. Ibid., 18 July 1916.   77. Ibid., 18 July 1916.
71. Ibid., 14 June 1916.   78. Ibid., 5 January 1930.
72. Ibid., 13 April 1916.   79. Ibid., 12 June 1930.
80. HRS Scrapbook 94:1; also published in *The Living Church*.
81. HRS Diary, end of 1930.
82. Ibid., 30 January 1933.
83. Ibid., 13 October 1926.
84. Ibid., 4 September 1925.
85. Malden *Evening News*, 8 June 1931.
86. HRS Diary, 30 August 1931.
87. Martha Abbott to HRS, n.d., pasted in HRS Diary, 3 November 1928.
88. Poughkeepsie (New York) *Star*, 26 June 1933.
89. HRS Diary, 16 June 1933.   94. Ibid., 8, 20 January 1936.
90. Ibid., 30 June 1933.   95. Ibid., 11 June 1936.
91. Ibid., 29 October 1933.   96. Ibid., 16 July 1936.
92. Ibid., 5 January 1934.   97. Ibid., 22–23 January 1937.
93. Ibid., 15 March 1934.   98. Ibid., 24 March 1937.

BIBLIOGRAPHY

A NOTE ON SOURCES

This book is based primarily on the personal papers of Harriet Hanson Robinson and, to a lesser extent, on those of her daughter Harriette Lucy (Hattie) Robinson Shattuck. These papers are housed in the Arthur and Elizabeth Schlesinger Library on the History of Women in America, at Radcliffe College, Cambridge, Massachusetts. The collection was reprocessed by Madeleine Bagwell Perez and microfilmed to provide greater access to the material without further wear on the old papers.

Harriet Robinson's twenty-seven volumes of daily diaries were the most useful part of the collection for this study. Beginning in 1852, in two miscellaneous volumes that record several years apiece—often in retrospect—the diaries are hastily written, careless of punctuation, often in pencil, and have some leaves torn out and others loosened though left in. Sometimes pages torn from another notebook are pasted on the pages of almanacs; sometimes small clippings from newspapers or other little items are pasted or pinned in. From 1863 to 1873 Robinson wrote conscientiously in a series of small similar books, some leather, some black-cloth bound. Another series of contiguous diaries in small similar books ran from 1892 to 1904. The first three volumes of this series had only brief notations. A travel journal dating from early 1874 appears to be lost, but the concluding remarks about the Robinsons' European trip are in the collection. The journals of 1888 and 1908, which were written after several years of silence, are particularly large, full, and valuable for information on the Robinsons' institutional activities and their perceptions of the world.

Shattuck's diaries begin in 1867, and the first seven volumes overlap her mother's in time, often providing two views of the same event. The first seventeen volumes are written in pencil on loose and now crumbling sheets of old "nickle tablets." Some pages are missing and some dates unrecorded, and the books, which cover parts of different years rather than a single year each, have been tied together with string. These diaries are more personal and introspective than Robinson's diaries, and less effort was made to preserve them in good condition. Shattuck also filled sixteen uniform cloth-bound books for the years between 1921 and 1937 with news clippings on world affairs and her comments. Together, the diary collections of Shattuck and Robinson provide some form of comment daily from 1852 to 1937.

Robinson's preserved correspondence documents her interaction with suffrage leaders and mill workers. This correspondence is one-sided, though she did make copies of certain significant letters of her own. The family correspondence—primarily the letters of Harriet Robinson and her husband, William Stevens Robinson, to other members of the family, without replies—describes homely detail and perceptions of family relations. The charming courtship correspondence of Harriet and William has recently come to light in a private collection, and is being edited for publication by Susan Sutton Smith of the State University of New York at Oneonta. The only letters of Shattuck's that have been preserved in the Schlesinger Collection are those few included in her scrapbooks.

The scrapbooks comprise the ordered miscellany of the Robinson lives. Harriet Robinson's scrapbooks are housed in a wide variety of ill-matched volumes; some of these volumes were designed to be scrapbooks, others were published books in which clippings were pasted over the print. Some scrapbooks tend to be chronological, with the programs, tickets, clippings, greeting cards, and other papers of a particular year. Others are topical, filled with clipped obituaries, club-work items, travel mementos, and published reviews. There are fifteen volumes of suffrage-news clippings. The collection testifies to Robinson's ready pair of scissors, a handy paste pot, and frequent sessions of putting her papers in order. When pasted material made the volumes too thick, she severed the remaining empty pages. Robinson paginated some of the volumes, but not all. She made several attempts over the years at indexing, but none of these indexes is very useful. Most of the scrapbooks are tied together with string, and all of them are now ragged.

Robinson arranged her husband's papers in a similar way, pasting his collected essays and columns into scrapbooks and interspersing personal material when it came to hand. The thirty-two volumes of William Robinson's scrapbooks are available in the Boston Public Library, Department of Rare Books & Mss., to which Harriet Robinson donated them.

Hattie Shattuck's scrapbooks are more artistic than her mother's. She bought a matched set of books, eight and a half by eleven inches, with black paper covers and leather corners and bindings, and numbered them on the back with cut-out newspaper numerals. The pages are decorated with embossed stickers, greeting cards, pressed flowers, newspaper illustrations, and samples of dress fabrics. Each scrapbook deals with approximately one year. She included photographs, with comments written in while making the books and later while rereading them. The scrapbooks documenting her later years are more businesslike than her earlier books, with programs of different events—especially club programs—clippings of her newspaper pieces, bills and accounts, and correspondence. Each of these now worn scrapbooks is approximately eighty pages long. Shattuck indexed and numbered some of them.

Along with the diaries, correspondence, and scrapbooks there is other miscellaneous Robinson matter that is arranged in folders and indexed in the library catalogue of the papers.

The Works of Harriet Hanson Robinson

Cambridge, Mass. Arthur and Elizabeth Schlesinger Library on the History of Women in America, Radcliffe College. Collection A-80. Robinson-Shattuck papers.

Captain Mary Miller. Boston: W. H. Baker & Co., 1887.

"Nicholas Browne of Reading and some of His Descendants," *The Historical and Genealogical Register* 44 July 1890): 281–86.

Early Factory Labor in New England. Boston: Wright & Potter Printing Co., 1883.

"The Life of the Early Mill-Girls." *Journal of Social Science* 16 (1882): 127–40.

Loom and Spindle, Or Life Among the Early Mill Girls, with a Sketch of "The Lowell Offering" and Some of Its Contributors. Boston: Thomas Y. Crowell & Co., 1898.

The Lowell "Offering" (leaflet for the Old South Church). Boston: Directors of the Old South Work, 1904.

Massachusetts in the Woman Suffrage Movement: A General Political, Legal and Legislative History from 1774–1881. Boston: Roberts Brothers, 1881.

Memoir of "Warrington" in *"Warrington" Pen-Portraits*, by William Stevens Robinson. Boston: Mrs. W. S. Robinson, 1877.

Compiler and corrector, "Names and Noms de Plume of the Writers in the *Lowell Offering.*" Malden, Mass., 1902, in the library of the University of California, Berkeley.

The New Pandora: A Drama. New York: G. P. Putnam's Sons, 1889.

"William S. Robinson ('Warrington')." *The Historical and Genealogical Register* 39 (October 1885): 313–24.

The Works of Harriette Lucy (Hattie) Robinson Shattuck

Cambridge, Mass. Arthur and Elizabeth Schlesinger Library on the History of Women in America, Radcliffe College. Collection A-80. Robinson-Shattuck papers.

Little Folks East and West; comprising "Prairie Stories," "Mother Goose Stories," "Fairy Stories" and "True Stories." Boston: Lee & Shepard, 1892.

Our Mutual Friend. A Comedy in Four Acts. Dramatized from Charles Dickens. Boston: W. H. Baker, 1870.

Shattuck's Advanced Rules for Large Assemblies; A Supplement to the Woman's Manual of Parliamentary Law. Boston: Lee & Shepard, 1898.

Shattuck's Parliamentary Answers, Alphabetically Arranged for All Questions Likely to Arise in Women's Organizations. Boston: Lothrop, Lee & Shepard Co., 1914.

The Story of Dante's Divine Comedy. New York: J. B. Alden, 1887.

Woman's Manual of Parliamentary Law, With Practical Illustrations Especially Adapted to Women's Organizations. Boston: Lee & Shepard, 1891.

The Works of William Stevens Robinson

Boston, Mass. Boston Public Library, Department of Rare Books & Mss. Scrapbooks.

[Warrington.] *A Conspiracy to Defame John A. Andrew, Being a Review of the Proceedings of Joel Parker, Linus Child, Leverett Saltonstall at the People's Convention (so called) Held in Boston, Oct. 7, 1862.* Boston: Wright & Potter, 1862.

"The Dred Scott Decision and the Judiciary, Feb. 27, 1858." Manuscript [Malden, 1876?], a copy written and signed by Harriet Hanson Robinson.

"General Butler's Campaign." *The Atlantic Monthly* 28 (December 1871): 745–51.

Manual for the Use of the General Court. Boston: Massachusetts General Court, 18—.

The Salary Grab: A History of the Passage of the Act Increasing the Salaries of Members of Congress; with Full Lists of the Yeas and Nays in Both Branches; with a Sketch of the Debates and a Review of the Apologies for the Bill; with Special Reference to the Responsibility of Gen. B. F. Butler Therefore Not Neglecting, However, Senator Carpenter and the Other Accomplices . . . Boston: Lee & Shepard, 1873.

Statement to the Public in Reference to the Act of the Legislature to Remove the Dam Across the Concord River at Billerica. Lowell: Stone & Huse, 1860.

"Twenty Years of Massachusetts Politics," Boston, December 1858. Manuscript. (Malden: 1876?) A copy written and signed by Harriet Hanson Robinson.

Harriet Hanson Robinson, ed. *"Warrington" Pen-Portraits: A Collection of Personal and Political Reminiscences from 1848 to 1876 from the Writings of William Stevens Robinson.* Boston: Mrs. W. S. Robinson, 1877.

Warrington's Manual: A Manual for the Information of Officers and Members of Legislatures, Conventions, Societies, Corporations [etc., etc.] *According to the Parliamentary Law and Practice in the United States.* Boston: Lee & Shepard, 1875.

Other Works

Abbott, Edith. *Women in Industry: A Study in American Economic History.* New York: D. Appleton and Co., 1910.

Abbott, Richard H. *Cobbler in Congress: The Life of Henry Wilson, 1812–1875.* Lexington, Ky.: University of Kentucky Press, 1972.

Adams, Charles Francis. *Massachusetts, Its Historians and Its History: An Object Lesson.* Boston: Houghton Mifflin Co., 1893.

Adams, John G. *Fifty Notable Years: Views of the Ministry of Christian Universalism During the Last Half Century, with Biographical Sketches.* Boston: Universalist Publishing House, 1882.

Addison, Daniel Dulany. *Lucy Larcom: Life, Letters, and Diary.* Boston: Houghton Mifflin Co., 1895.

Albright, Raymond. *Focus on Infinity: A Life of Phillips Brooks.* New York: Macmillan Co., 1961.

Anderson, Godfrey T. "The Slavery Issue in Massachusetts Politics from the Compromise of 1850 to the Outbreak of the Civil War." Ph.D. dissertation, University of Chicago, 1944.

Anderson, Michael. *Family Structure in Nineteenth Century Lancashire.* Cambridge: Cambridge University Press, 1971.

Aries, Phillippe. *Centuries of Childhood: A Social History of Family Life.* New York: Vintage Books, 1960.

Baird, Robert H. *The American Cotton Spinner.* Philadelphia: H. C. Baird, 1887.

Ballou, Hosea. *Notes on the Parables of the New Testament.* Randolph, Vt.: Sereno Wright, 1804.

Banks, J. A., and Banks, Olive. *Feminism and Family Planning in Victorian England.* New York: Schocken Books, 1964.

Balthazar, Henry Meyer. *History of Transportation in the United States Before 1860*. Washington, D.C.: Carnegie Institution of Washington, 1917.

Barber, J. W. *Massachusetts Towns: An 1840 View*. Barre, Mass.: Barre Publishers, 1963.

Bean, W. G. "The Transformation of Parties in Massachusetts from 1848 to 1860." Ph.D. dissertation, Harvard University, 1922.

————. "Puritan Versus Celt, 1850–1860." *New England Quarterly* 7 (1934): 70–89.

Beecher, Catharine E. *The True Remedy for the Wrongs of Women, with a History of an Enterprise Having That for Its Object*. Boston: Phillips, Sampson, 1851.

———— and Stowe, Harriet Beecher. *The American Woman's Home*. Hartford: Stowe-Day Foundation, 1975.

Bishop, Robert R. *The Senate of Massachusetts*. Boston: Press of G. H. Ellis, 1882.

Boutwell, George S. *Reminiscences of Sixty Years in Public Affairs*. 2 vols. New York: McClure, Phillips & Co., 1902.

Bowen, James L. *Massachusetts in the War, 1861–1865*. Springfield, Mass.: C. W. Bryan & Co., 1889.

Bradford, Gamaliel, *Damaged Souls*. Boston: Houghton Mifflin Co., 1923.

Brauer, Kinley J. *Cotton Versus Conscience: Massachusetts Politics and Southwestern Expansion, 1843–1848*. Lexington, Ky.: University of Kentucky Press, 1967.

Bremner, Robert, ed. *Children and Youth in America: A Documentary History*. 2 vols. Cambridge: Harvard University Press, 1970–71.

Briggs, Asa. "Middle-Class Consciousness in English Politics, 1780–1846." *Past and Present* 9 (April 1956): 65–74.

———— "The Language of 'Class' in Early Nineteenth Century England." In *Essays in Labour History*, edited by Asa Briggs and John Saville. London: Macmillan & Co., 1960.

Brunet, Michael. "The Secret Ballot Issue in Massachusetts Politics from 1851 to 1853." *New England Quarterly* 25 (1952): 354–62.

Burgy, Jacob Herbert. *The New England Cotton Textile Industry: A Study in Industrial Geography*. Baltimore: Waverly Press, 1932.

Butler, Benjamin. *Autobiography and Personal Reminiscences of Major General Benjamin Franklin Butler: Butler's Book*. Boston: A. M. Thayer & Co., 1892.

Calhoun, Arthur W. *A Social History of the American Family*. 3 vols. Cleveland: Clark, 1917.

Cary, Thomas Greaves. *Profits on Manufactures at Lowell*. Boston: C. C. Little & J. Brown, 1845.

Cassara, Ernest. *Hosea Ballou: The Challenge to Orthodoxy*. Boston: Universalist Historical Society, 1961.

Catt, Carrie Chapman, and Shuler, Nettie Rogers. *Woman Suffrage and Politics*. New York: C. Scribner's Sons, 1923.

Cheetham, Henry H. *Unitarianism and Universalism: An Illustrated History*. Boston: Beacon Press, 1962.

Cheney, Ednah Dow. *Reminiscences of Ednah Dow Cheney*. Boston, Lee & Shepard, 1908.

Chickering, Jesse. *A Statistical View of the Population of Massachusetts from 1765 to 1840.* Boston: C. C. Little & J. Brown, 1846.

Coburn, Frederick W. *History of Lowell and Its People.* 3 vols. New York: Lewis Historical Publishing Co., 1920.

Congdon, Charles T. *Reminiscences of a Journalist.* Boston: J. R. Osgood and Co., 1880.

Conklin, Edwin P. *Middlesex County and Its People: A History.* New York: Lewis Historical Publishing Co., 1927.

Conlin, Joseph R. *Big Bill Haywood and the Radical Union Movement.* Syracuse, N.Y.: Syracuse University Press, 1969.

Coolidge, John Phillips. *Mill and Mansion: A Study of Architecture and Society in Lowell, Massachusetts, 1820–1865.* New York: Russell & Russell, 1942.

Cott, Nancy. *Bonds of Womanhood.* New Haven: Yale University Press, 1976.

————, ed. *Root of Bitterness: Documents of the Social History of American Women.* New York: E. P. Dutton & Co., 1972.

Cowley, Charles. *Illustrated History of Lowell.* Boston: Lee & Shepard, 1868.

Croly, Jennie June. *The History of the Woman's Club Movement in America.* New York: Henry G. Allen & Co., 1898.

Daniels, Jonathan. *They Will Be Heard: America's Crusading Newspaper Editors.* New York: McGraw-Hill, 1965.

Darling, Arthur B. *Political Change in Massachusetts, 1824–1848: A Study of Liberal Movements in Politics.* New Haven: Yale University Press, 1925.

Davis, Rebecca Harding. "Life in the Iron Mills." *The Atlantic Monthly* 4 (April 1861): 126–72.

Dean, Paul. *Discourse Delivered Before the First Universalist Society, in Boston, on the Character and Death of the Rev. John Murray, Their Late Senior Pastor.* Boston: T. W. White, 1815.

————. *Sermon Before Gen'l Convention of Universalists at the Installation of Robert Bartlett in Hartland, Vt.* September 2, 1825.

————. *120 Reasons for Being a Universalist, Or a Conversation Between a Believer in the Final Restoration and a Sincere Inquirer after Truth.* Providence: Christian Telescope Office, 1827.

————. *Course of Lectures in Defence of the Final Restoration. Delivered in the Bulfinch Street Church, Boston, in the Winter of Eighteen Hundred and Thirty-Two.* Boston: Edwin M. Stone, 1832.

Demos, John. *A Little Commonwealth: Family Life in the Plymouth Colony.* New York: Oxford University Press, 1970.

Donald, David Herbert. *Charles Sumner and the Coming of the Civil War.* New York: Alfred A. Knopf, 1960.

Drake, Samuel Adams. *History of Middlesex County.* 2 vols. Boston: Estes and Lauriat, 1880.

Duberman, Martin. *Charles Francis Adams, 1807–1886.* Boston: Houghton Mifflin Co., 1961.

Dublin, Thomas. "Women, Work, and Protest in the Early Lowell Mills: 'The Oppressing Hand of Avarice Would Enslave Us.'" *Labor History* 16 (winter 1975): 99–116.

————. "Women, Work, and the Family: Female Operatives in the Lowell Mills, 1830–1860." *Feminist Studies* 3 (fall 1975): 30–39.

————. *Women at Work: The Transformation of Work and Community in Lowell, Massachusetts, 1826–1860.* New York: Columbia University Press, 1979.

Eddy, Richard. *Universaliam in America.* 2 vols. Boston: Universalist Publishing House, 1886.

Edson, Theodore. *An Address Delivered at the Opening of the Colburn Grammar School in Lowell, December 13, 1848.* Lowell, Mass.: James Atkinson, City Printer, 1849.

Ehrenreich, Barbara, and English, Deirdre. *Complaints and Disorders: The Sexual Politics of Sickness.* Old Westbury, N.Y.: Feminist Press, 1973.

Eisler, Benita, ed. *The Lowell Offering: Written by New England Mill Women (1840–1845).* Philadelphia: Lippincott, 1977.

Ely, Richard T. *The Labor Movement in America.* New York: Crowell & Co., 1886.

Endicott, William Crowninshield. *Endicott's Letter: A Refutation of Some of General Butler's Recent Mis-statements to the People of Massachusetts.* Boston, 1878.

Farber, Bernard. *Guardians of Virtue: Salem Families in 1800.* New York: Basic Books, 1972.

Fishbein, Morris. *Fads and Quackery in Healing.* New York: Covici, Friede, 1932.

Flexner, Eleanor. *A Century of Struggle: The Woman's Rights Movement in the United States.* Cambridge: Harvard University Press, 1959.

Flower, Benjamin Orange. *Progressive Men, Women, and Movements of the Past Twenty-five Years.* Boston: The New Arena, 1914.

Foner, Eric. *Free Soil, Free Labor, Free Men: The Ideology of the Republican Party Before the Civil War.* New York: Oxford University Press, 1970.

Foner, Philip S. *History of the Labor Movement in the United States.* 4 vols. New York: International Publishers, 1947–65.

————, ed. *The Factory Girls: A Collection of Writings on Life and Struggles in the New England Factories of the 1840s by the Factory Girls Themselves, and the Story, in Their Own Words, of the First Trade Unions of Women Workers in the United States.* Urbana, Ill.: University of Illinois Press, 1977.

Forster, E. M. *Marianne Thornton: A Domestic Biography, 1797–1887.* New York: Harcourt Brace Jovanovich, 1956.

Francis William Bird: A Biographical Sketch by His Children. Boston: privately printed, 1897.

Gatell, Frank O. *John Gorham Palfrey and the New England Conscience.* Cambridge: Harvard University Press, 1963.

Giele, Janet. "Social Change in the Feminine Role, 1870–1920." Ph.D. dissertation, Radcliffe College, 1961.

The Glad Tidings and Ladies' Universalist Magazine (title varies). Pittsburgh: Universalist Publishing Co., 1836–40.

Goodman, Paul. "The Eclipse of a Whig Elite: Politics and Social Change in Massachusetts, 1830–1877." In *Uprooted Americans: Essays to Honor Oscar Handlin,* edited by Richard L. Bushman *et al.* Boston: Little, Brown, 1979.

Gravely, William. *Gilbert Haven, Methodist Abolitionist: A Study in Race, Religion, and Reform, 1850–1880*. Nashville: Abingdon Press, 1973.

Greven, Philip. *Four Generations: Population, Land, and Family in Colonial Andover, Massachusetts*. Ithaca, N.Y.: Cornell University Press, 1970.

Grizzell, Emit D. *Origin and Development of the High School in New England Before 1865*. New York: Macmillan Co., 1923.

Gross, Robert A. *The Minutemen and Their World*. New York: Hill and Wang, 1976.

Guernsey, Egbert. *Homeopathic Domestic Practice, Containing Also an Abridged Materia Medica*. New York: Boericke & Tafel, 1856.

Gutman, Herbert G. *Work, Culture, and Society in Industrializing America*. New York: Alfred A. Knopf, 1976.

Haight, Gordon S. *Mrs. Sigourney, the Sweet Singer of Hartford*. New Haven: Yale University Press, 1930.

Hale, Sarah Josepha. *Housekeeping and Keeping House*. New York: Harper & Bros., 1845.

Hall, Mrs. Walter A.; Leach, Mrs. Joseph S.; and Smith, Mrs. Frederick G., *Progress and Achievement: A History of the Massachusetts State Federation of Women's Clubs*. Norwood, Mass.: 1932.

Hareven, Tamara K. "The History of the Family as an Interdisciplinary Field." *Journal of Interdisciplinary History* 2 (October 1971): 399–414.

————. "The Family as Process: The Historical Study of the Family Cycle." *Journal of Social History* 7 (spring, 1974): 322–29.

Harrington, Fred H. *Fighting Politician: Major General Nathaniel P. Banks*. Philadelphia: University of Pennsylvania Press, 1948.

Haskell, W. G. *Historical Sketch of the Second Universalist Society of Lowell, Massachusetts*. Lowell, 1874.

Hayes, John Lord. *American Textile Machinery*. Cambridge: Cambridge University Press, 1879.

Herlihy, Elizabeth M., ed. *Fifty Years of Boston: A Memorial Volume*. Boston: Tercentenary Committee, 1932.

Hewitt, Margaret. *Wives and Mothers in Victorian Industry*. London: Rockliff, 1958.

Higginson, Mary Thacher. *Thomas Wentworth Higginson: The Story of His Life*. Boston: Houghton Mifflin Co., 1914.

Higginson, Thomas Wentworth, *Cheerful Yesterdays*. Boston: Houghton, Mifflin Co., 1898.

Hill, Reuben. "Methodological Issues in Family Development." *Family Process* 3 (spring 1964): 186–205.

————. *Family Development in Three Generations*. Cambridge, Mass.: Schenkman Publishing Co., 1970.

Hoar, George Frisbie. *Autobiography of Seventy Years*. 2 vols. New York: Charles Scribner's Sons, 1903.

Hogeland, Ronald W. "'The Female Appendage'; Femine Life-styles in America, 1820–1860." *Civil War History* 17 (June 1971): 101–14.

Holmes, Oliver Wendell. *Homeopathy and Its Kindred Delusions*. Boston: Ticknor & Fields, 1842.

Holt, Michael. "The Politics of Impatience: The Origins of Know-Nothingism." *Journal of American History* 60 (September 1973): 309–31.

Holzman, Robert S. *Stormy Ben Butler*. New York: Macmillan Co., 1954.

Hooker, Richard. *The Story of an Independent Newspaper: 100 Years of the Springfield "Republican," 1824–1924*. New York: Macmillan Co., 1924.

Howe, Daniel Walker. *The Unitarian Conscience: Harvard Moral Philosophy, 1805–1861*. Cambridge: Harvard University Press, 1970.

Howe, Julia Ward. *Reminiscences*. Boston: Houghton Mifflin Co., 1899.

———, ed. *Sketches of Representative Women of New England*. Boston: New England Historical Publishing Co., 1904.

Howells, William Dean. "The Country Printer." *Scribner's Magazine* 13 (May 1893): 539–58.

Horwitz, Richard P. "Architecture and Culture: The Meaning of the Lowell Boarding House." *American Quarterly* 25 (March 1973): 64–82.

Hudson, Alfred S. *The History of Concord, Massachusetts*. Concord, Mass.: The Erudite Press, 1904.

Huggins, Nathan I. *Protestants Against Poverty: Boston's Charities, 1870–1900*. Westport, Conn.: Greenwood Publishing Corp., 1971.

Hurd, Duane Hamilton, ed., *History of Middlesex County, Massachusetts, with Biographical Sketches of Many of Its Pioneers and Prominent Men*. 3 vols. Philadelphia: J. W. Lewis & Co., 1890.

Jackson, Patrick Tracy. *Report on the Production and Manufacture of Cotton*. Boston: Friends of Domestic Industry, J. T. & E. Buckingham, 1832.

James, Edward, and James, Janet, eds. *Notable American Women*. 3 vols. Cambridge: Harvard University Press, 1971.

Jeffrey, Kirk. "Marriage, Career, and Feminine Ideology in Nineteenth-Century America: Reconstructing the Marital Experience of Lydia Maria Child, 1828–1874." *Feminist Studies* 2 (nos. 2–3, 1975): 113–30.

Johnson, Edward. *Hydropathy: The Theory, Principles, and Practice of the Water Cure*. London: Marshall & Co., 1846.

Josephson, Hannah. *The Golden Threads: New England's Mill Girls and Magnates*. New York: Duell, Sloan and Pearce, 1949.

Katz, Michael. *The Irony of Early School Reform: Educational Innovation in Mid-nineteenth Century Massachusetts*. Cambridge: Harvard University Press, 1968.

Kaufman, Polly. "Boston Women and City School Politics, 1872–1905: Nurturers and Protectors in Public Education." Unpublished Ph.D. dissertation, Boston University, 1978.

Kenney, Carol Jean. "An Analysis of Political Alignments in Massachusetts as Revealed in the Constitutional Convention of 1853." M. A. thesis, Smith College, 1951.

Kenngott, George F. *The Record of a City: A Social Survey of Lowell, Massachusetts*. New York: Macmillan Co., 1912.

Kerber, Linda. "Daughters of Columbia: Educating Women for the Republic, 1787–1805." In *The Hofstadter Aegis*, edited by Stanley Elkins and Eric McKitrick. New York: Random House, 1974.

Kett, Joseph. "Growing Up in Rural New England." In *Anonymous Americans*, edited by Tamara K. Hareven. Englewood Cliffs, N.J.: Prentice-Hall, 1971.

Kingsbury, Susan, ed. *Labor Laws and Their Enforcement, with Special Reference to Massachusetts*. New York: Longmans, 1911.

Kirkland, Edward C. *Men, Cities and Transportation: A Study in New England History, 1820–1900.* 2 vols. Cambridge: Harvard University Press, 1948.

Knights, Peter. *The Plain People of Boston, 1830–1860.* New York: Oxford University Press, 1971.

Kraditor, Aileen S. *The Ideas of the Woman Suffrage Movement, 1890–1920.* New York: Columbia University Press, 1965.

––––––. *Up from the Pedestal.* New York: Quadrangle Books, 1968.

Larcom, Lucy. *An Idyl of Work.* Boston: J. R. Osgood and Co., 1875.

––––––. "Among Lowell Mill-Girls: A Reminiscence." *The Atlantic Monthly* 48 (November 1881): 593–612.

––––––. *A New England Girlhood: Outlined from Memory.* Boston: Houghton Mifflin Co., 1889.

Lasch, Christopher. *Haven in a Heartless World: The Family Besieged.* New York: Basic Books, 1977.

Laslett, Peter. *The World We Have Lost.* New York: Scribners, 1965.

––––––, ed. *Household and Family in Past Time.* Cambridge: Cambridge University Press, 1972.

Layer, Robert George. *Earnings of Cotton Mill Operatives, 1825–1914.* Cambridge, Mass.: Committee on Research in Economic History, 1955.

Loubert, J. Daniel. "The Orientation of Henry Wilson, 1812–1856." Ph.D. dissertation, Boston University, 1956.

Lowell, Massachusetts, Trades and Labor Council. *Lowell: A City of Spindles.* Lowell, Mass.: Lawler & Co., 1900.

The Lowell "Offering": A Repository of Original Articles, Written Exclusively by Females Actively Employed in the Mills. 5 vols. Lowell, Mass.: Powers and Bagley, 1840–45.

Luther, Seth. *An Address to the Workingmen of New England on the State of Education, and on the Condition of the Producing Classes in Europe and America.* Boston: Seth Luther, 1834.

MacFarlane, Alan. *The Family Life of Ralph Josselin, a Seventeenth-Century Clergyman: An Essay in Historical Anthropology.* Cambridge: Cambridge University Press, 1970.

McGovern. James R. *Yankee Family.* New Orleans: Polyanthos, 1975.

McKay, Ernest A. "Henry Wilson and the Coalition of 1851." *New England Quarterly* 36 (1963): 338–58.

––––––. "Henry Wilson: Unprincipled Know-Nothing." *Mid-America* 46 (1964): 29–37.

McKitrick, Eric L. *Andrew Johnson and Reconstruction.* Chicago: University of Chicago Press, 1960.

McLoughlin, William G. *The Meaning of Henry Ward Beecher: An Essay on the Shifting Values of Mid-Victorian America, 1840–1870.* New York: Alfred A. Knopf, 1970.

Malden Historical Society Register No. 1, 1910–1911. Lynn, Mass.: Malden, Mass., 1910.

Malden, Massachusetts. *The Bi-Centennial Book of Malden.* Boston: G. C. Rand & Co., 1850.

Mann, Arthur. *Yankee Reformers in the Urban Age.* Cambridge: Harvard University Press, 1954.

Martineau, Harriet. *Society in America*. 2 vols. London: Saunders and Otley, 1837.

Merriam, George Spring. *The Life and Times of Samuel Bowles*. 2 vols. New York: The Century Co., 1885.

Meserve, H. C. *Lowell: An Industrial Dream Come True*. Boston: The National Association of Cotton Manufacturers, 1923.

Meyer, Annie Nathan, ed. *Women's Work in America*. New York: H. Holt and Co., 1891.

Miles, Henry A. *Lowell: As It Was and As It Is*. Lowell, Mass.: Nathaniel L. Dayton, 1847.

Mind Amongst the Spindles: A Miscellany, Wholly Composed by the Factory Girls. Selected from the Lowell "Offering." Boston: Jordan, Swift & Wiley, 1845.

Modell, John, and Hareven, Tamara K. "Urbanization and the Malleable Household: An Examination of Boarding and Lodging in American Families." *Journal of Marriage and the Family* 35 (August 1973): 467–79.

Monroe, Paul. *Founding of the American Public School System: A History of Education in the United States from the Early Settlements to the Close of the Civil War Period*. New York: Macmillan Co., 1840.

Montgomery, David. *Beyond Equality: Labor and the Radical Republicans, 1862–1872*. New York: Alfred A. Knopf, 1967.

Morgan, Edmund S. *The Puritan Family*. New York: Harper & Row, 1966.

Mulkern, John R. "The Know-Nothing Party in Massachusetts." Ph.D. dissertation, Boston University, 1963.

Murray, John. *Universalism Vindicated*. Charlestown, Mass.: J. Lamson, 1798.

Nash, Howard P., Jr. *Stormy Petrel: The Life and Times of General Benjamin F. Butler, 1818–1893*. Rutherford, N.J.: Fairleigh Dickinson University Press, 1969.

Nevins, Allan, *Ordeal of the Union*. New York: Scribners, 1947.

O'Connor, Thomas. *Lords of the Loom: The Cotton Whigs and the Coming of the Civil War*. New York: Scribners, 1968.

O'Neill, William. *Everyone Was Brave: The Rise and Fall of Feminism in America*. Chicago: Quadrangle, 1968.

Our Famous Women: Comprising the Lives and Deeds of American Women Who Have Distinguished Themselves. Hartford: A. D. Worthington, 1884.

Pattee, Fred Lewis. *The Feminine Fifties*. New York: D. Appleton-Century Co., 1940.

Pearson, Henry G. *The Life of John A. Andrew*. 2 vols. Boston: Houghton Mifflin Co., 1904.

Pessen, Edward. *Riches, Class and Power Before the Civil War*. Lexington, Mass.: D. C. Heath, 1973.

Pickering, David, ed. *The Gospel Preacher: Original Sermons by Universalist Ministers*. Providence: John S. Greene, 1827.

Pierce, Edward L. *Memoir and Letters of Charles Sumner*. 4 vols. Boston: Roberts Brothers, 1877–94.

Pollard, Sidney. "Factory Discipline in the Industrial Revolution." *Economic History Review* 16 (1963): 254–71.

Prentice, George. *The Life of Gilbert Haven, Bishop of the Methodist Episcopal Church*. New York: Phillips and Hunt, 1883.

Riley, Glenda Gates. "The Subtle Subversion: Changes in the Traditionalist Image of the American Woman." *Historian* 32 (February 1970): 210–27.

Schouler, William. *A History of Massachusetts in the Civil War.* 2 vols. Boston: E. P. Dutton & Co., 1868–71.

Schwartz, Harold. *Samuel Gridley Howe, Social Reformer.* Cambridge: Harvard University Press, 1956.

Scott, Clinton Lee. *The Universalist Church of America: A Short History.* Boston: Universalist Historical Society, 1957.

Sennett, Richard. *Families Against the City: Middle Class Homes of Industrial Chicago, 1872–1890.* Cambridge: Harvard University Press, 1970.

Sennett, Richard, and Cobb, Jonathan. *The Hidden Injuries of Class.* New York: Alfred A. Knopf, 1972.

Shapiro, Samuel. "The Conservative Dilemma: The Massachusetts Constitutional Convention of 1853." *New England Quarterly* 33 (June 1960): 207–24.

————. *Richard Henry Dana, Jr., 1815–1882.* East Lansing, Mich.: Michigan State University Press, 1961.

Shryock, Richard H. *Medicine and Society in America, 1660–1860.* New York: New York University Press, 1960.

Silloway, Thomas W. *An Historical Discourse, Delivered in the First Universalist Meeting-House, Boston, Sunday May 29, 1864, on the Occasion of Taking Final Leave of the Premises.* Boston: Dakin & Metcalf, 1864.

Sinclair, Andrew. *The Better Half: The Emancipation of the American Woman.* New York: Harper & Row, 1965.

Skinner, Clarence R. *Social Implications of Universalism.* Boston: Universalist Publishing House, 1915.

Sklar, Kathryn Kish. *Catharine Beecher: A Study in American Domesticity.* New York: W. W. Norton & Co., 1973.

Smith, Harriette Knight. *The History of the Lowell Institute.* Boston: Lamson, Wolff & Co., 1898.

Sprague, Julia A. *History of the New England Woman's Club from 1868 to 1893.* Boston: Lee and Shepard, 1894.

Stanton, Elizabeth Cady; Anthony, Susan B.; Gage, Matilda Joslyn; and Harper, Ida H. *History of Woman Suffrage.* 6 vols. New York: Fowler & Wells, 1881–1922.

Stearns, Frank P. *Cambridge Sketches.* Freeport, N.Y.: Books for Libraries Press, 1968.

Stone, Lawrence. *The Family, Sex, and Marriage in England, 1500–1800.* New York: Harper & Row, 1977.

Swan, Susan Burrows. *Plain and Fancy: American Women and Their Needlework, 1700–1850.* New York: Holt, Rinehart and Winston, 1977.

Taylor, William R., and Lasch, Christopher. "Two 'Kindred Spirits': Sorority and Family in New England, 1839–1846." *New England Quarterly* 36 (March 1963): 23–41.

Thompson, E. P. *The Making of the English Working Class.* London: Gollancz, 1963.

Trefousse, Hans. *The Radical Republicans.* New York: Alfred A. Knopf, 1969.

————. *Ben Butler: The South Called Him Beast.* New York: Twayne Publishers, 1957.

Tyler, Alice Felt. *Freedom's Ferment: Phases of American Social History from the Colonial Period to the Outbreak of the Civil War*. Minneapolis: University of Minnesota Press, 1944.

Vincus, Martha, ed. *Suffer and Be Still: Women in the Victorian Age*. Bloomington, Ind.: Indiana University Press, 1972.

Ware, Edith. *Political Opinion in Massachusetts During the Civil War and Reconstruction*. New York: Columbia University Press, 1916.

Ware, Norman. *The Industrial Worker, 1840–1860: The Reaction of American Industrial Society to the Advance of the Industrial Revolution*. Boston: Houghton Mifflin Co., 1924.

Watson, Frank D. *The Charity Organization Movement in the United States*. New York: Macmillan Co., 1922.

Webb, Robert. *Harriet Martineau: A Radical Victorian*. New York: Columbia University Press, 1960.

Wells, Kate Gannett. "The Boston Club Woman." *Arena* 6 (July 1892): 371–82.

Werlich, Robert. *"Beast" Butler: The Incredible Career of Major General Benjamin Franklin Butler*. Washington, D.C.: Quaker Press, 1962.

Wheeler, Ruth R. *Concord: Climate for Freedom*. Concord, Mass.: Concord Antiquarian Society, 1967.

Willard, Frances E., and Livermore, Mary A., eds. *A Woman of the Century*. Buffalo: Charles Wells Moulton, 1893

Wilson, Henry. *History of the Rise and Fall of the Slave Power in America*. Boston: J. R. Osgood & Co., 1872–77.

Wilson, James Harrison. *Life of Charles A. Dana*. New York: Harper & Brothers, 1907.

Winchester, Elhanan. *The Universal Restoration*. Worcester: Isaiah Thomas, Jun., 1803.

Winsor, Justin. *The Memorial History of Boston, Including Suffolk County, Massachusetts, 1630–1880*. 4 vols. Boston: J. R. Osgood & Co., 1880–81.

Wishy, Bernard. *The Child and the Republic*. Philadelphia: University of Pennsylvania Press, 1968.

Wolfe, Allis Rosenberg. "Letters of a Lowell Mill Girl and Friends, 1845–1846." *Labor History* 17 (1976): 96–102.

Wood, Ann Douglas. "The 'Scribbling Women' and Fanny Fern: Why Women Wrote." *American Quarterly* 23 (spring 1971): 3–24.

———. "Mrs. Sigourney and the Sensibility of the Inner Space." *New England Quarterly* 45 (June 1972): 163–81.

Wood, Mary I. *The History of the General Federation of Women's Clubs for the First Twenty-two Years of Its Organization*. New York: General Federation of Women's Clubs, 1912.

Woody, Thomas. *A History of Women's Education in the United States*. 2 vols. New York: Octagon Books, 1966.

Wright, Helena. "Sarah G. Bagley: A Biographical Note." *Labor History* 20 (summer 1979): 398–413.

INDEX

LIBRARY OF CONGRESS CATALOGING IN PUBLICATION DATA

Bushman, Claudia L.
  "A good poor man's wife."
  Bibliography: p.
  Includes index.
  1. Robinson, Harriet Jane Hanson, 1825–1911.
  2. Social reformers—Massachusetts—Biography.
  3. Massachusetts—Social conditions. I. Title.
  HQ1413.R58.B88   361.2'4'0924 [B]   80-54470
  ISBN 0-87451-193-8   AACR2